The UNIVERSITY OF CENTRAL FLORIDA

THROUGH TIME

KATE CUMISKEY

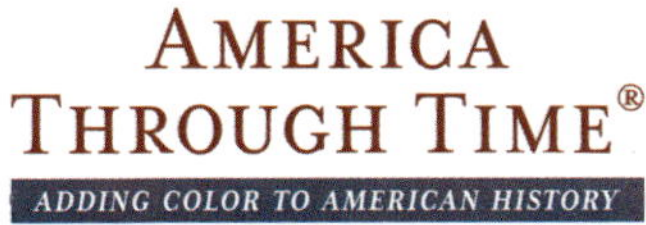

AMERICA THROUGH TIME is an imprint of Fonthill Media LLC

Fonthill Media LLC
www.fonthillmedia.com
office@fonthillmedia.com

First published 2015

ISBN 978-1-62545-085-2

Typeset in Mrs Eaves XL Serif Narrow
Printed and bound in England

Connect with us:
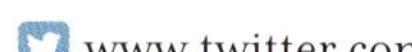 www.twitter.com/usathroughtime
www.facebook.com/AmericaThroughTime

Introduction

Images show us the where and the when of events; even the how. In the end it's the people who define an educational institution like the University of Central Florida. Without the unique faculty, staff, and students at the University all of the state of the art technology, sound and stately buildings, and native flora and fauna would be meaningless. This book is dedicated to one person among thousands who make up this institution of higher learning: the late Dr. Raymond "Bruce" Blake, who earned his PhD at UCF and was Coordinator of Education and Training Services at UCF's Center for Autism and Related Disabilities. Dr. Blake was as unique and vital and ever-changing as the University itself; constantly pushing himself to be a better human being and contributor to the betterment of his planet and those he served. Bruce believed each individual has not only a right and obligation to be a part of their community, but those we serve with exceptionalities are truly that; exceptional, and when listened to enrich us with their contributions to and interpretations of the world.

Education enlarges us. It opens us to the near environment and to those places and people far beyond us—it links us through history to the past; through imagination to the future. An important part of higher education is moving beyond the self and the known familiar, while learning one's own limits and how to expand them. UCF Stands for Opportunity. If opportunity is based in knowledge, knowing the self is the beginning of that journey. Students, here, have ample opportunity to explore aspects of self while taking steps toward recognition of and honoring the unfamiliar; diversity thrives, here. Therein lays the foundation education.

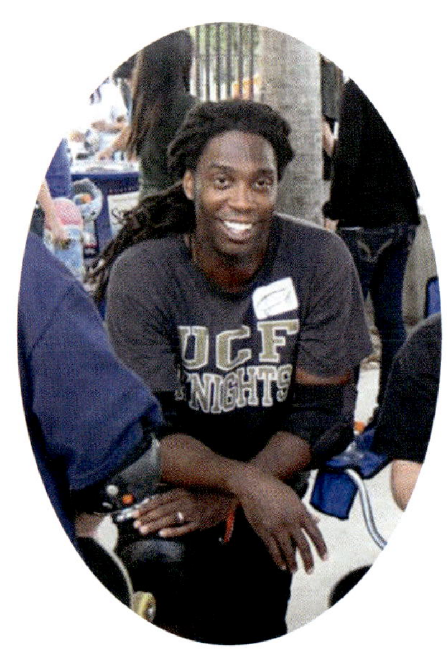

DEDICATION

This book is dedicated to my dear friend, the late Dr. Bruce Blake. Wherever he went, Bruce sported a UCF t-shirt. And, wherever he went, the needs of those exceptional individuals he served were constantly on his mind and in his heart. Fair winds, my friend. Until we meet again.

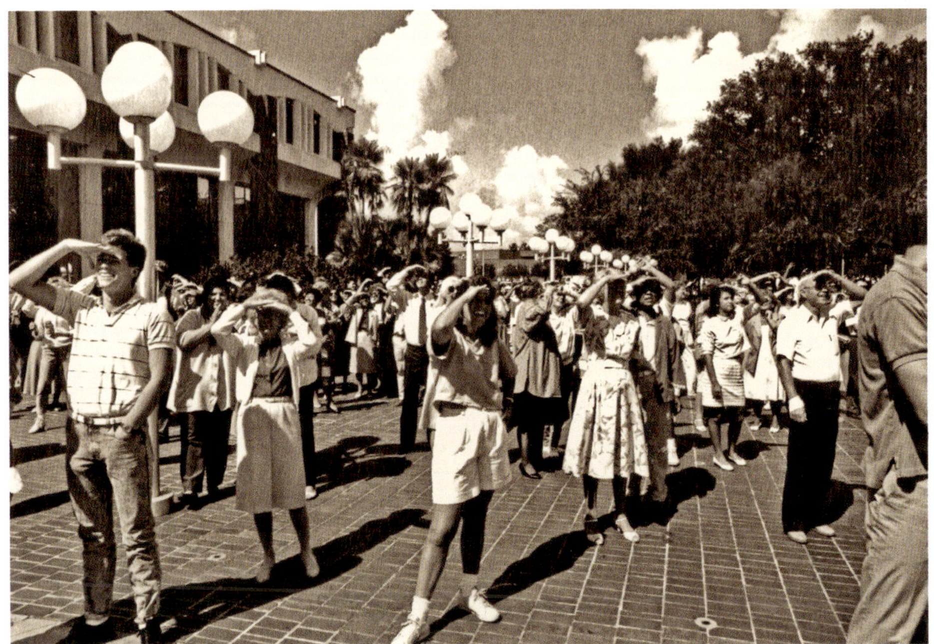

HIGH SCIENCE: Opportunities abound at UCF which are literally unique in the world: there is not another public university in America where students could step outside to view a Space Shuttle launch. Although the Shuttle program has ended, there are launches of other rockets on a regular basis, and the future of the United States Space Program is wide open. UCF, and its students, are a big part of both the history of and the future of space exploration.

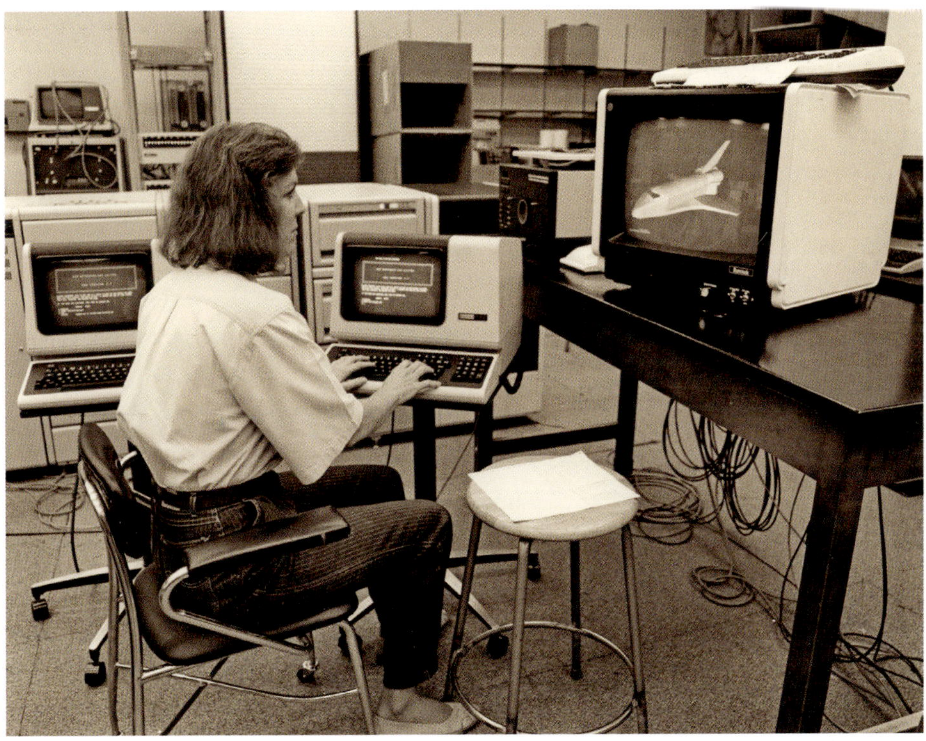

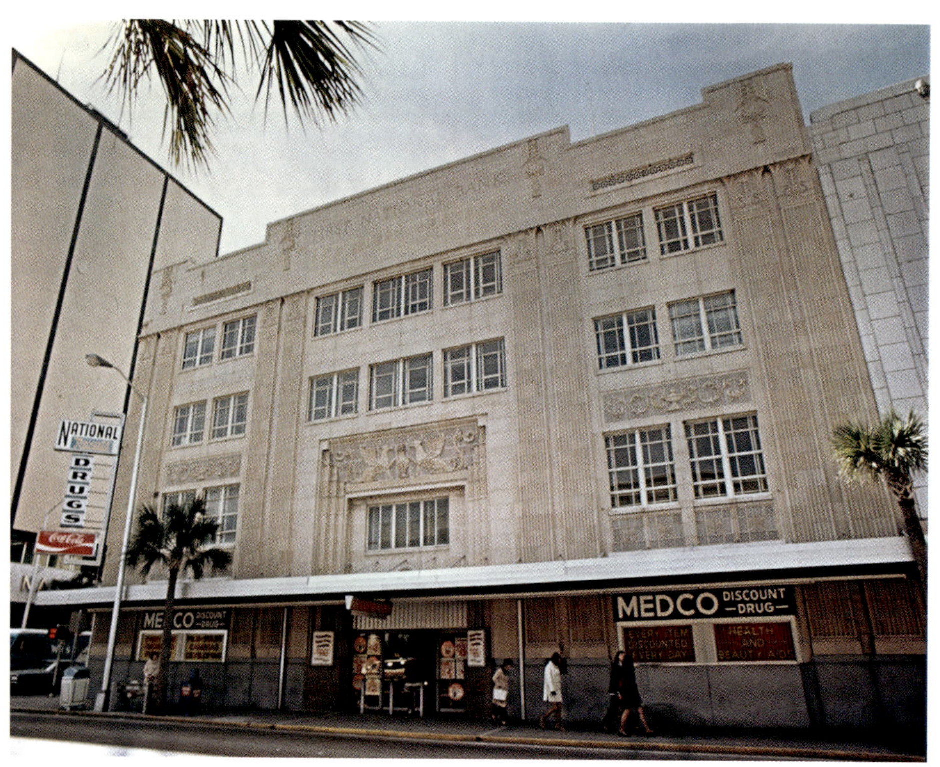

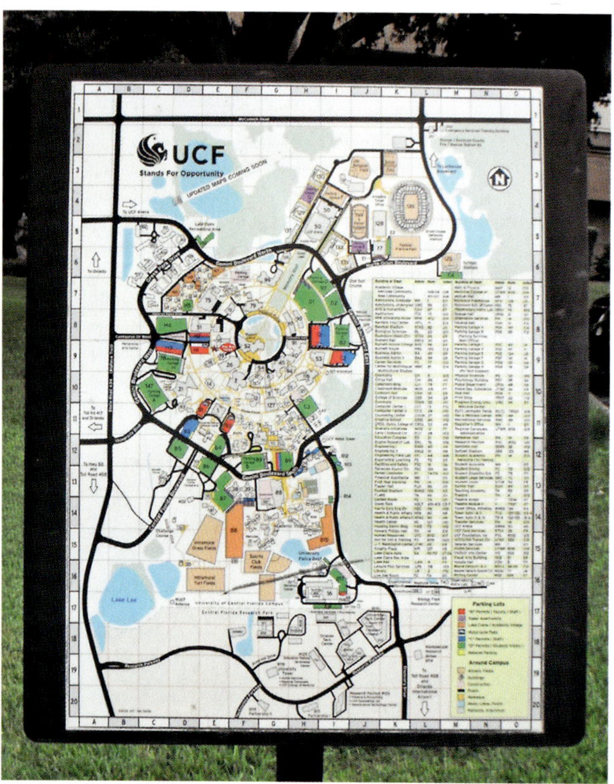

 As Florida Technological University, UCF began in this downtown building at One West Church Street, far from the current campus. It now houses Valencia Community College's downtown campus. With nine satellite campuses and a 1,415 acre main campus, UCF is the second largest university in the nation. Maps like this one are absolutely necessary, even for veteran students, on such a large campus.

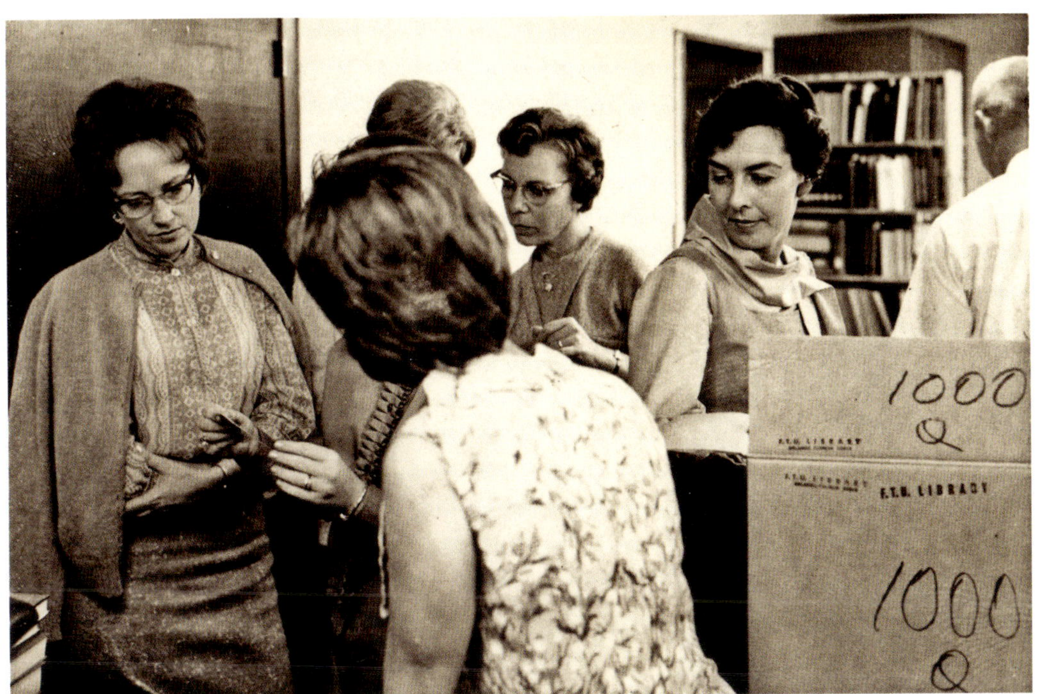

STARK CONTRAST: Ladies unpacking books at the downtown office, late 1960s. Steven Way looks sharp and wears a friendly smile, despite managing the extremely busy UCF bookstore. He's made it into much more than a business. Faculty, staff, students and visitors gather at the bookstore, located centrally near the library, keeping it hopping Steven is always willing to help with concerns large or small as well as pitching in to help his competent staff at any time.

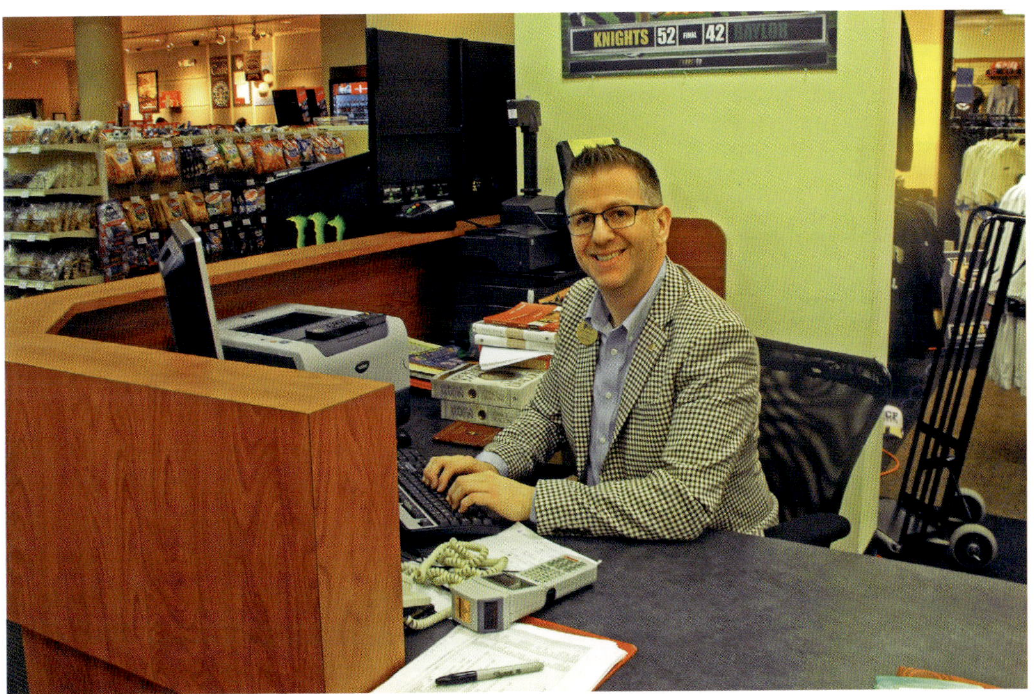

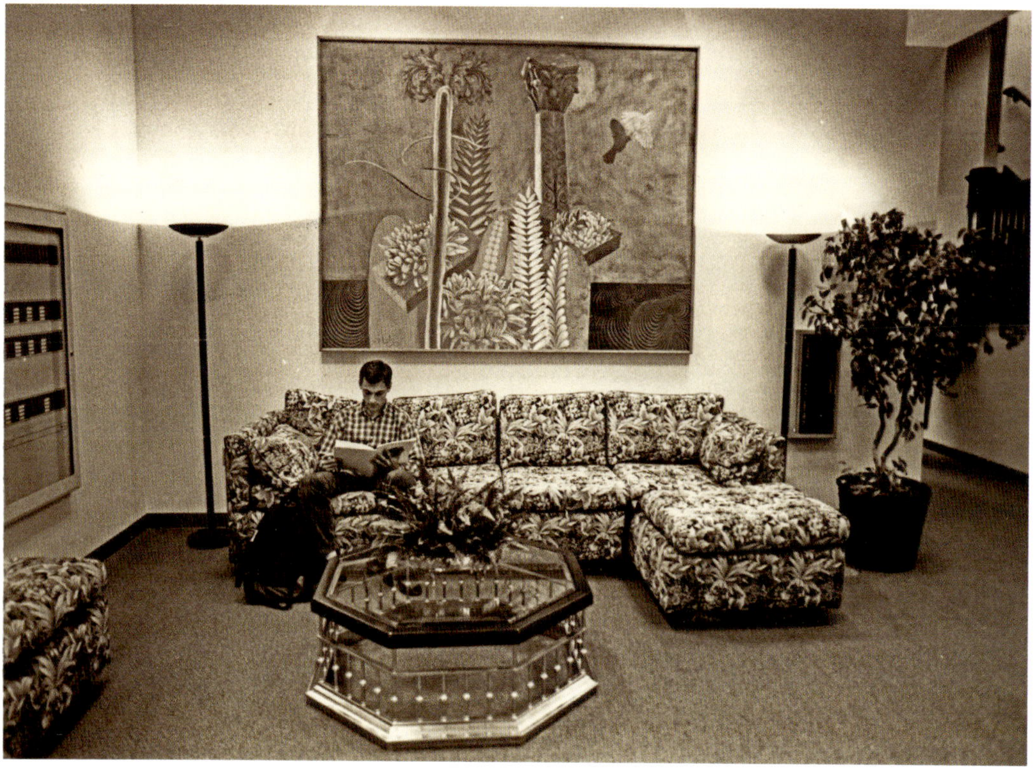

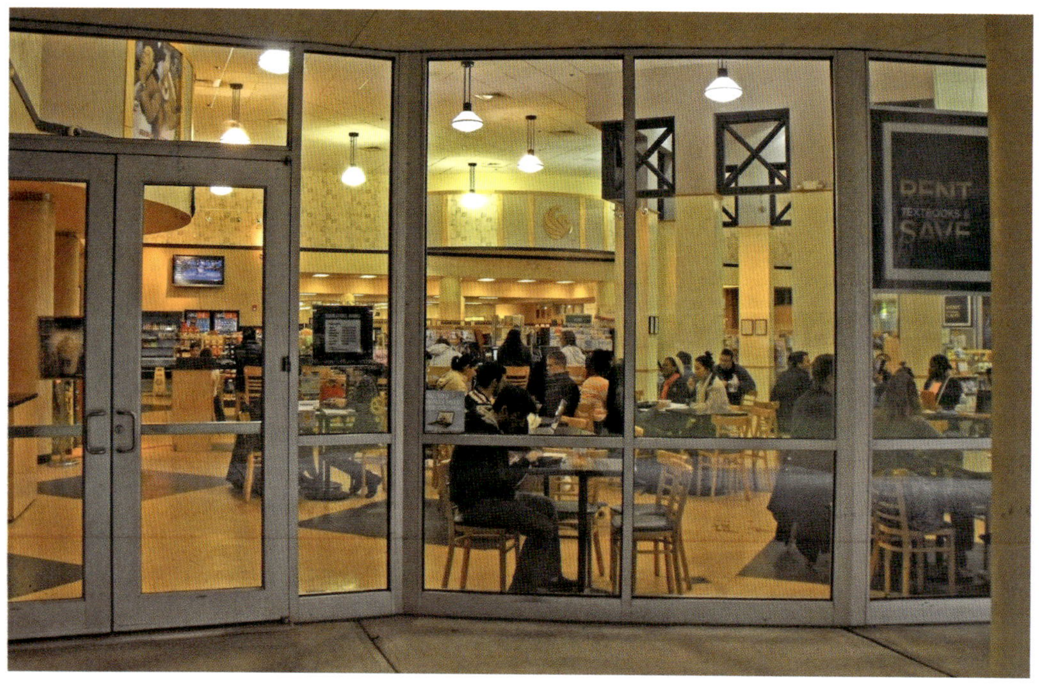

ADMINISTRATIVE SPACE: A student waits in the lobby of the old downtown offices in the early days of FTU beneath a painting by Professor Steven Lotz; fifty years later, students gather in one of the many coffee shops across the main campus. This one is located in the bookstore.

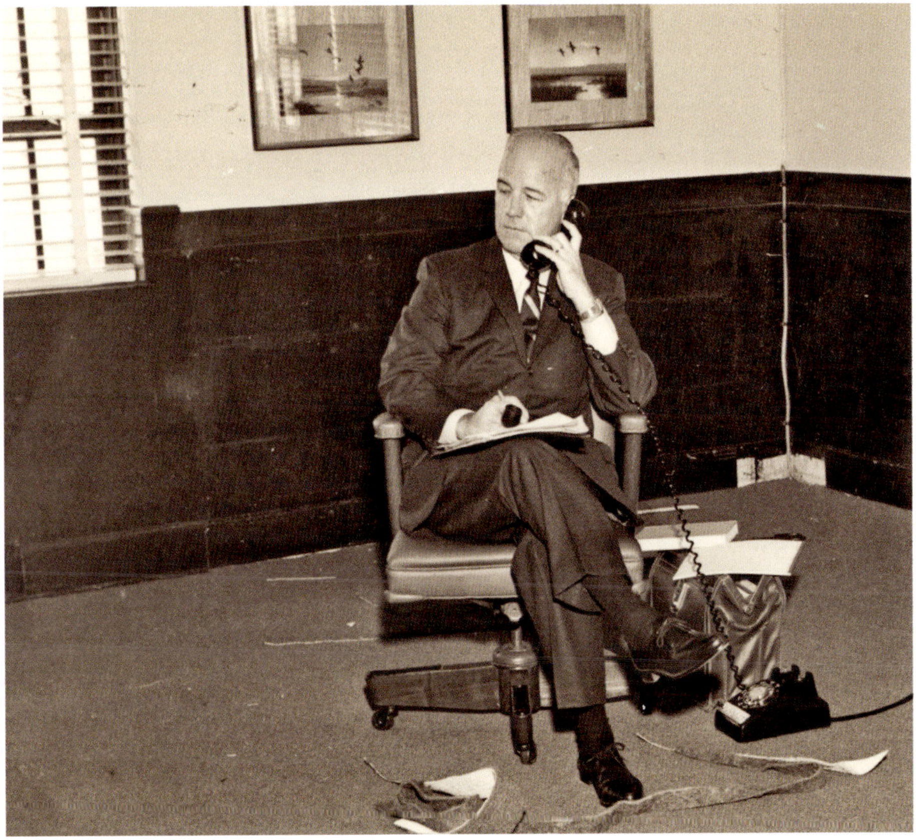

Dr. Charles Millican was appointed FTU's first president in 1965. He had to find buildings and staff, basically building the university. He was known as a very hands-on leader. This statue stands in front of Millican Hall on the main campus.

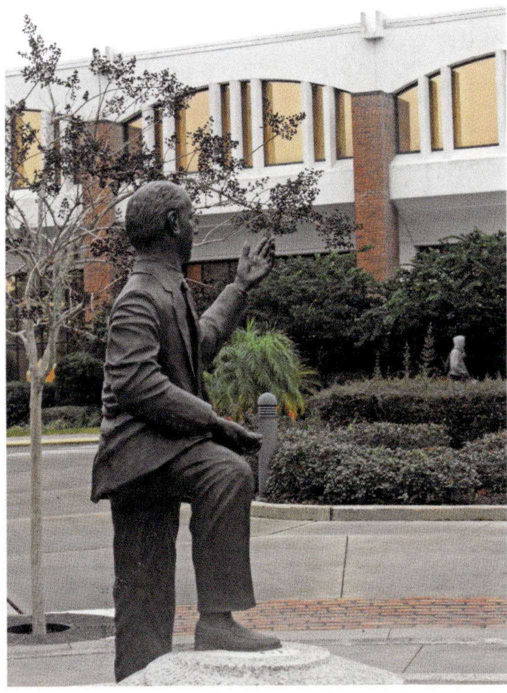

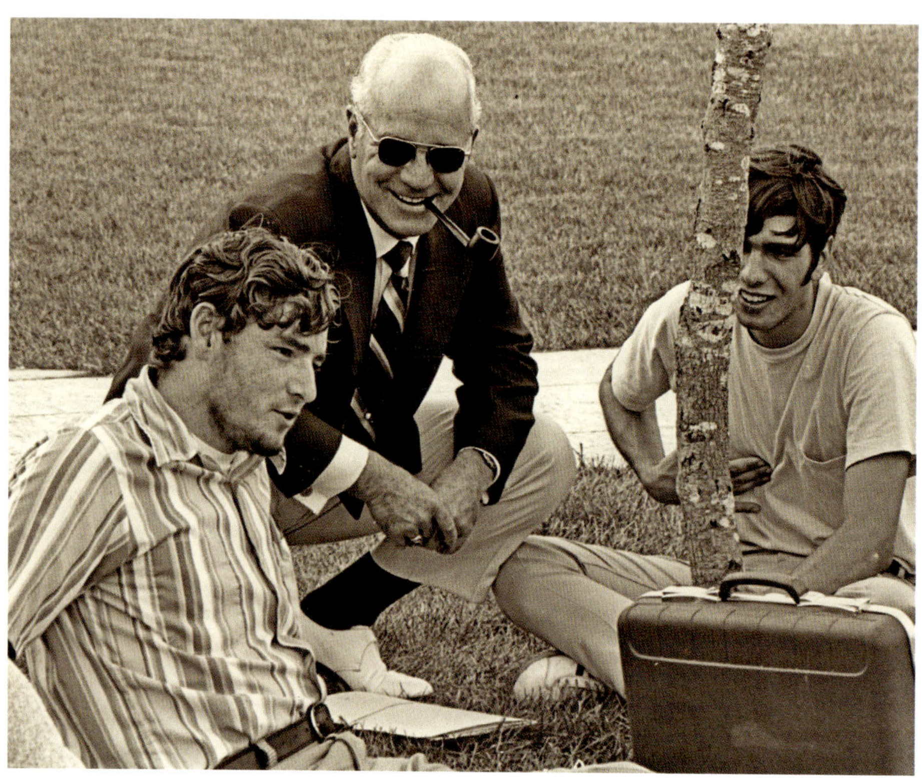

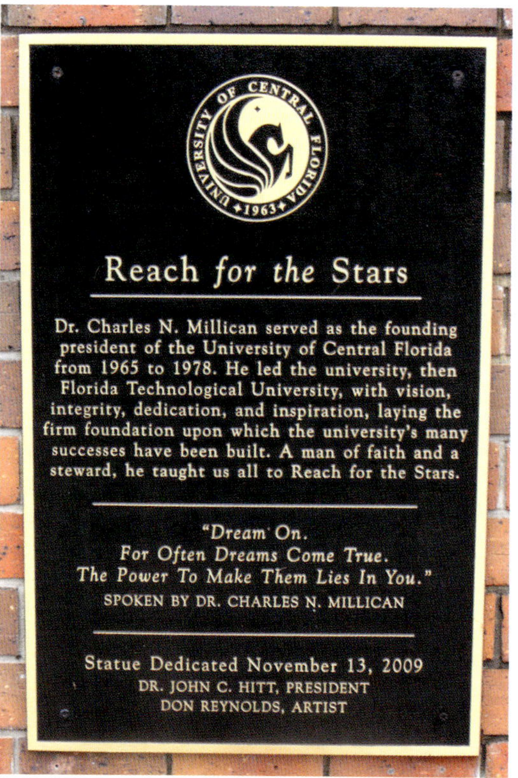

WORDS OF WISDOM: Dr. Millican believed in the value of the individual. That translated into his twin tenets for UCF, 'accent on the individual' and 'accent on excellence.' References to Millican abound throughout campus, and his motto of "reach for the stars" stands, today.

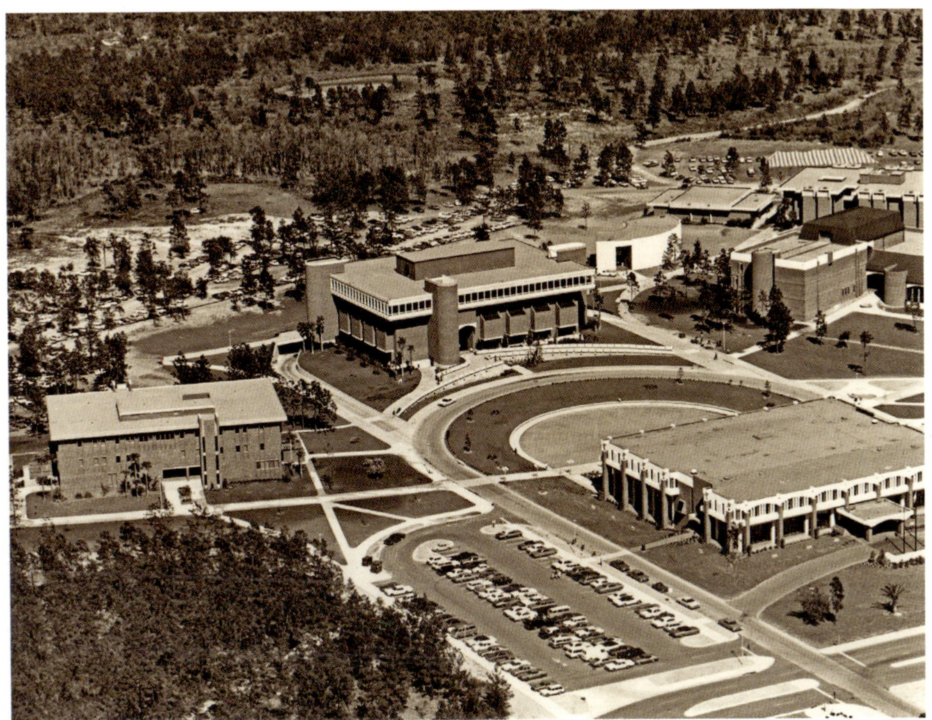

ROOM TO GROW: In 1971, the space for the reflecting pond between Millican Hall and the library was mapped out but incomplete. Note the car on the semi-circular road which, at present, is the surround for the pond. With UCF now the second largest per-capita public university in the U.S., open space is now at a premium, and transportation a real issue. Busses come and go nearly around the clock across campus and particularly at the pictured hub.

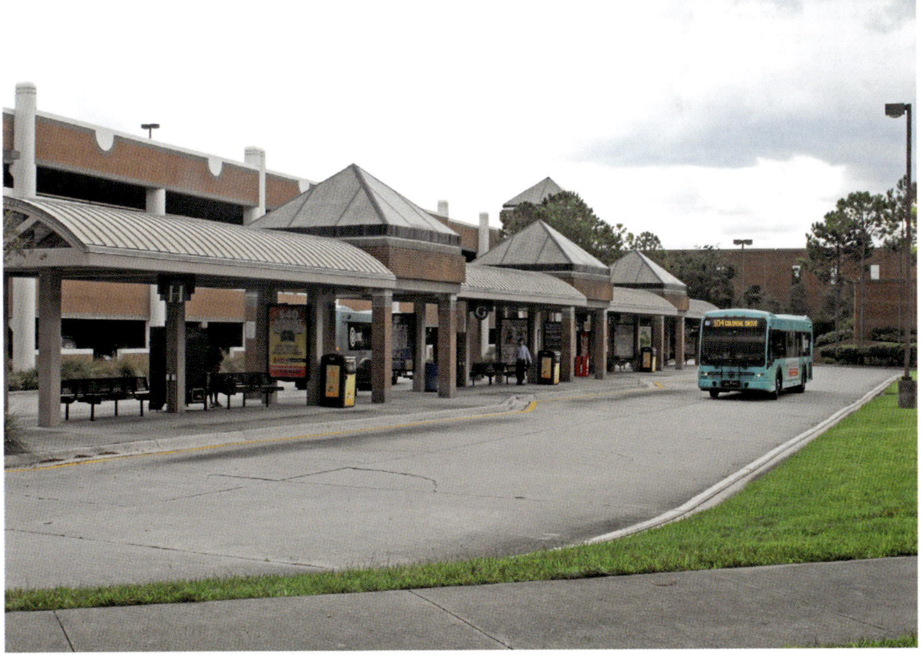

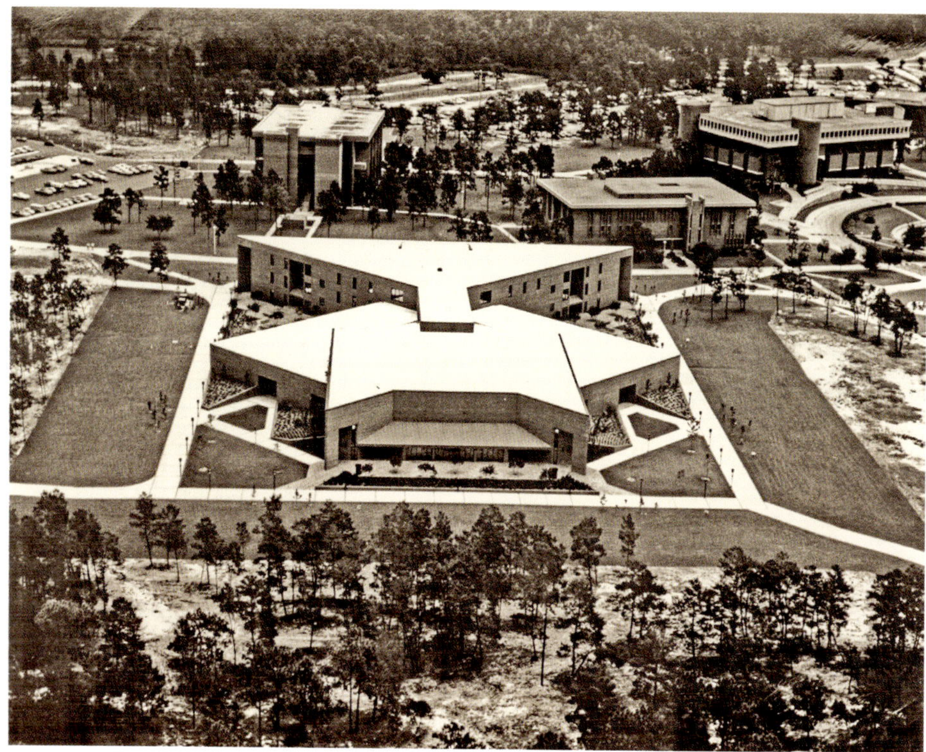

MODERN EDUCATION: Certainly modern, or at the very least mod, when designed and built in the early 1970s, the education building has become an education complex. Construction of new buildings continues on a regular basis, with architecture reflecting the times.

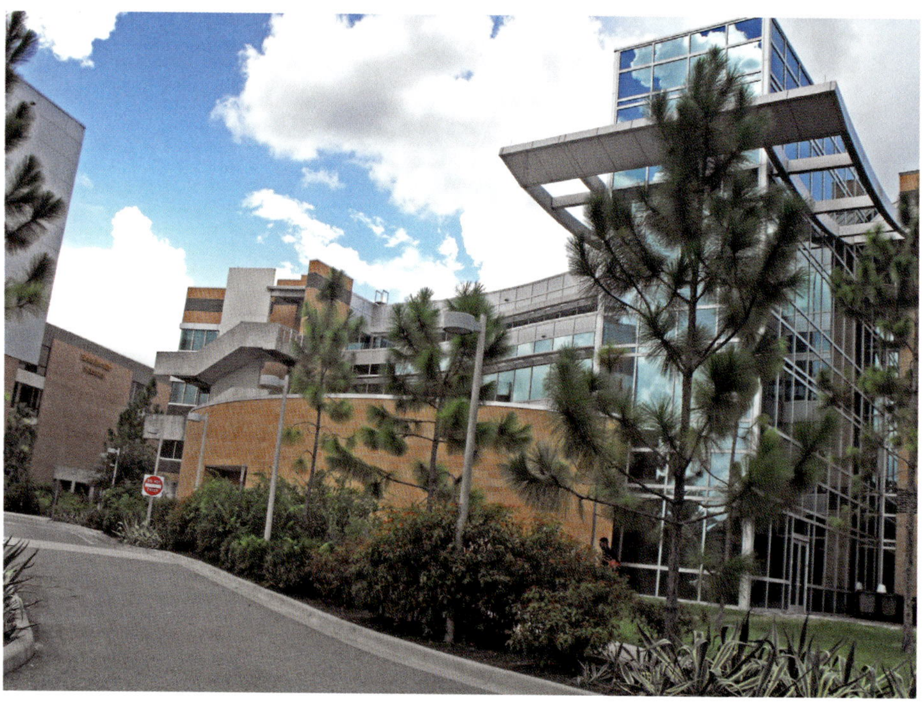

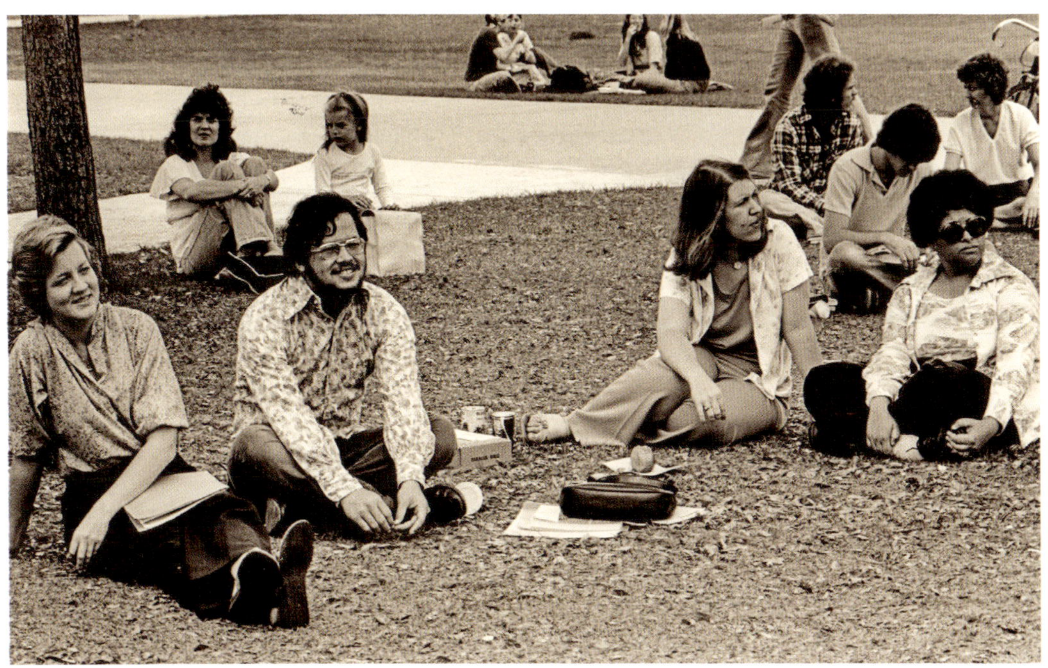

 Floridians make no bones about the fact that we enjoy our sunshine. Outdoor spaces are critical to, utilized by, and protected by UCF students, faculty, and staff. These days, it is more important than it used to be to protect oneself from heat and sunshine; but that doesn't mean we can't enjoy the beautiful weather.

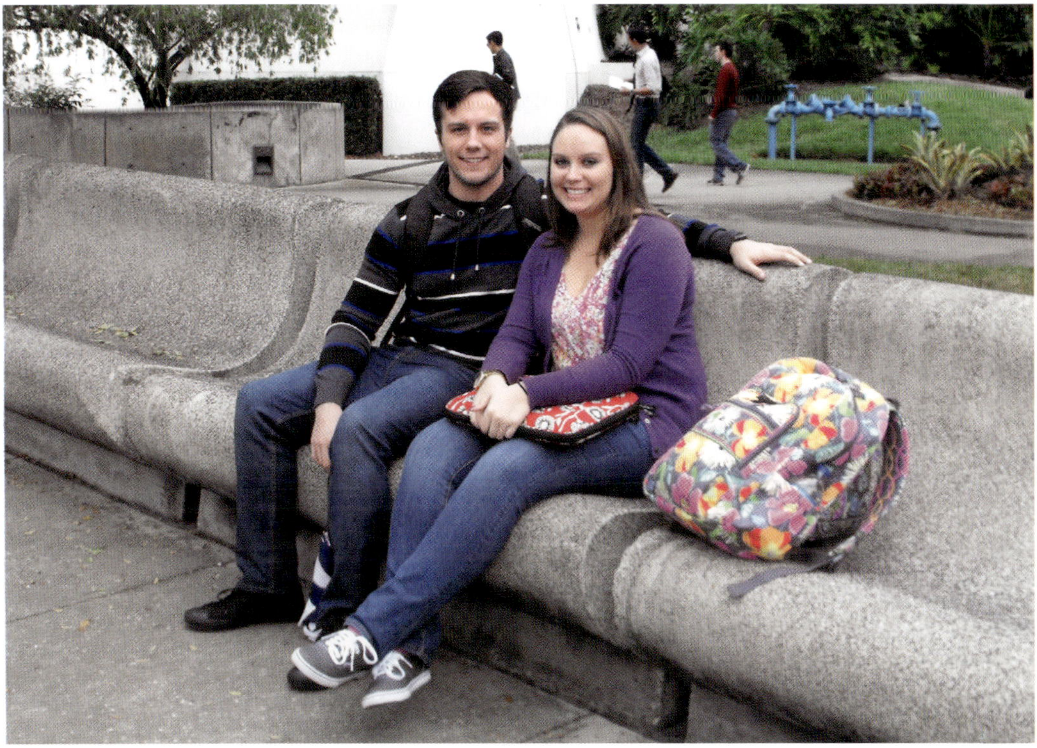

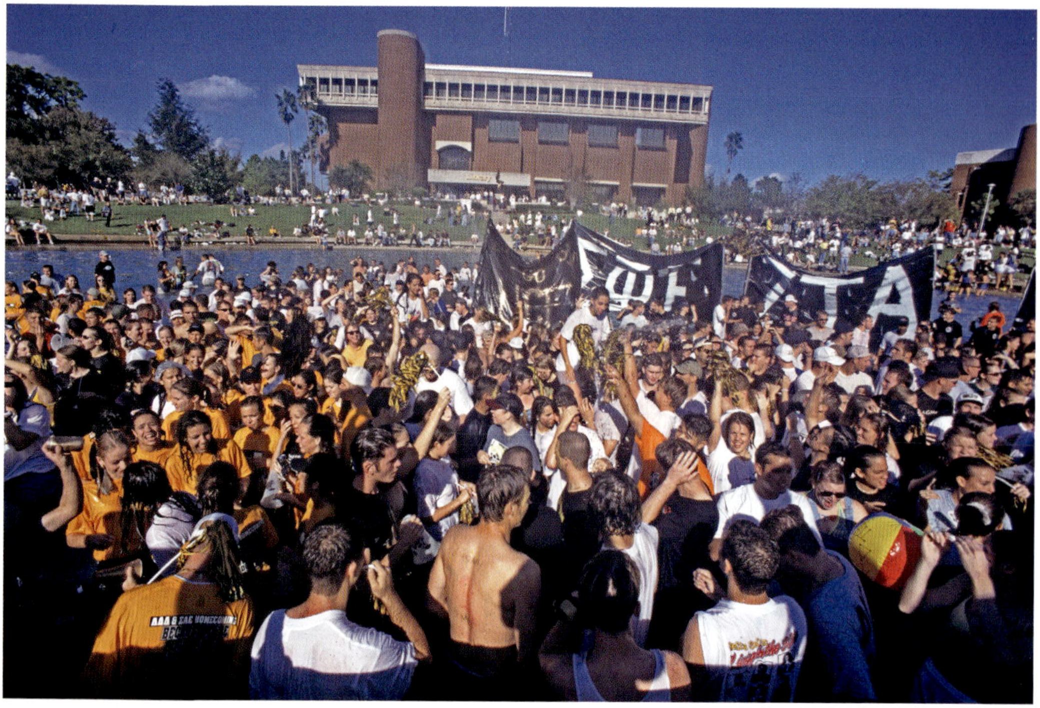

NOT ALL BOOKS AND PAPERS: Students crowd the reflecting pond, a hub on campus, during Greek Week. Social life is important to many students, but with the increase in adults with career experience and families returning to school, many avoid such crowded events and prefer to access the campus outdoor spaces during quieter times.

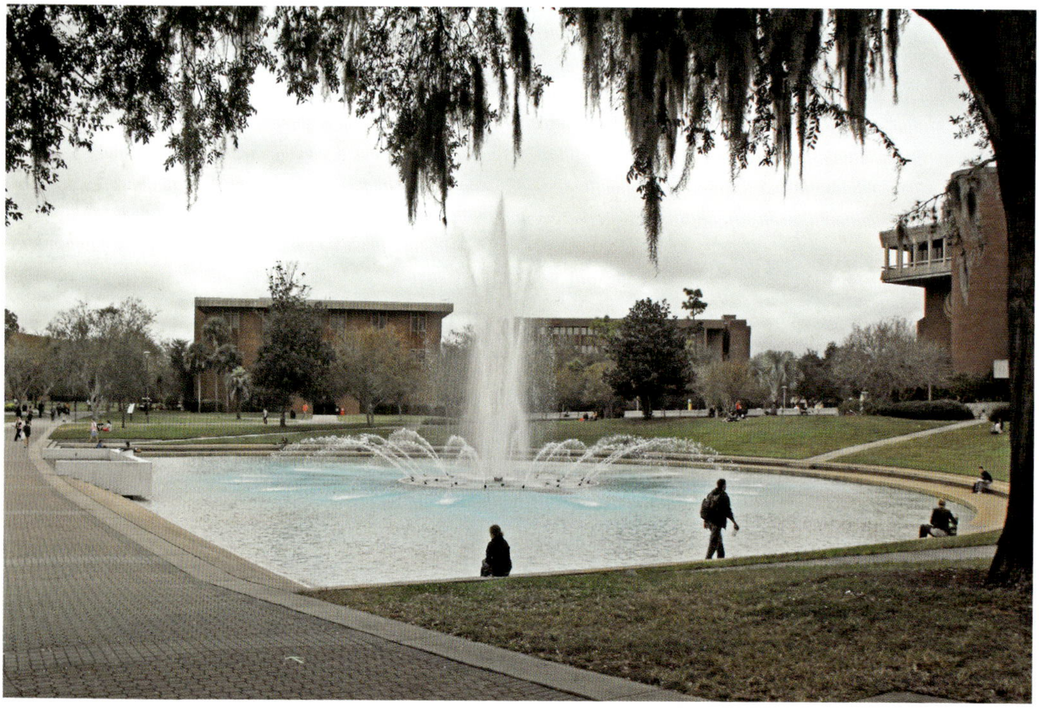

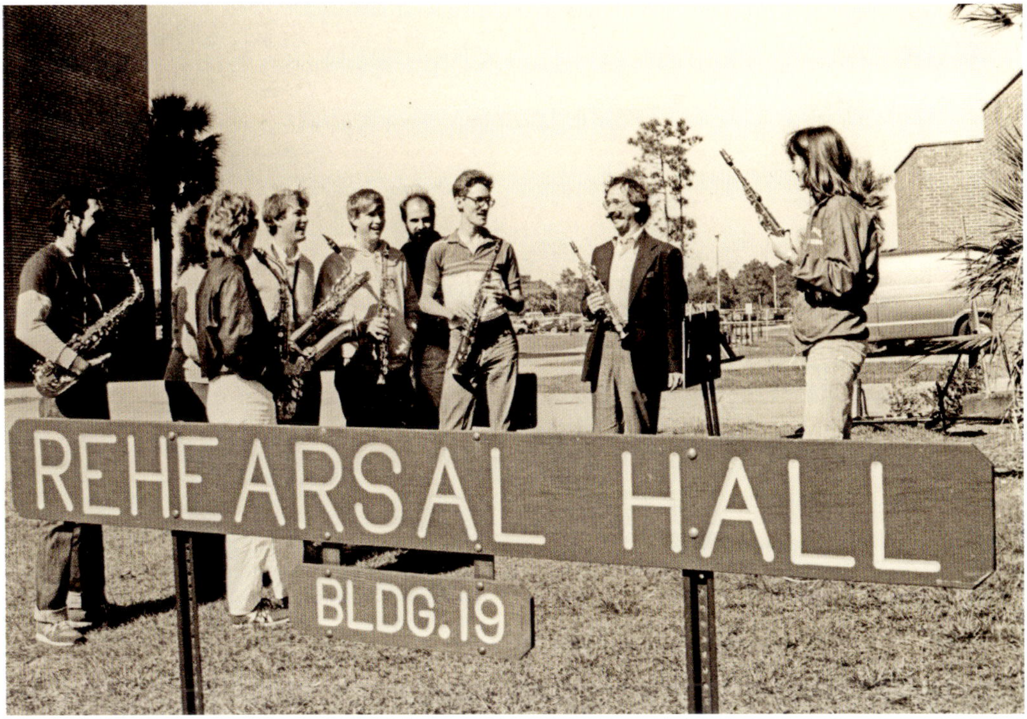

OUTDOOR ADVANTAGE: Believe it or not, this horn section gathered outside Building 19 is outdoors in the dead of winter, as evidenced by the jackets and long sleeves. This building remains a rehearsal hall to the present day.

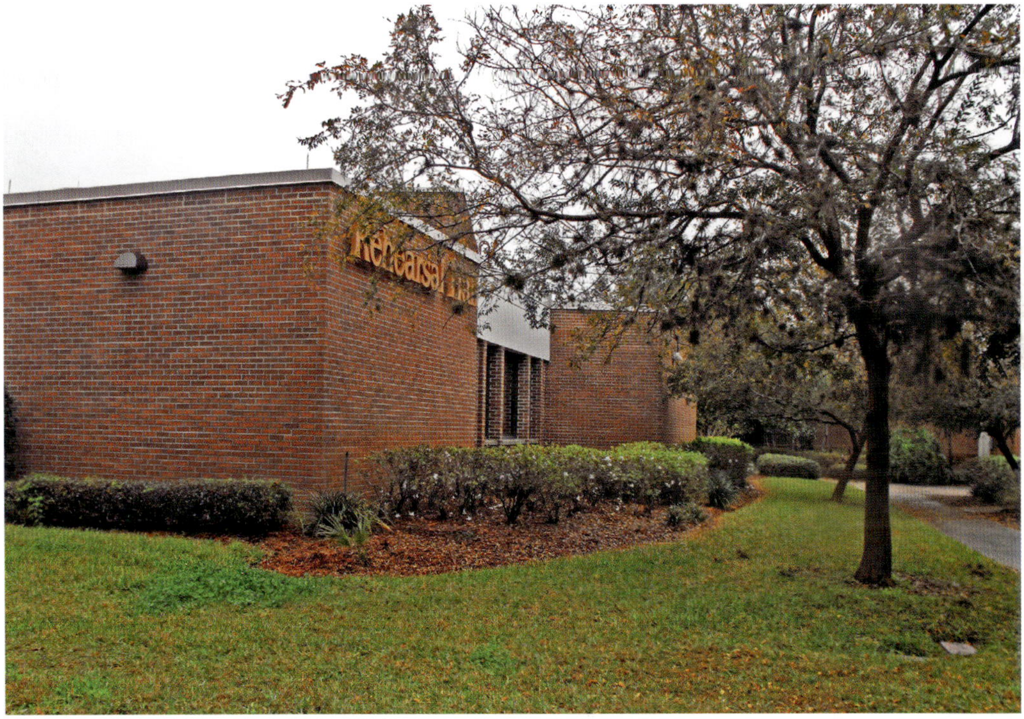

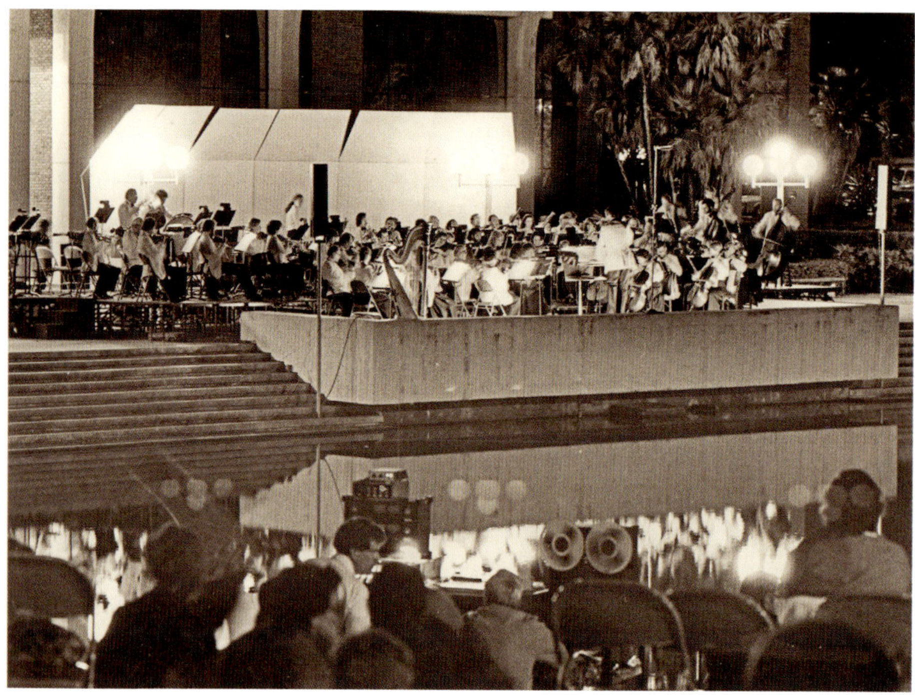

ARTS EVERYWHERE: The reflecting pond behind Millican Hall has long been a gathering space, formal and in, for the UCF Community. On a balmy night in 1981 the UCF community enjoys a performance by the Florida Symphony Orchestra. John C. Hitt Library, named for the current President of UCF, is directly across the pond from the performance area. When it is too hot outside, vast interior spaces provide a cool and stimulating study environment as well as a venue for visual art.

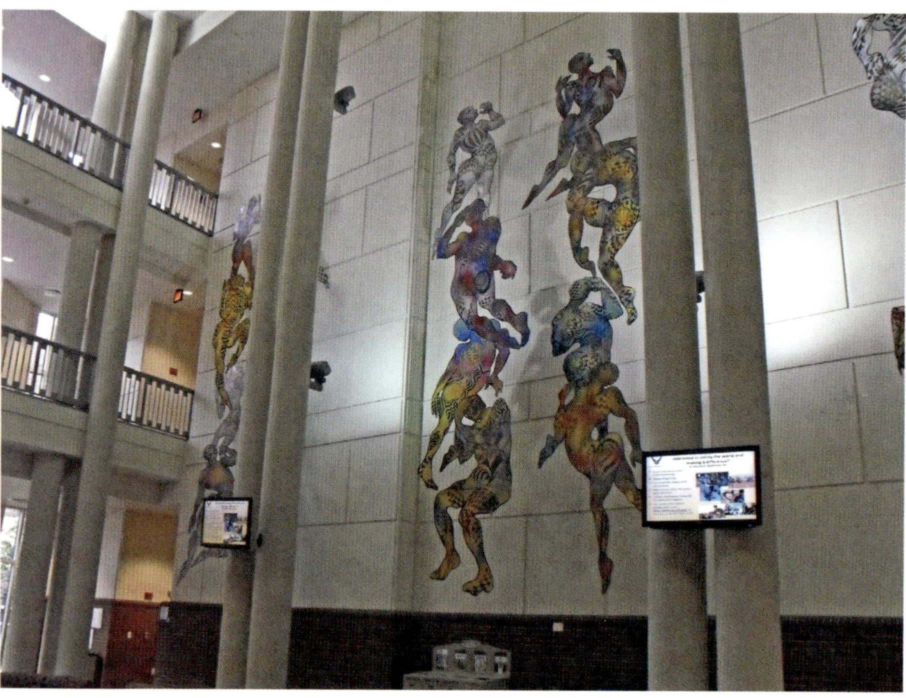

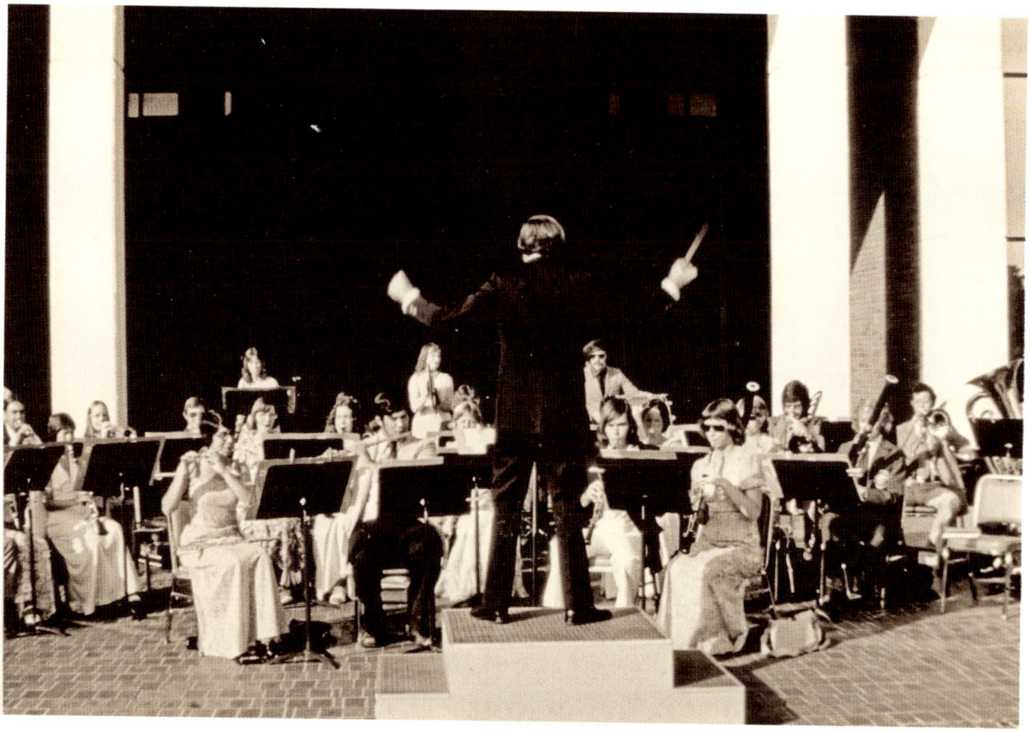

HAVE SUNGLASSES, WILL PLAY: An afternoon concert in 1977 in front of Millican Hall in bright sunlight requires creativity on the part of the musicians. Such performances demand long hours of class and even more of practice.

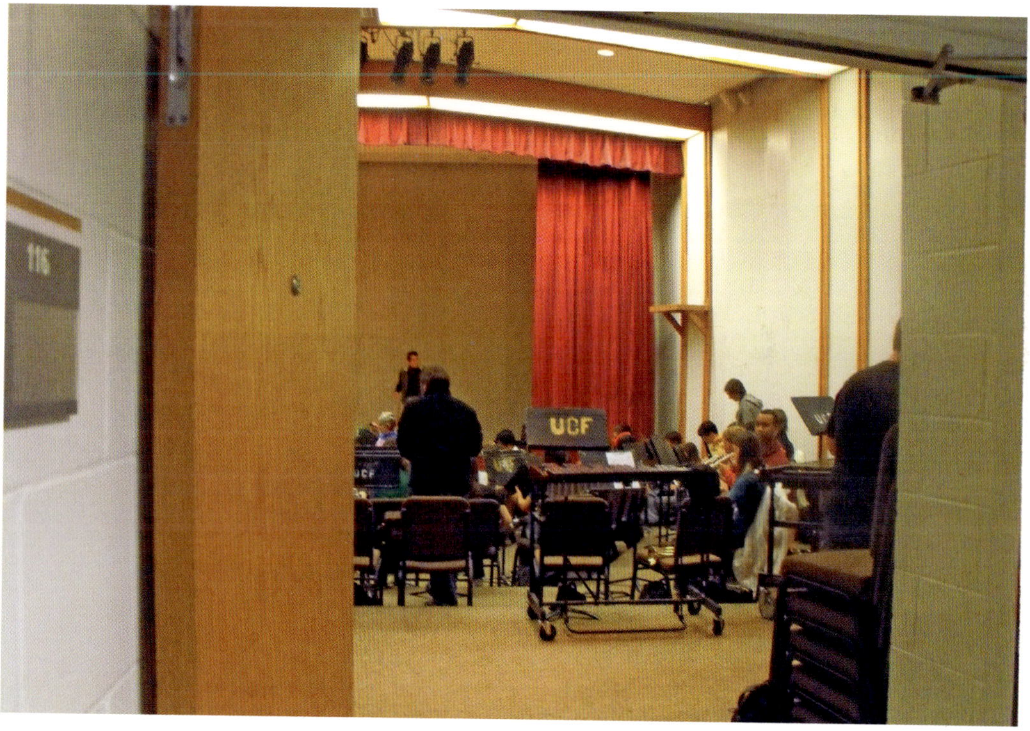

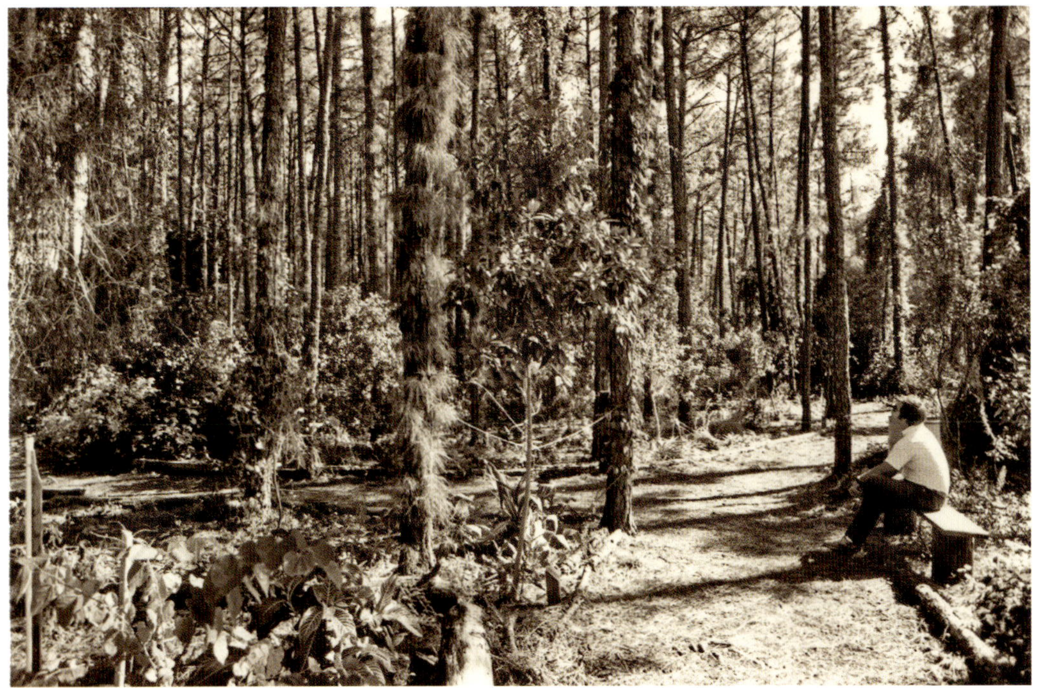

 Along the pathways through the Arboretum, one can contemplate the stark and the subtle changes in the Florida landscape over the years. It is easy to spend time here, imagining the lives of those Florida natives and pioneers who occupied the land long before UCF was dreamt of. Across campus, ancient live oak trees provide a lovely contrast between the old and the new; nature and the structures of man.

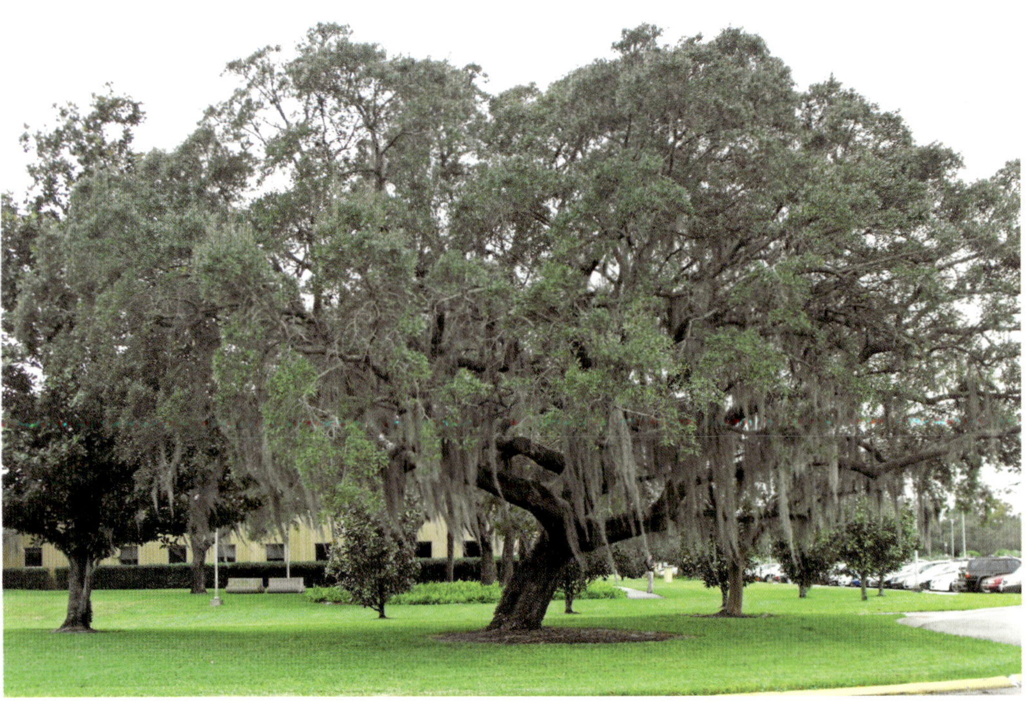

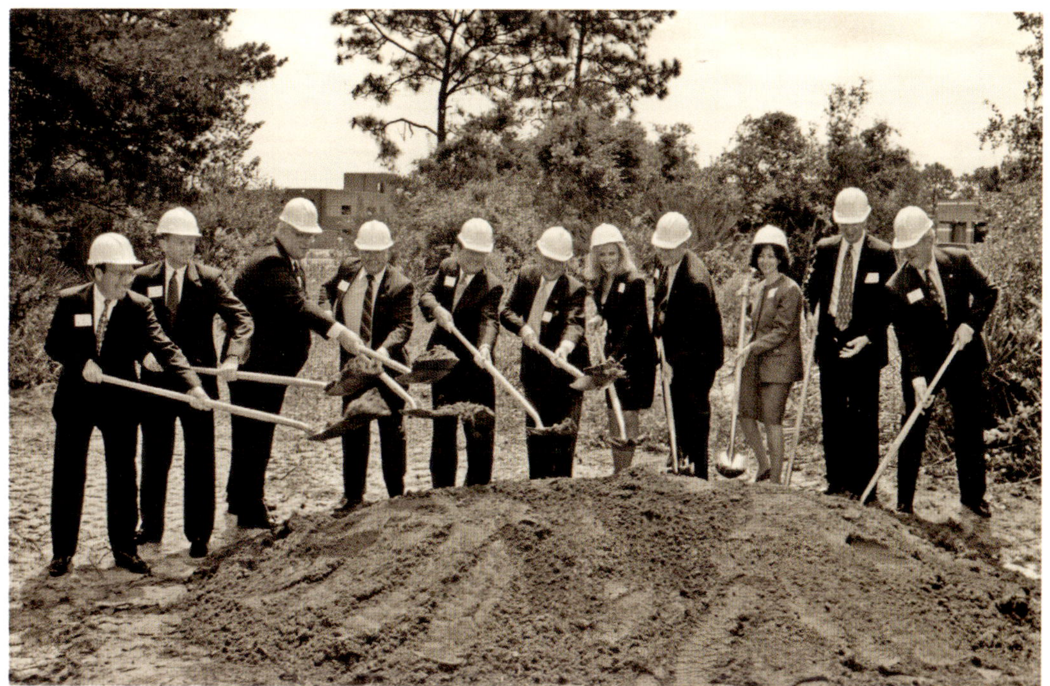

FAST PACE: UCF is one of the fastest-growing public universities in the nation. President John Hitt and other faculty happily lift shovels for the groundbreaking of the Communications Building in 1996. One of the earmarks of a relatively new, rapidly growing institution is a raw and unfinished look. In the last few years, UCF has pleasantly acquired a mature look in not only some of its buildings, but its landscaping and an abundance of much needed shade.

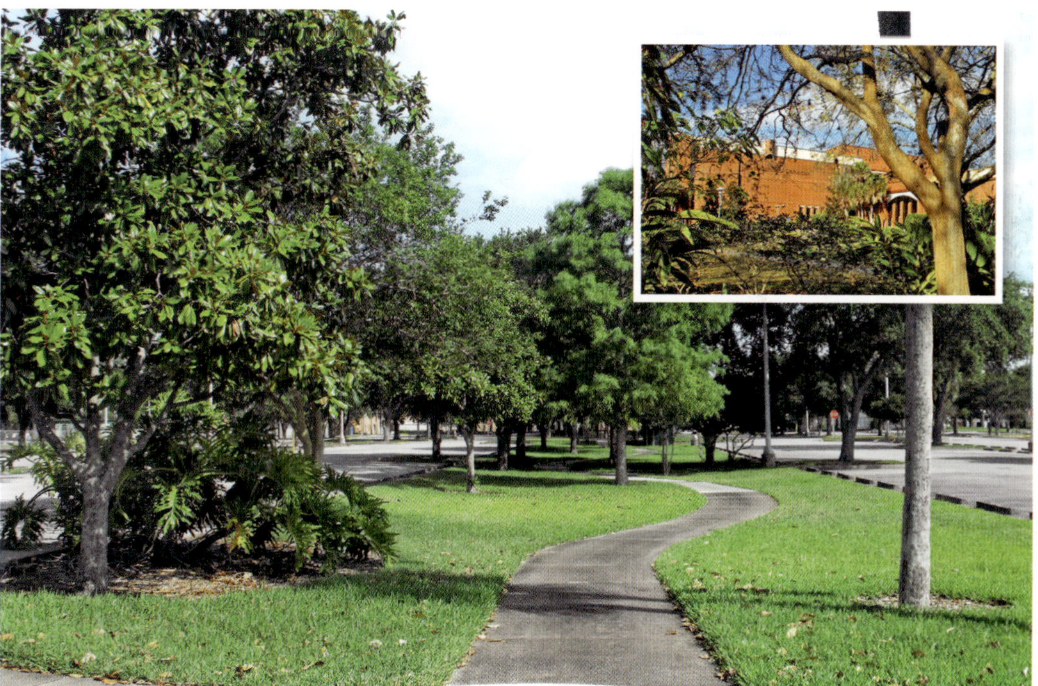

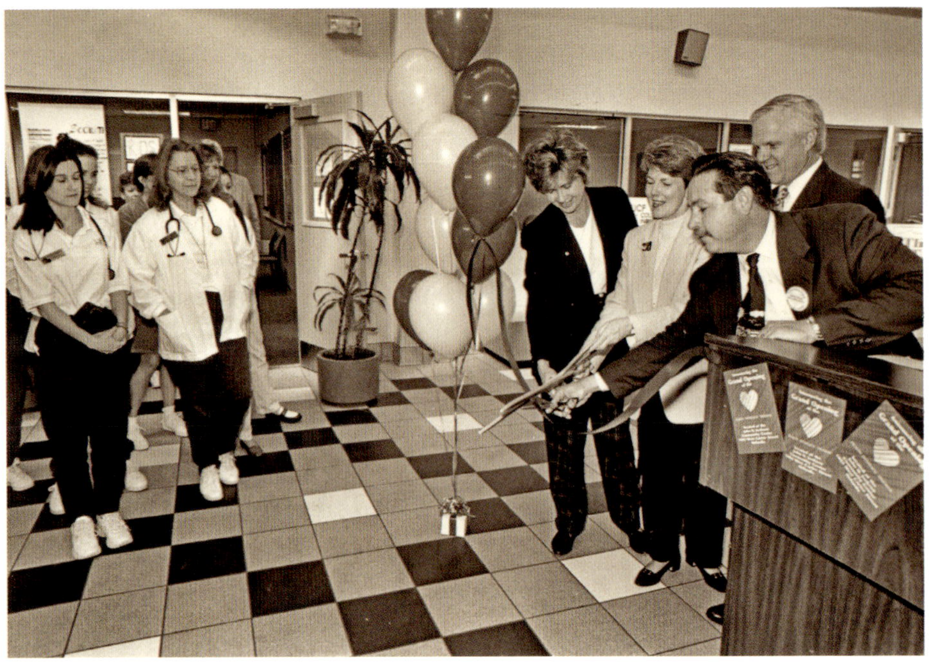

MARKING THE OCCASION: Students, faculty and community members celebrate the opening of the Jackson Community Center in Orlando in 1998. Mayor Glenda Hood and Dean McCarthy of the College of Health and Public Affairs share the scissors for the ribbon cutting. Good community relations and relationships are crucial to an excellent public university.

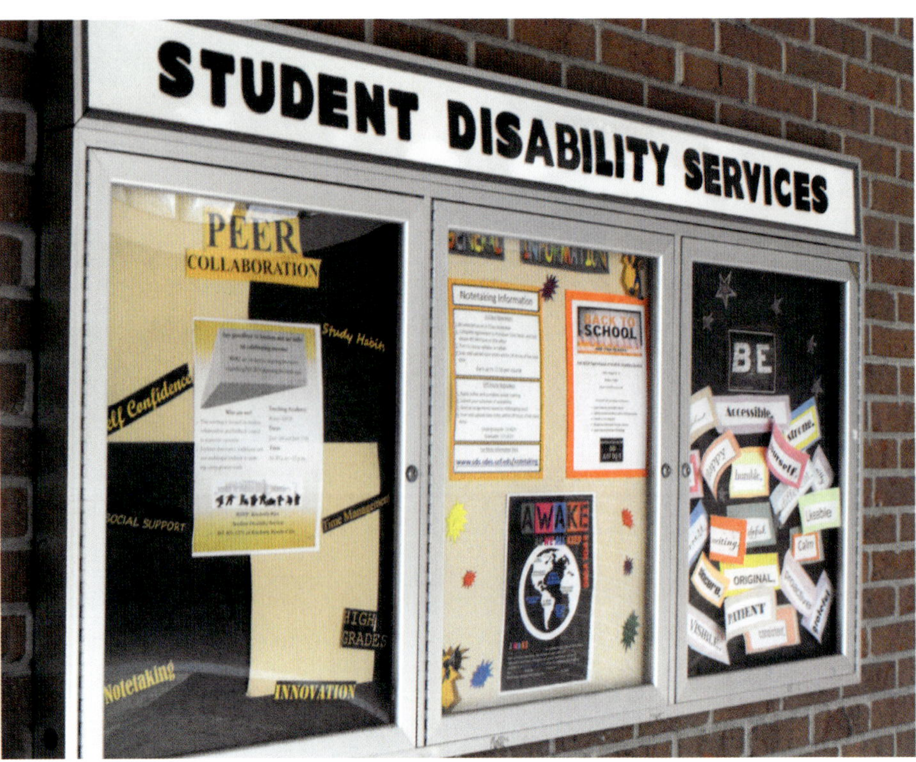

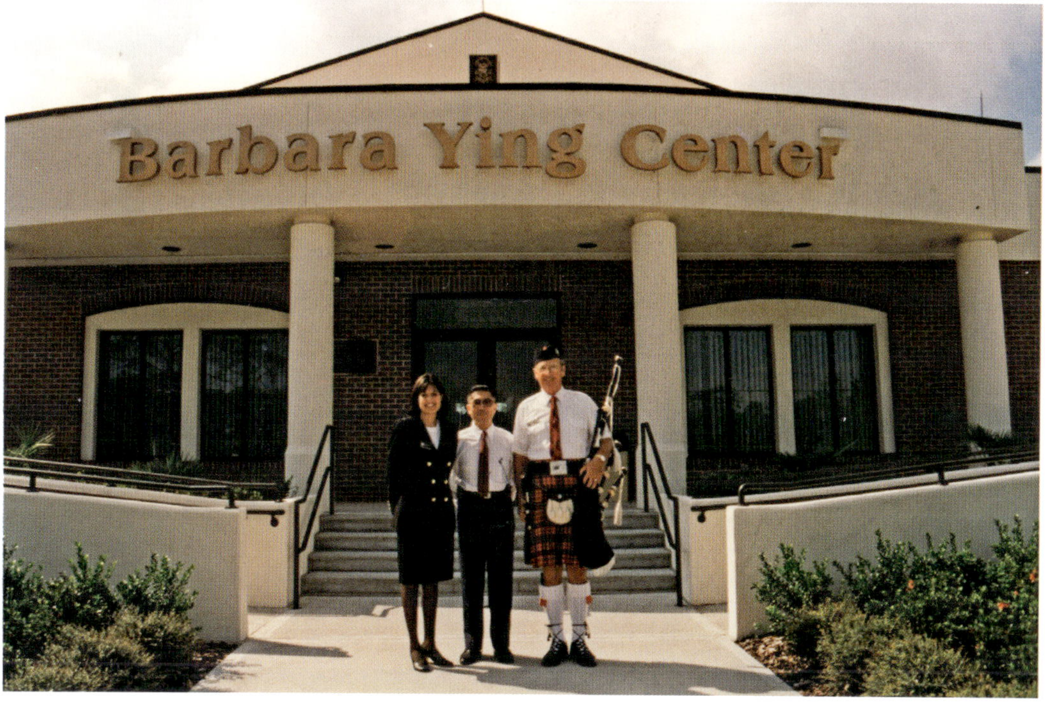

A LITTLE CLASS, A LITTLE FUN: A diversity of culture is honored through the international student center. College, for many students, is much more than an education. Having a designated place to go for information and activities can make the transition to a new land easier for international students. One of the newest places to hang out, Starbucks™ appeals to faculty and students alike.

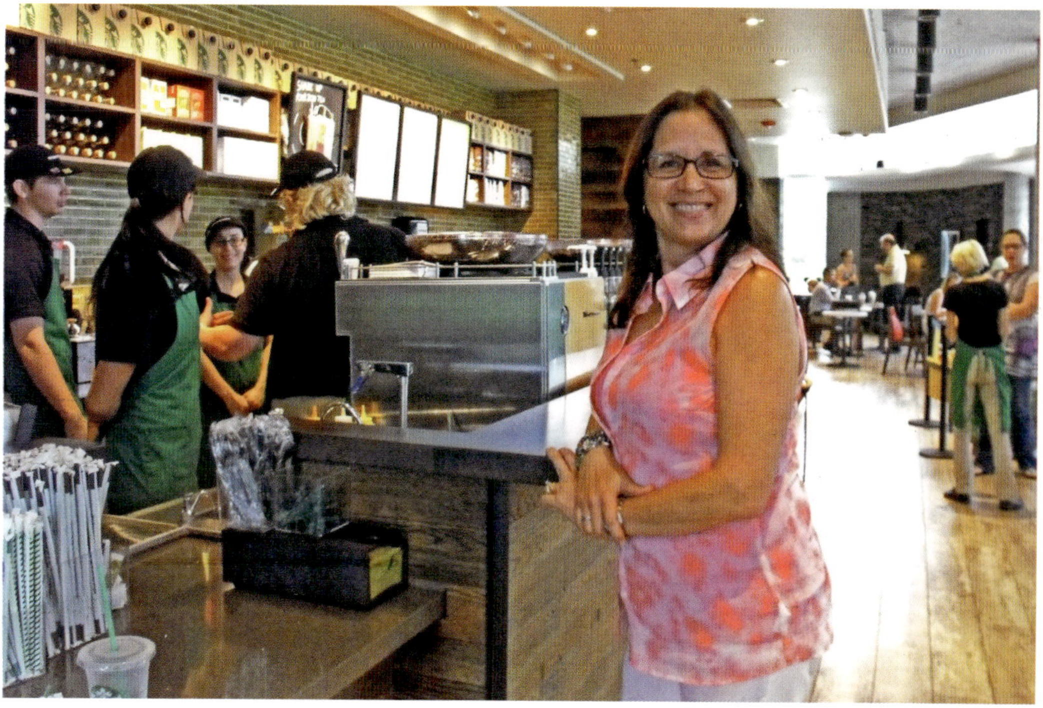

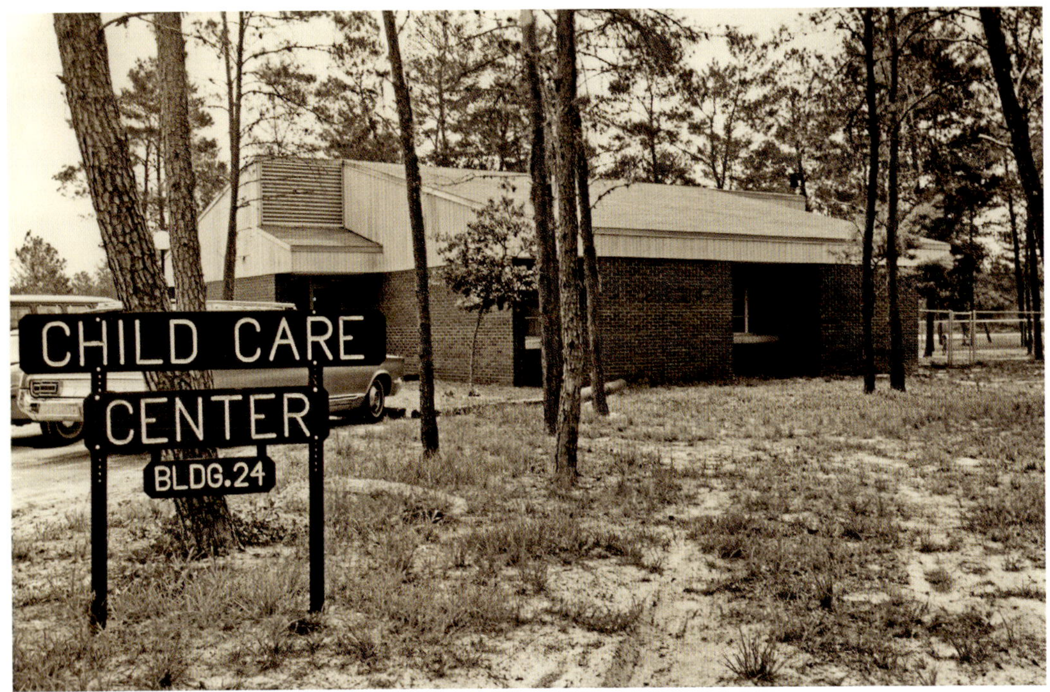

FAMILY IMPACT: University of Central Florida recognizes that many students have children of their own. The child care center is conveniently located not far from the recreation and wellness complex; sometimes busy college students can get in a workout or swim before picking up their children from daycare. A faculty member shares with her niece, visiting from Germany, some American cuisine at one of the many eateries on campus.

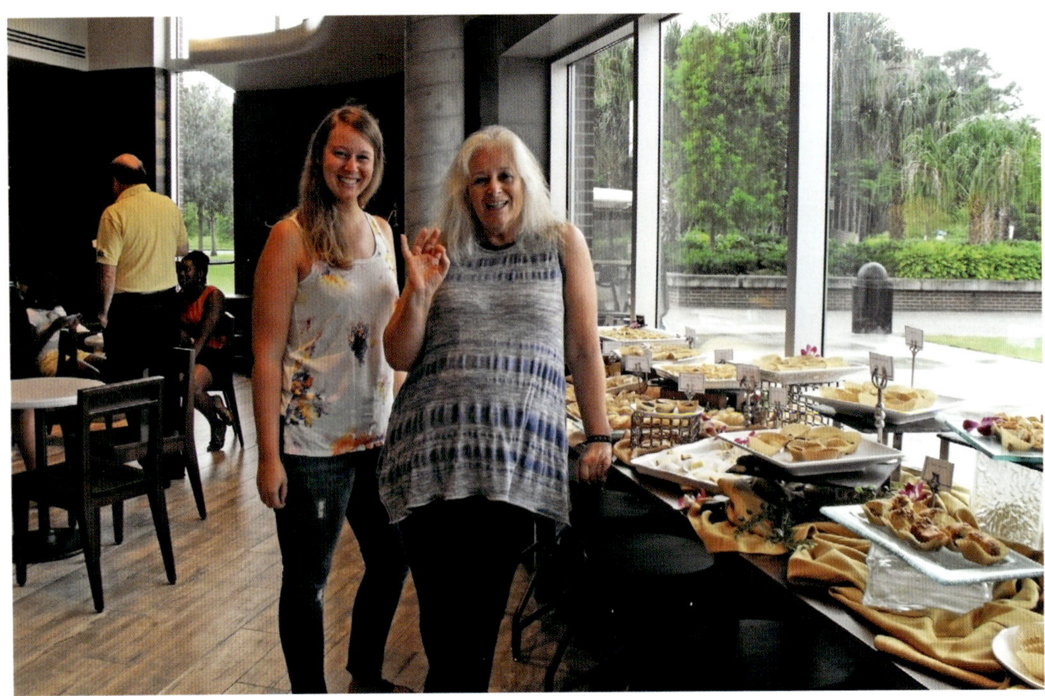

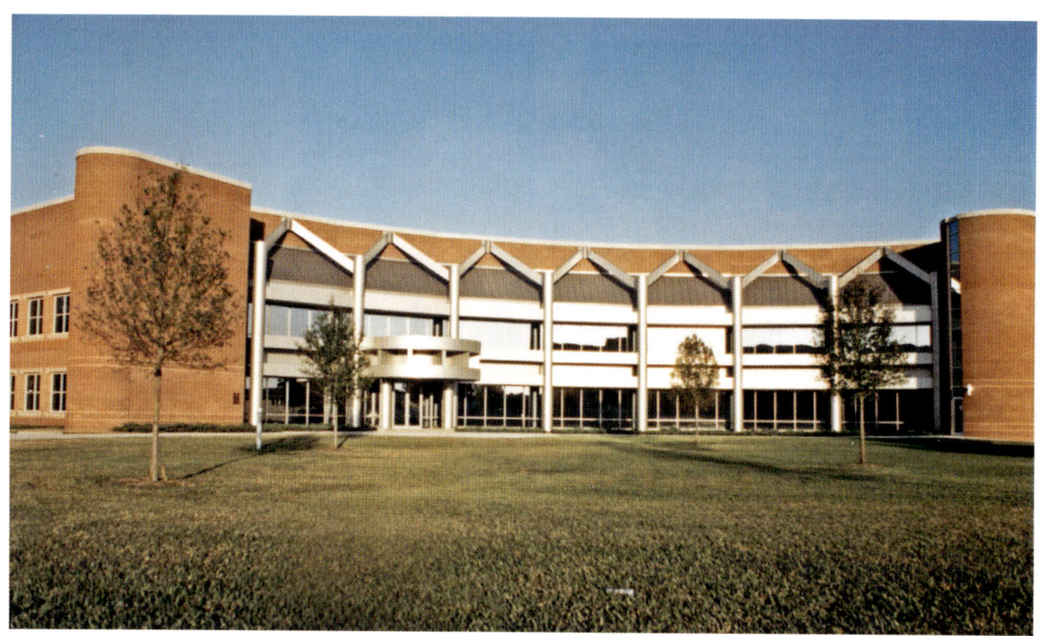

LEARNING CURVE: A beautifully curved classroom building on the main campus is contrasted with the high-rise view from one of the satellite locations; the higher education center at Daytona State College. Even the smaller, local campuses are growing rapidly to meet the needs of the Central Florida population.

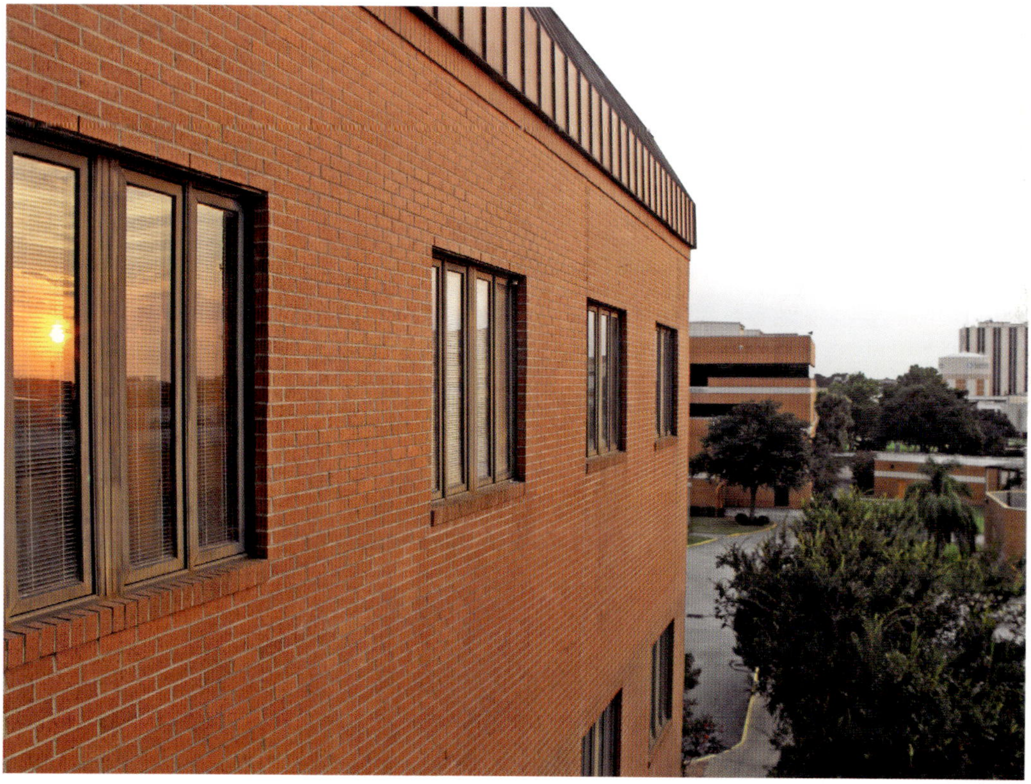

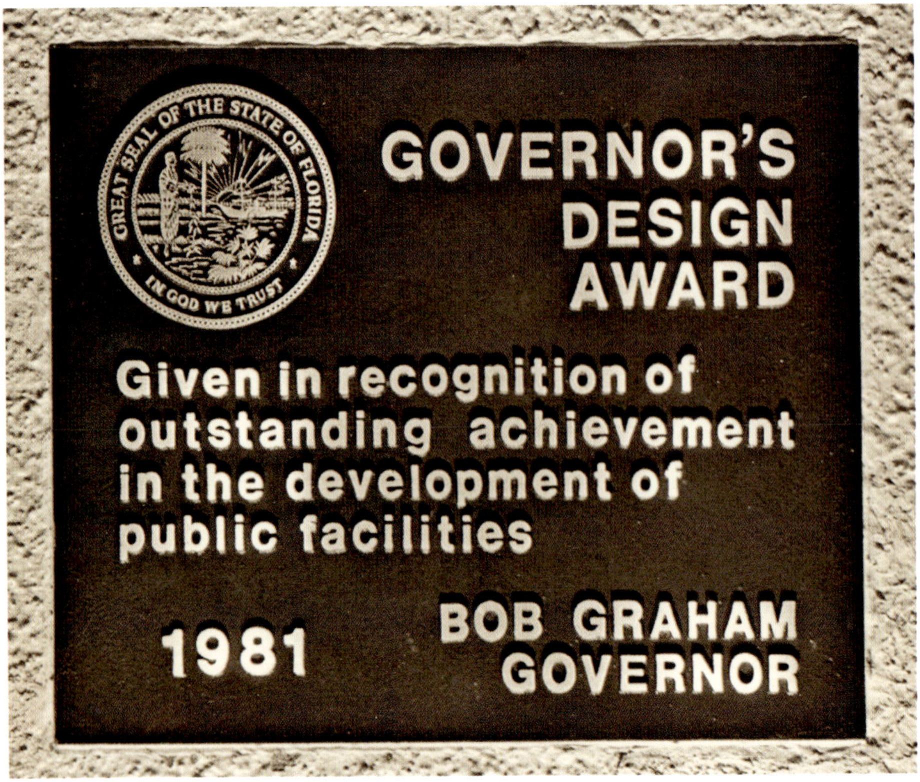

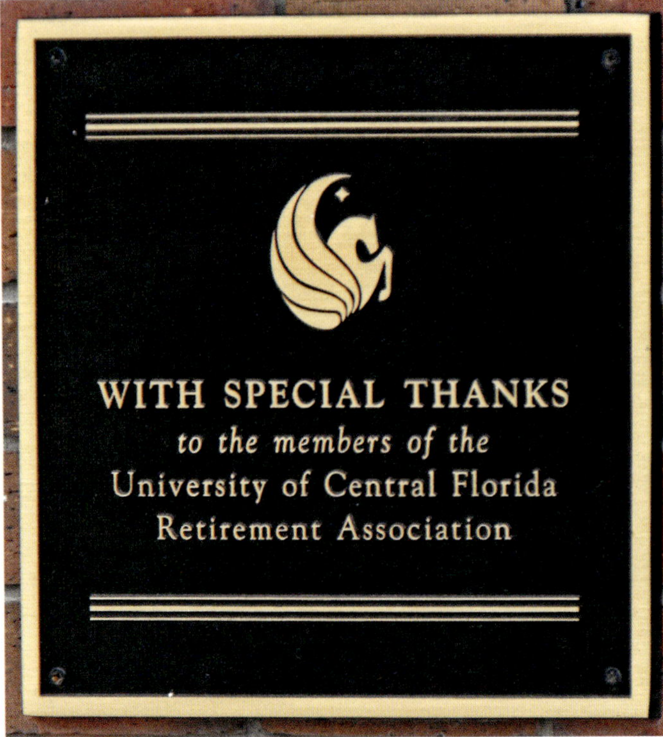

STATE OF EDUCATION: Plaques throughout campus not only acknowledge outstanding awards, but give recognition to the thousands of individuals and organizations which make up the UCF community.

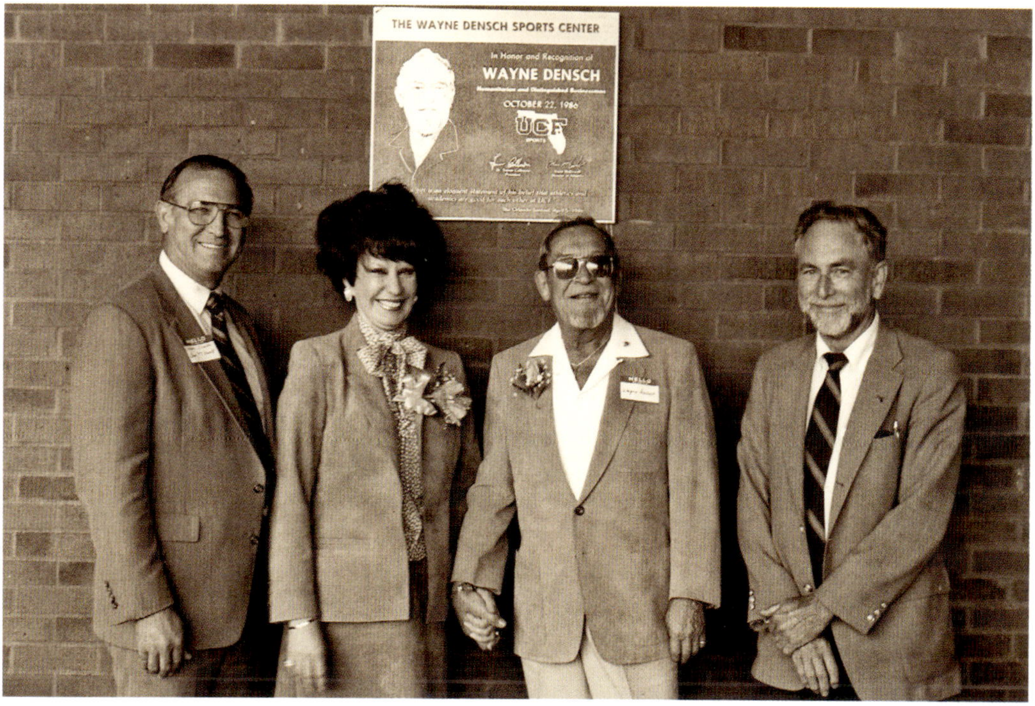

COMMUNITY IMPACT: Wayne and Ann Densch stand proudly with UCF dignitaries before a plaque designating the Wayne Densch Sports Complex on 22 October, 1988. Densch is a local philanthropist who believes strongly in academics and athletics for UCF. There's a strong sense of community at UCF, and throughout campus you will find standards bearing the national, state, and university flags.

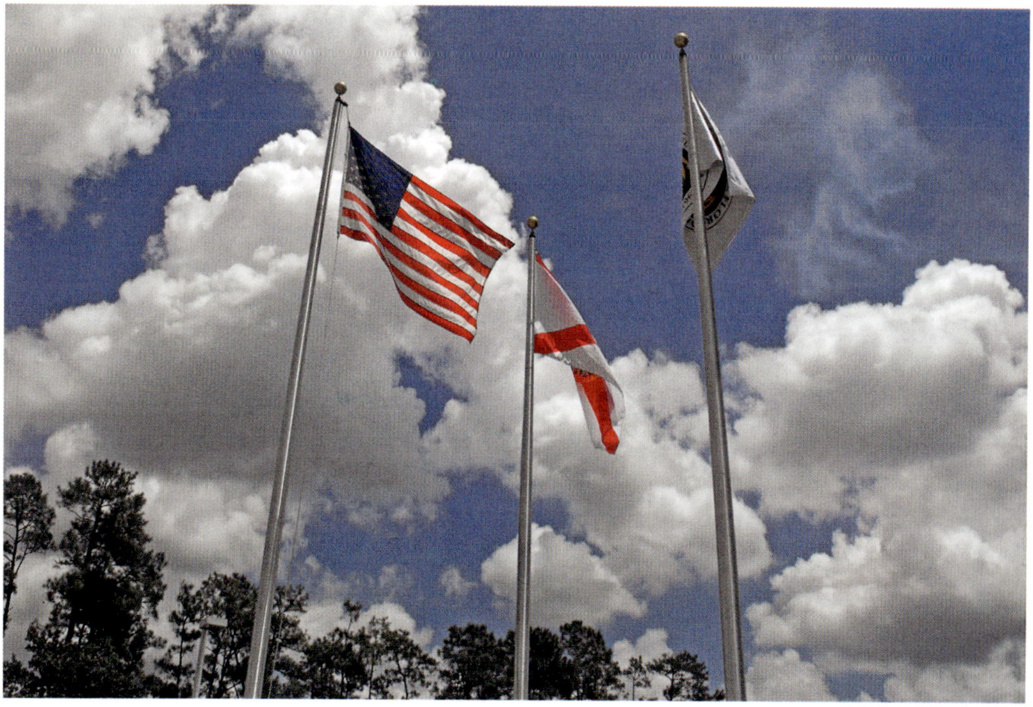

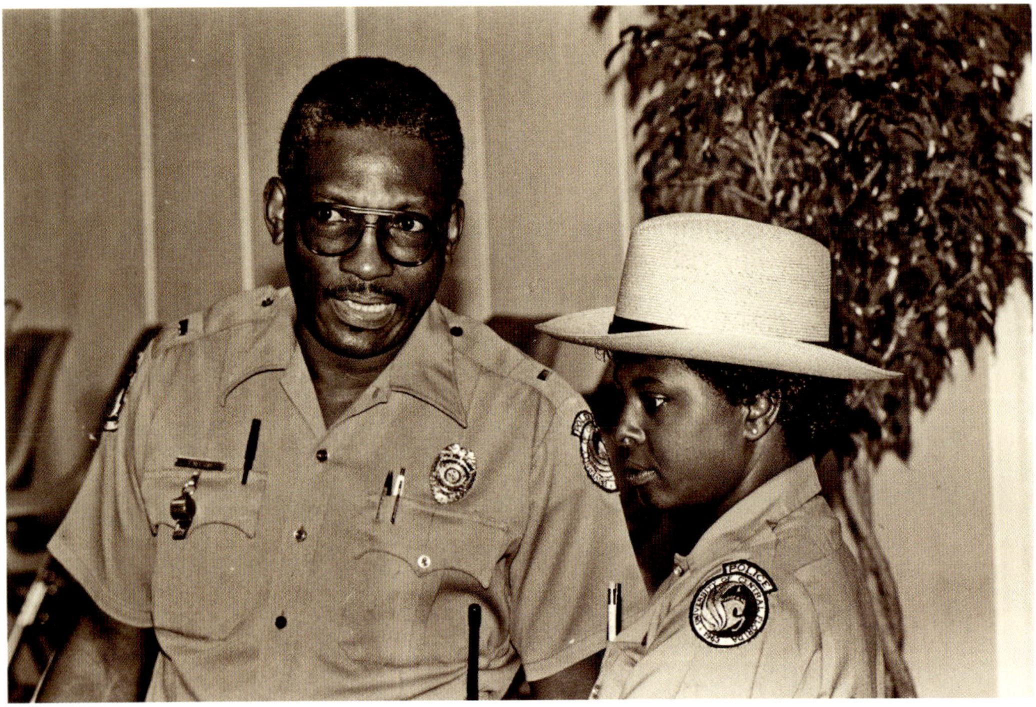

IN MEMORY: Campus police officers Tommie Nelson and Sandra McClindon hold a discussion. An impressive sculpture commemorates the service of Mario Jenkins and fellow officers in front of the UCF police department. Jenkins was killed in the line of duty at the UCF Citrus Bowl in 2005, working undercover to control illegal drinking.

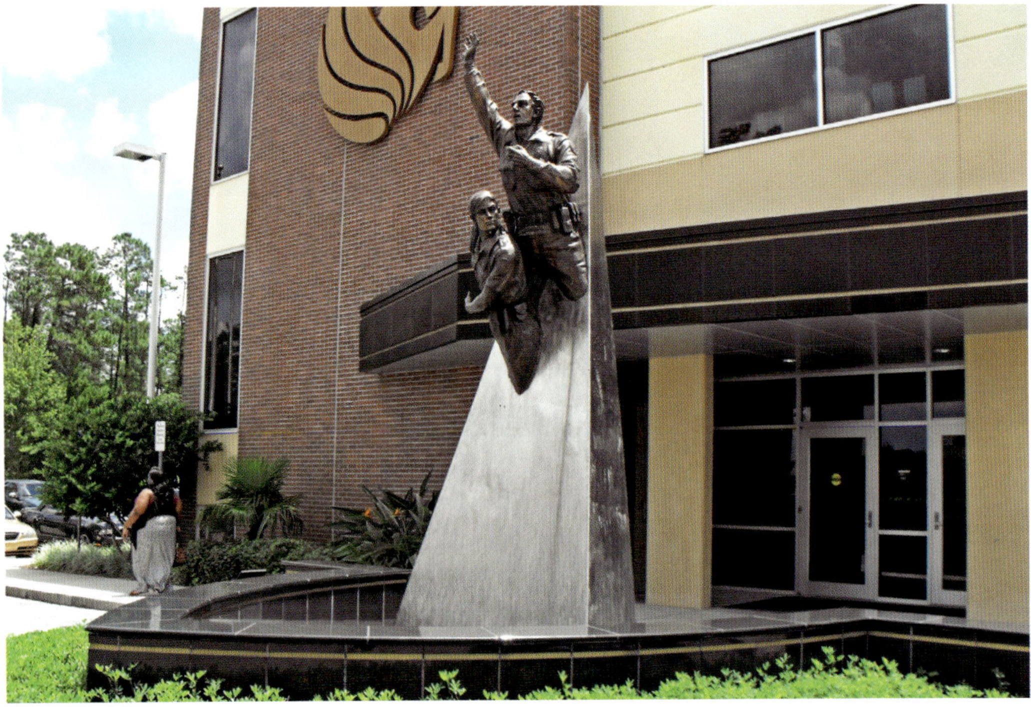

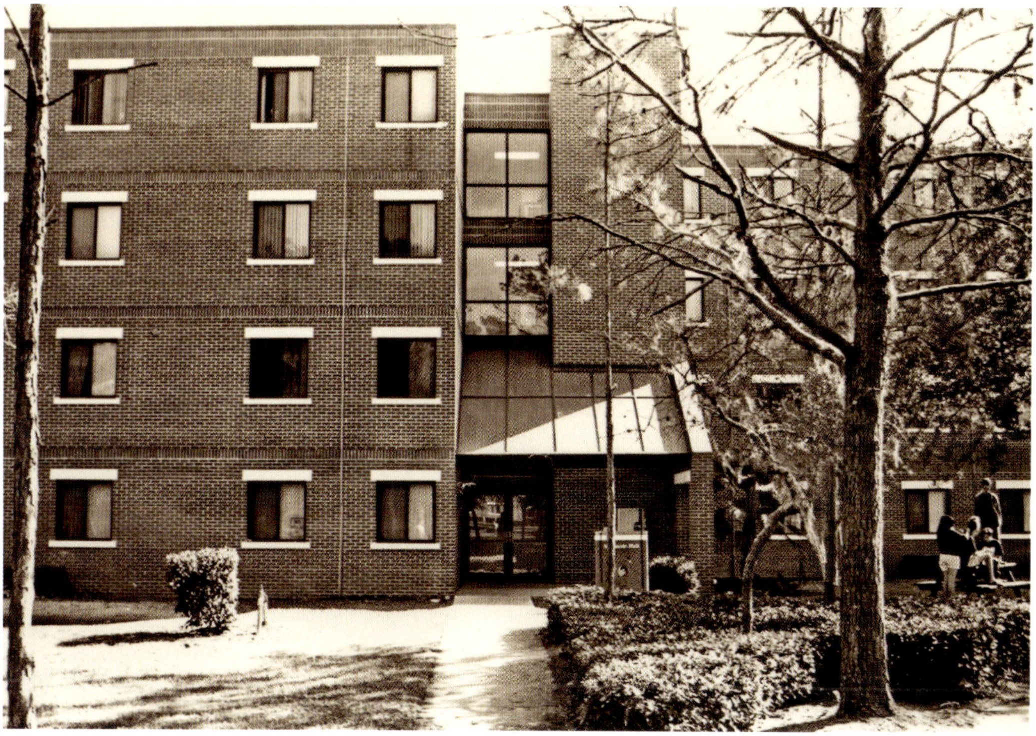

UPWARD BOUND: With the rapid growth of the UCF student body, it becomes necessary to increase the number of housing units on campus. One direction to go with new housing is up!

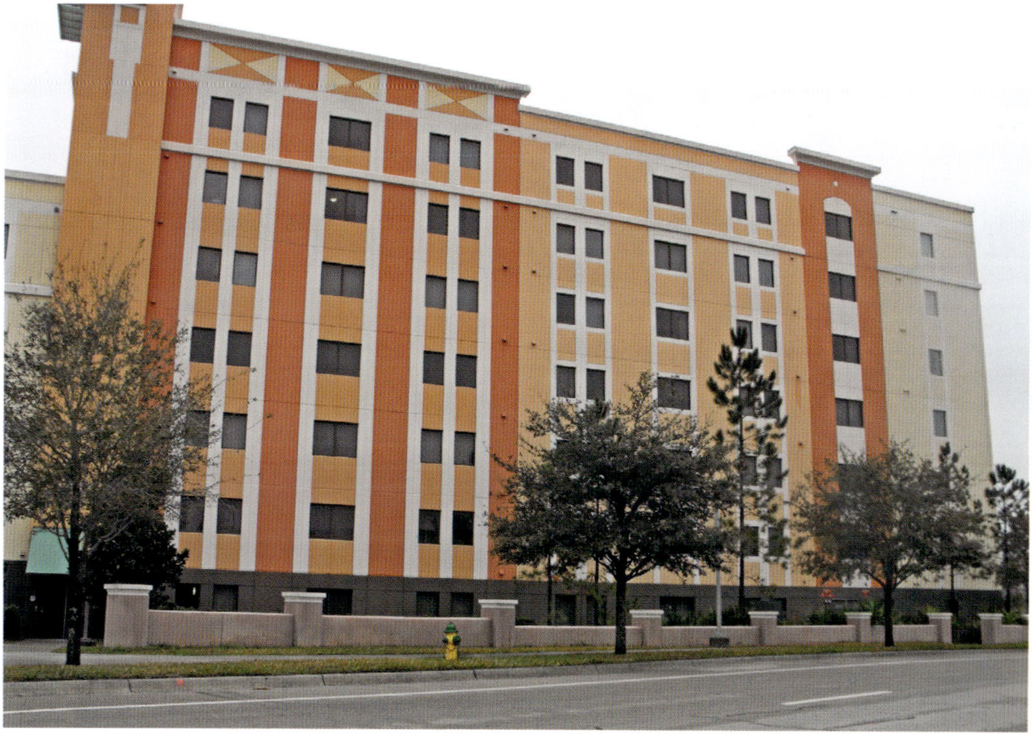

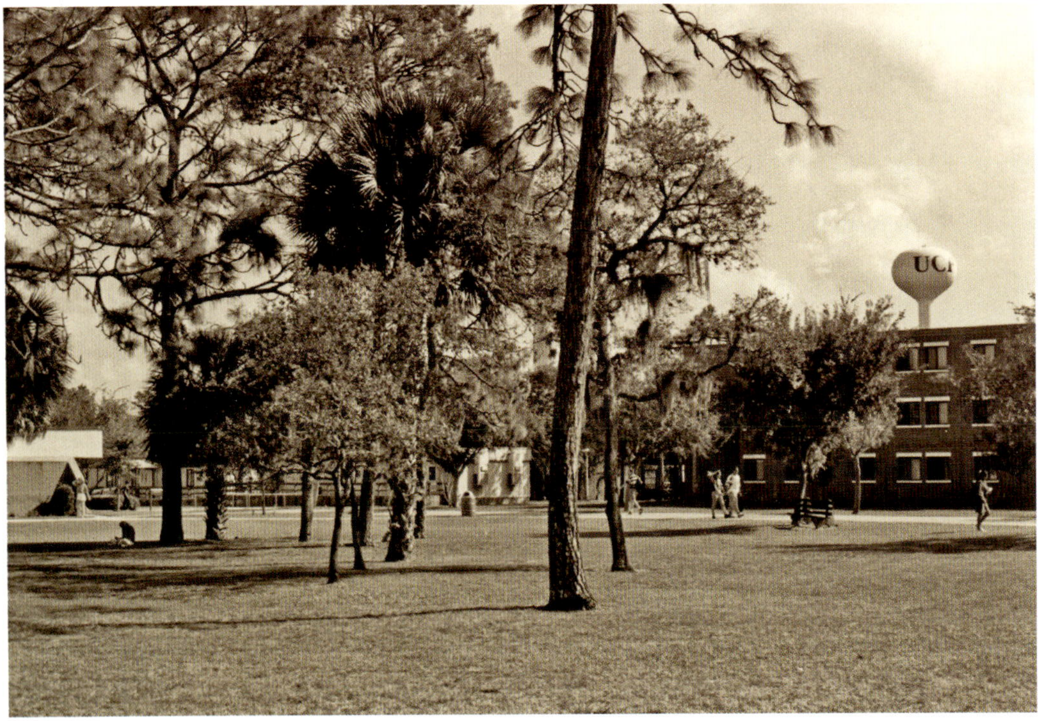

POINT OF NAVIGATION: It can be disorienting to navigate such a large campus. The water tower is a marker which can be seen for miles around, and is located on the south side of campus close to the police department.

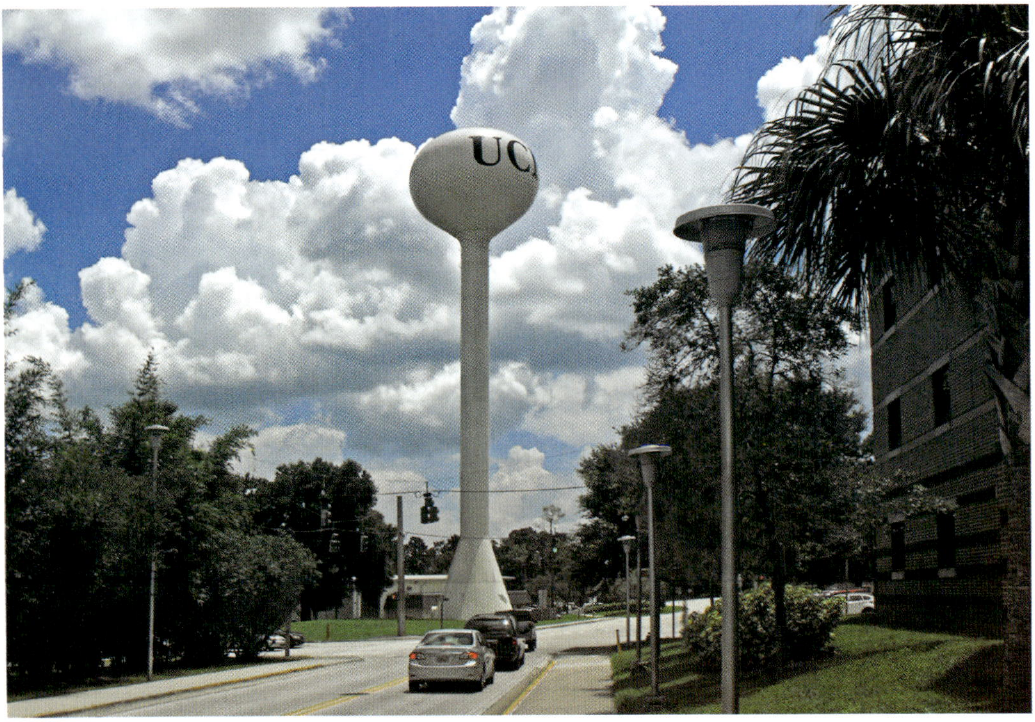

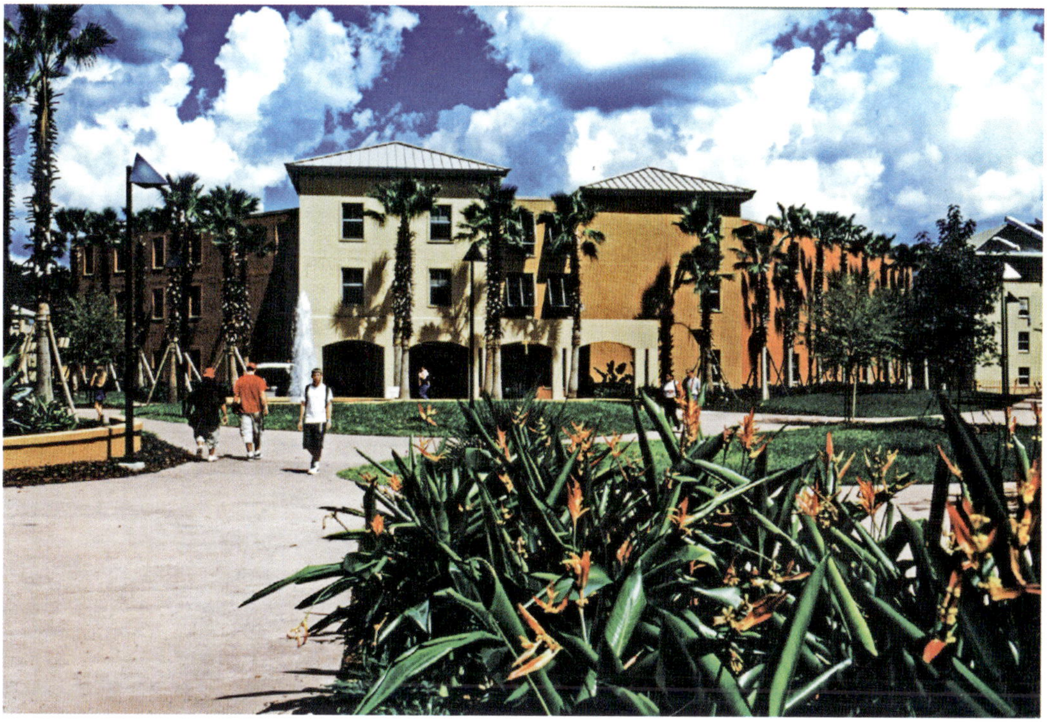

LUSH LIFE: Florida boasts a wide variety of natural plant life, including lovely birds-of-paradise, magnolia trees, and a wide variety of palm trees. Most of the young trees planted when main campus opened have become mature and help provide much-needed shade.

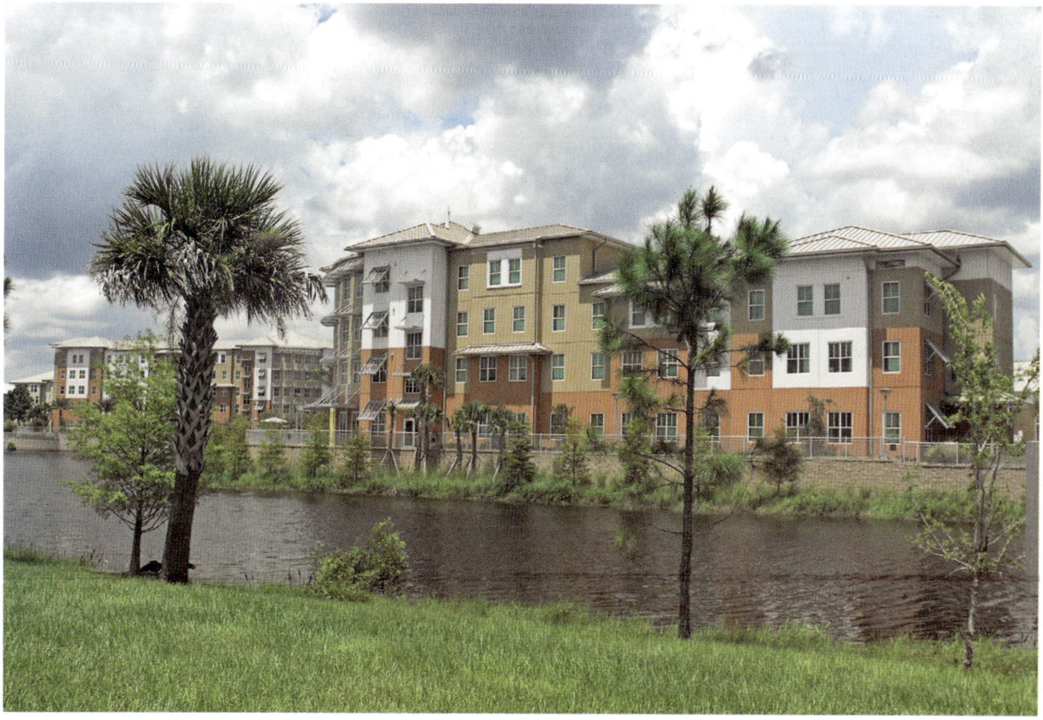

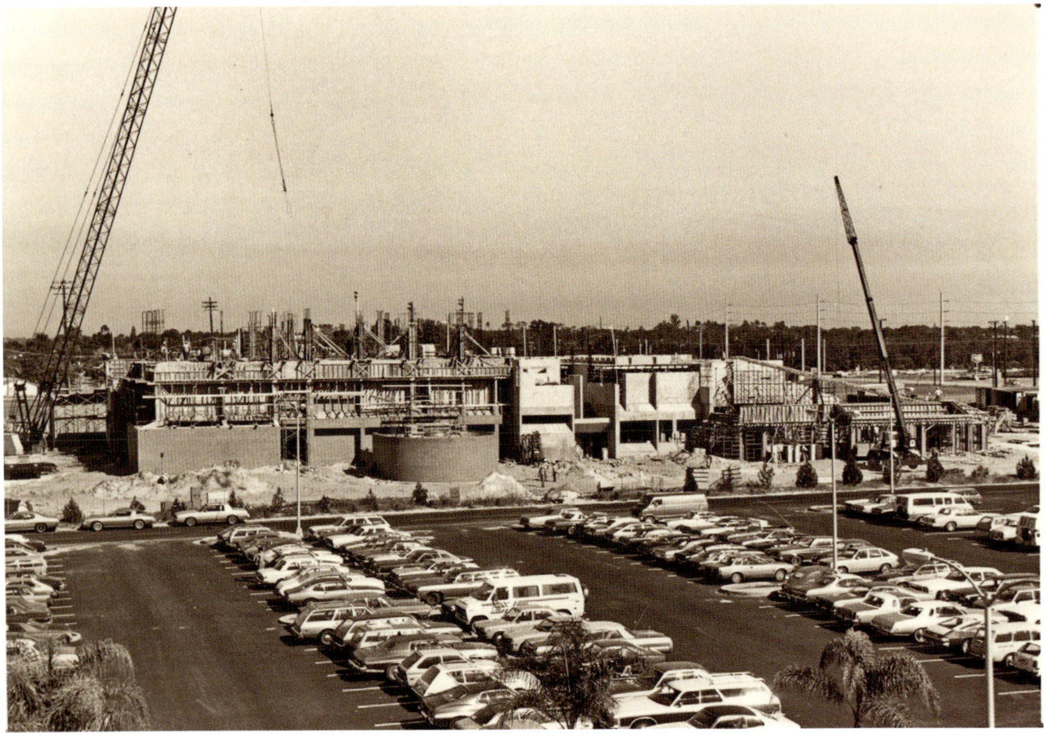

SMART ABOUT SPACE: The construction of the Brevard Campus and the finished Daytona Campus: note the huge canvas shade which covers the atrium, necessary under the hot Florida sun, of the rear building.

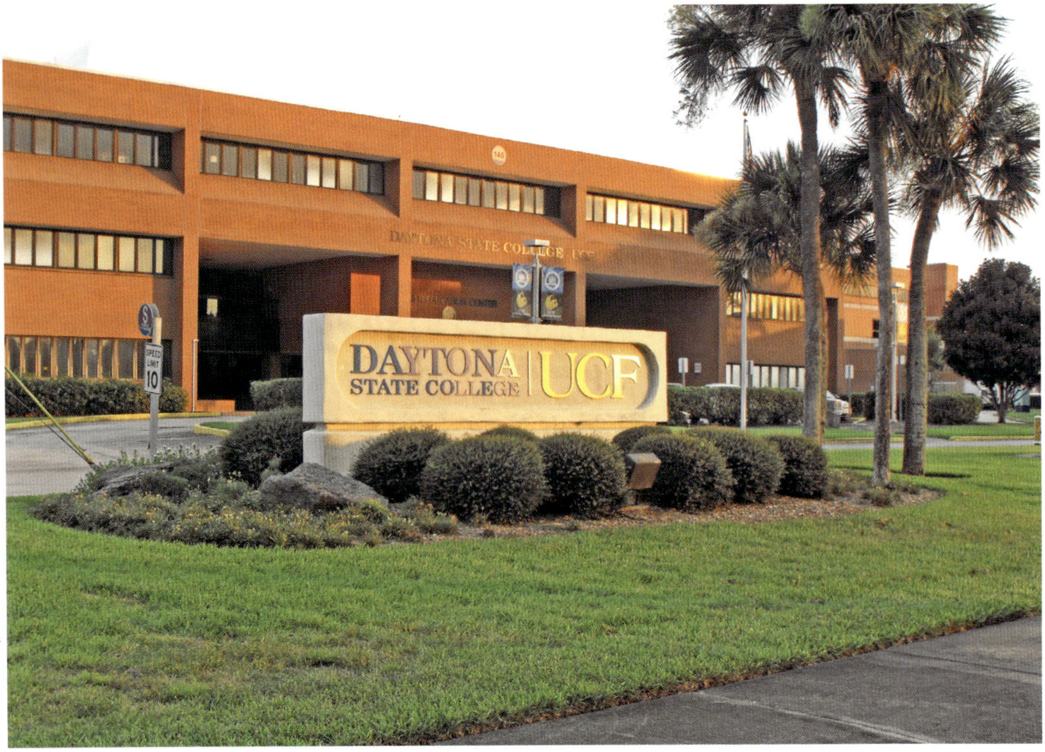

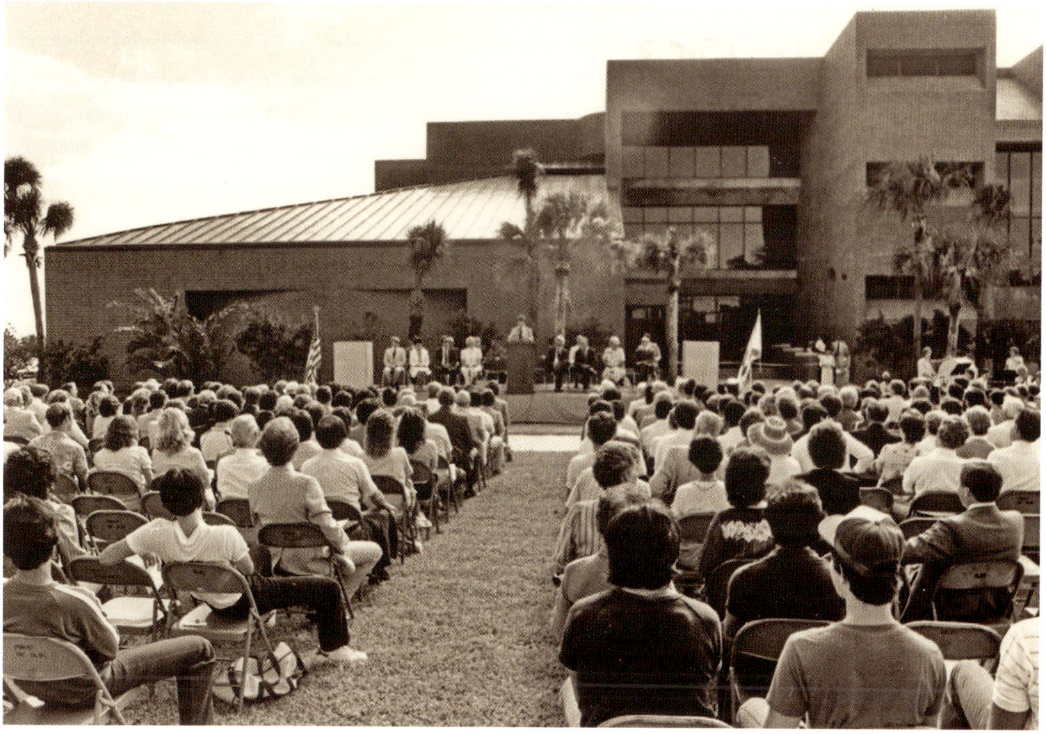

RAPID GROWTH: In much of the nation, most of education takes place indoors. In Florida, classes, and ceremonies, can take advantage of the year-round mild weather. It is a big plus.

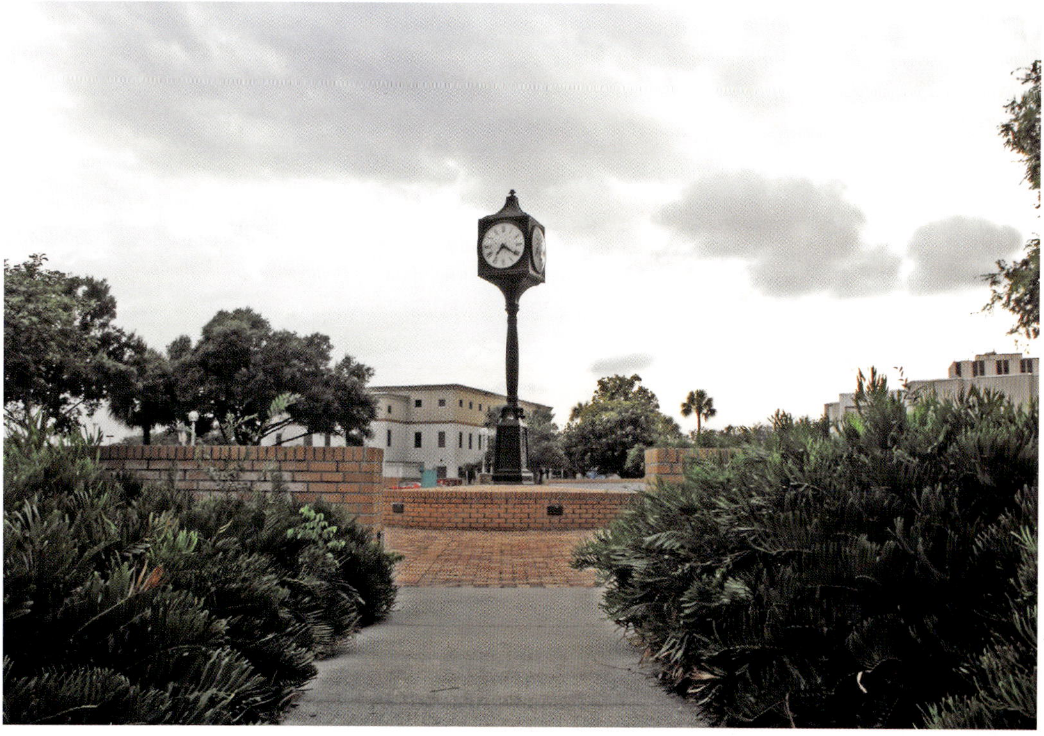

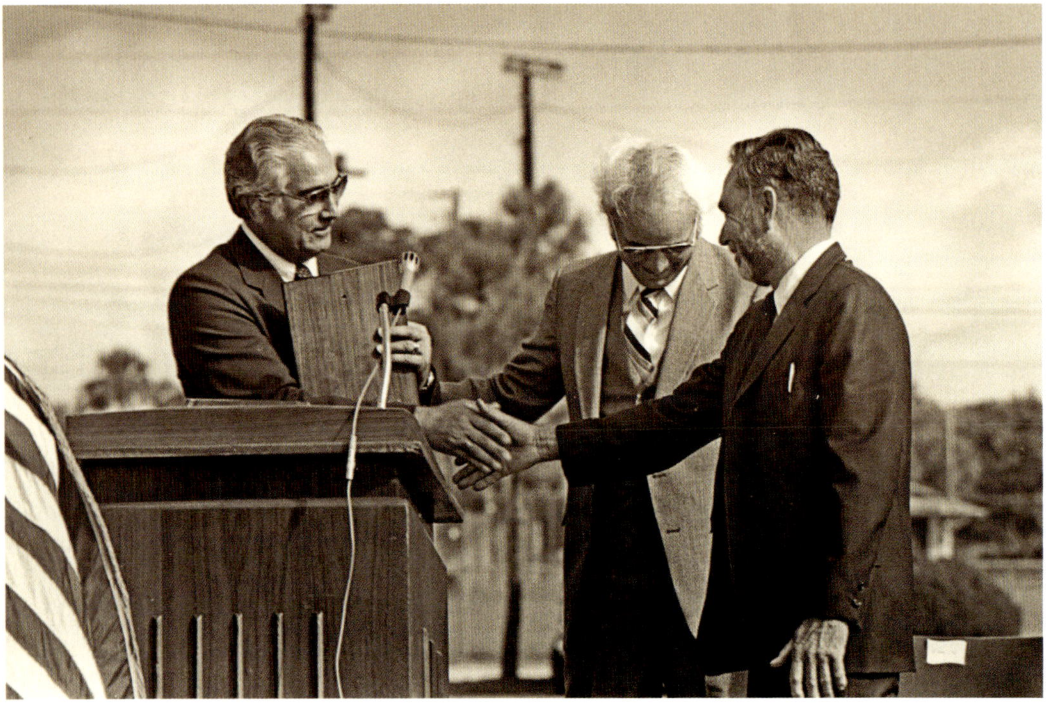

POMP AND CEREMONY: Three dignitaries celebrate the opening of the Clark Maxwell, Jr. Lifelong Learning Center at the Brevard campus on 2 October 1980: Dr. Tesori and Dr. Colbourn shake hands while Maxwell King of Brevard Community College looks on. Modern spaces to relax and to celebrate abound on all campuses.

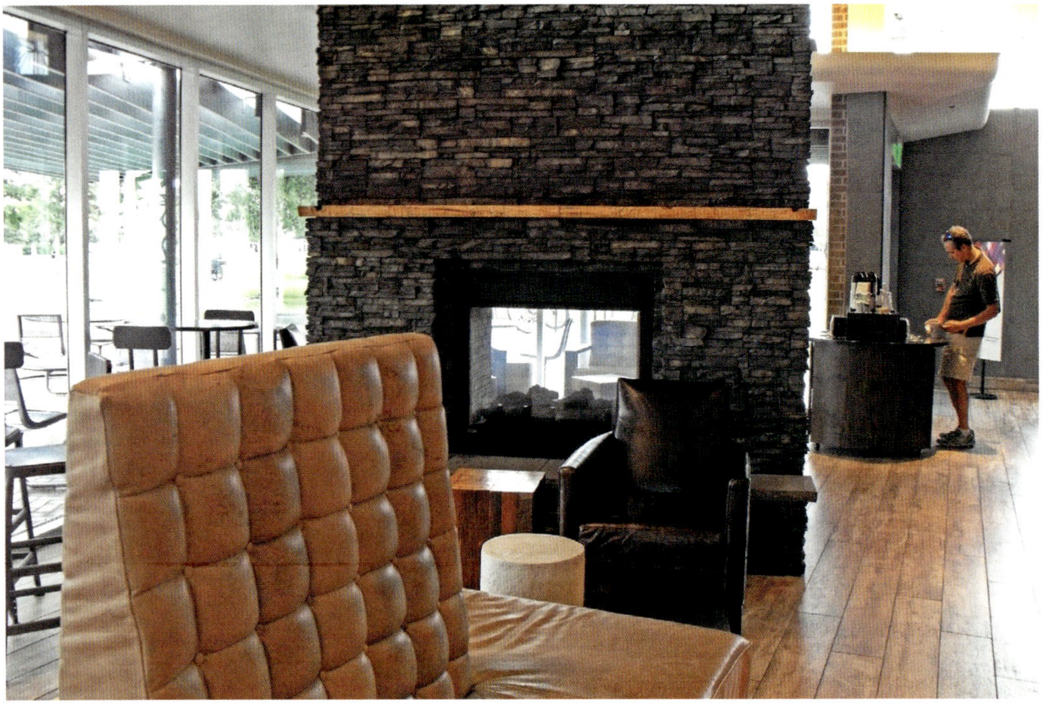

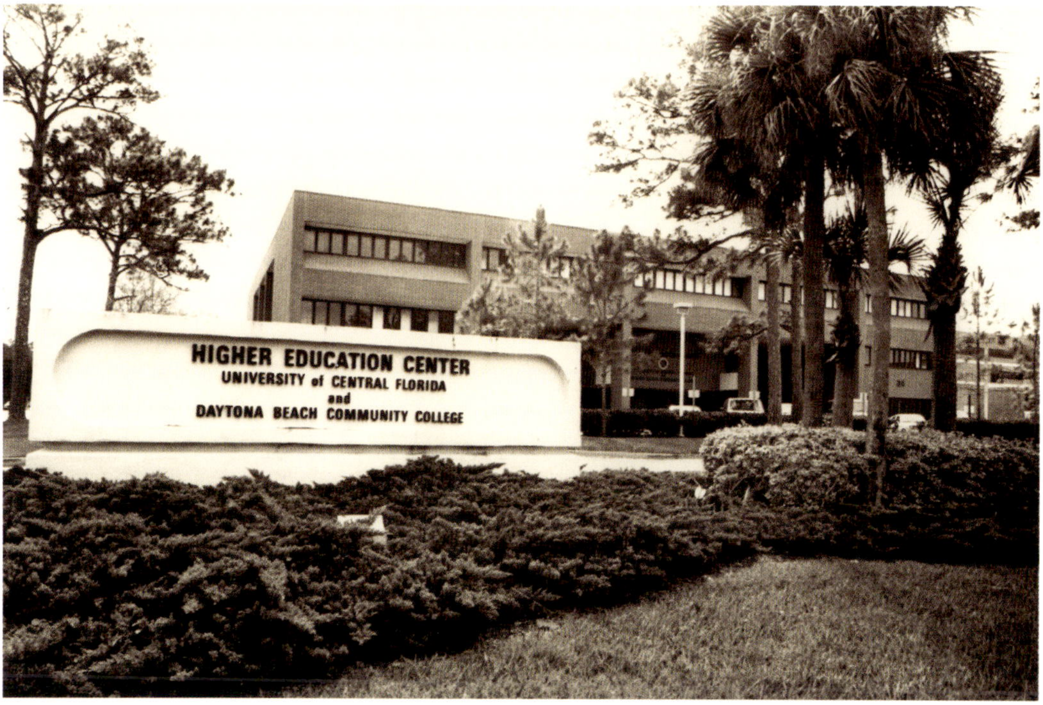

COMBINING FORCES: Daytona Beach Community College, formerly Daytona Junior College, is now Daytona State College. Just out in front of campus, on International Speedway Boulevard, the old is contrasted with the new: a sign for a college with a new name stands on one side of the street while an old entrance to a Daytona subdivision, built to mimic much older Spanish structures, stands opposite.

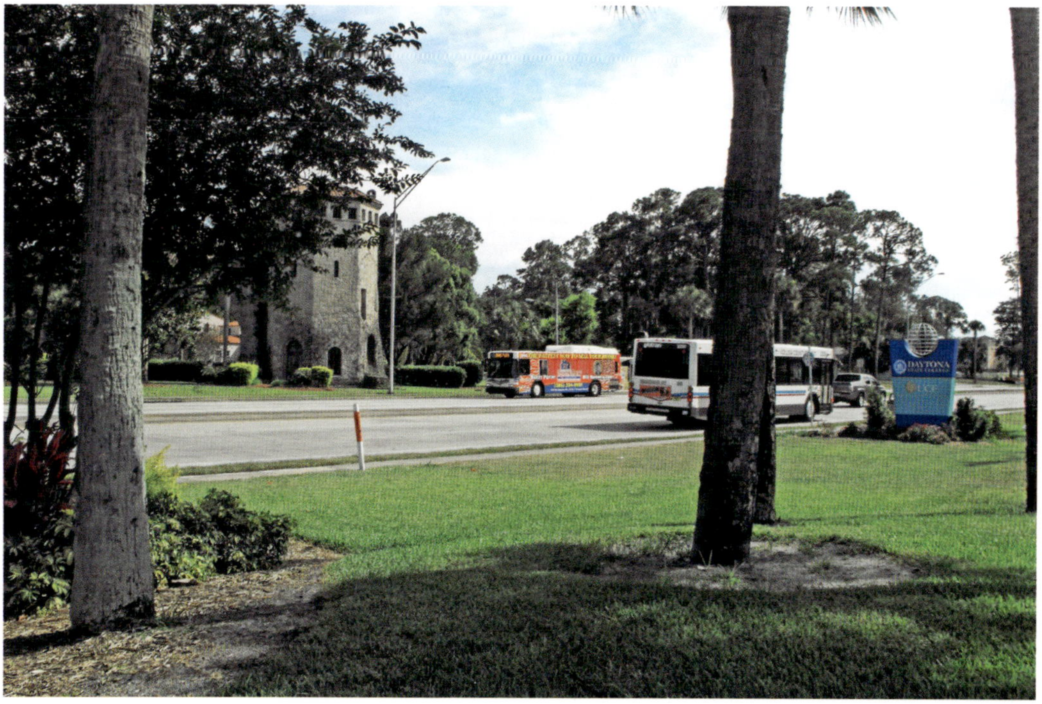

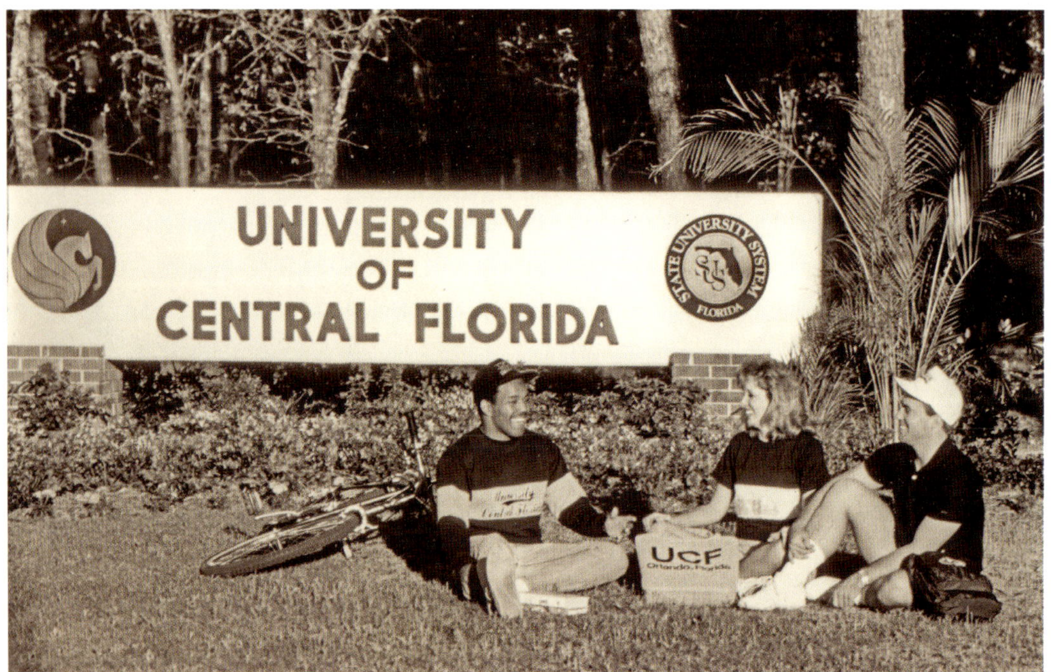

UPDATING: In 1978 Florida Technological University was renamed the University of Central Florida to reflect the academic focus expanding well beyond the original engineering and technology designed to support the nearby space program. UCF is now the second largest university, by enrollment population, in the United States.

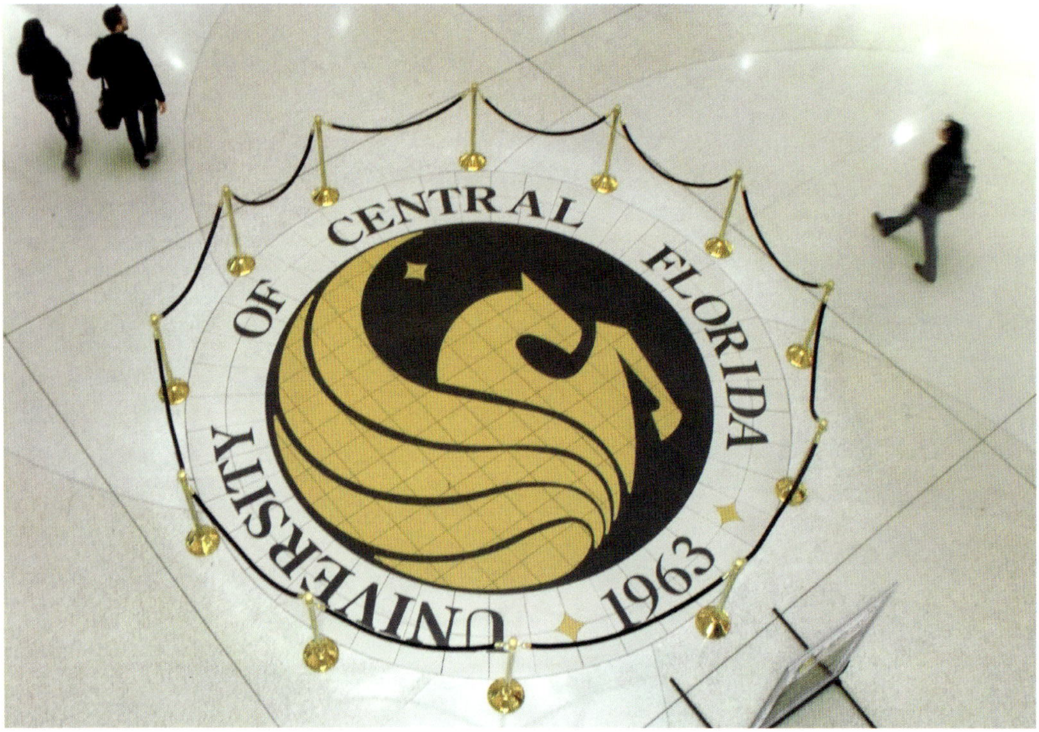

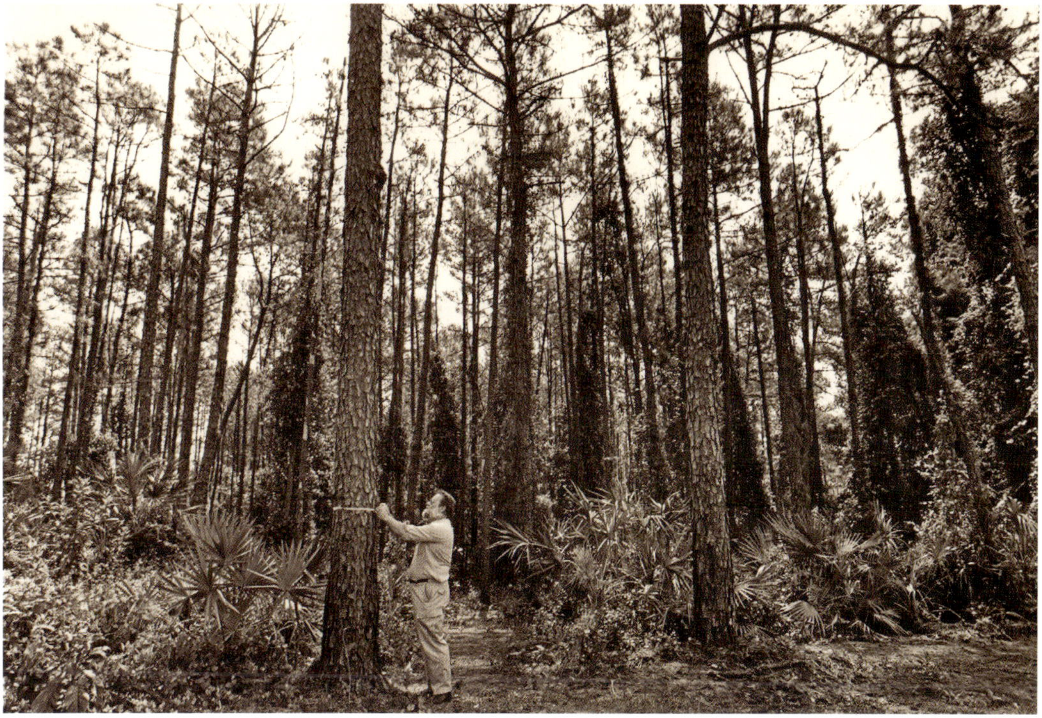

Beyond the classroom: The late Dr. Henry Whittier, botanist, measures the circumference of a tall pine not far from the courtyard at Ferrell Commons where students, staff, and faculty can pursue studies, eat, or just relax outdoors.

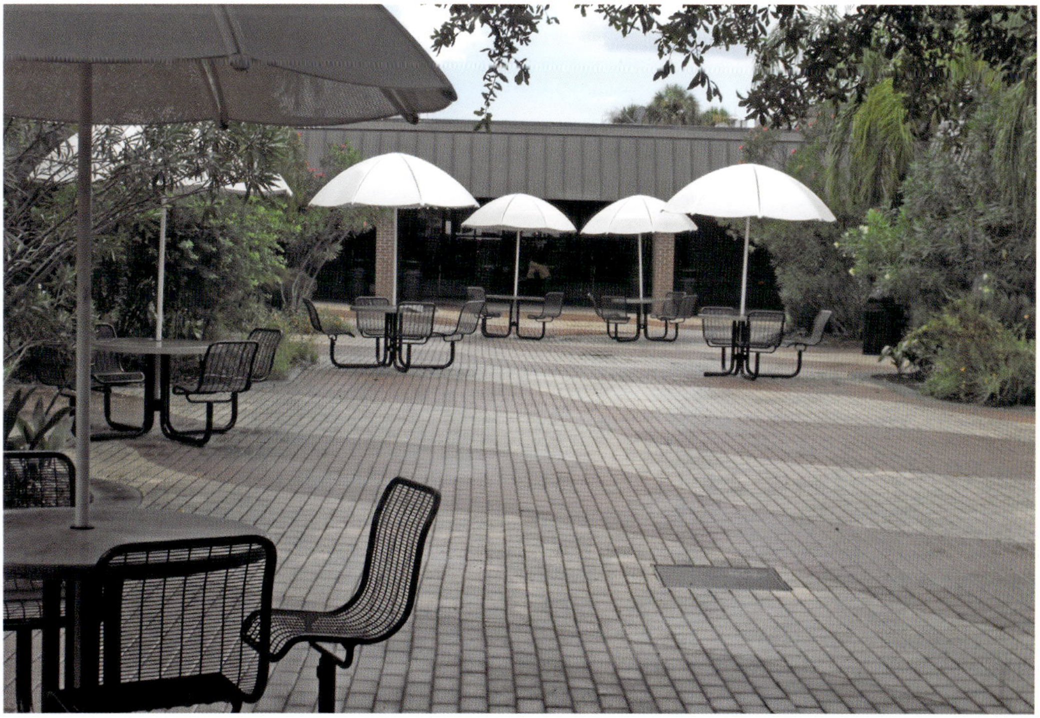

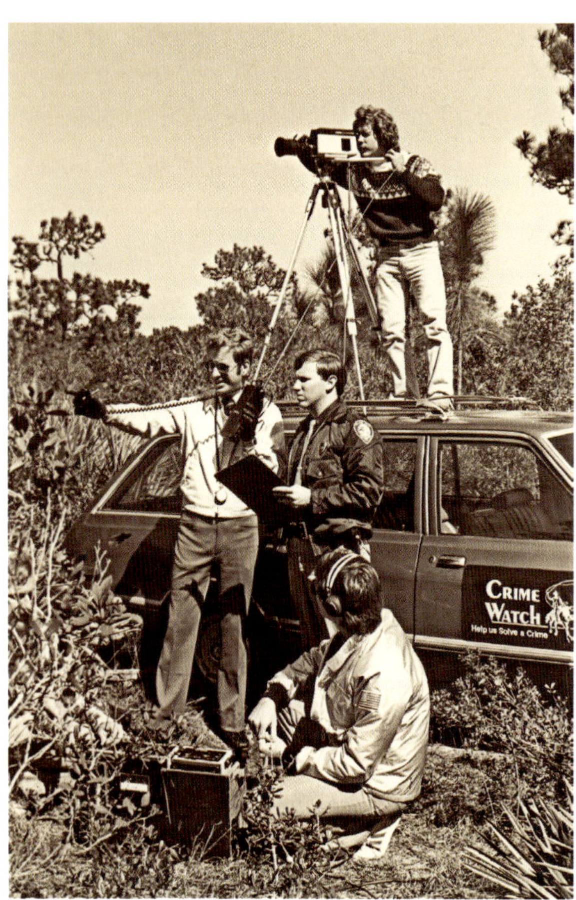

THE VALUE OF EXPERIENCE: Students need to gain experience in the real world to apply skills learned in the classroom. Changing times and technologies also mean changes in equipment. Modern digital recording devices would have been unimaginable just a few short years ago, and these bulky cameras now seem like, in fact are, artifacts.

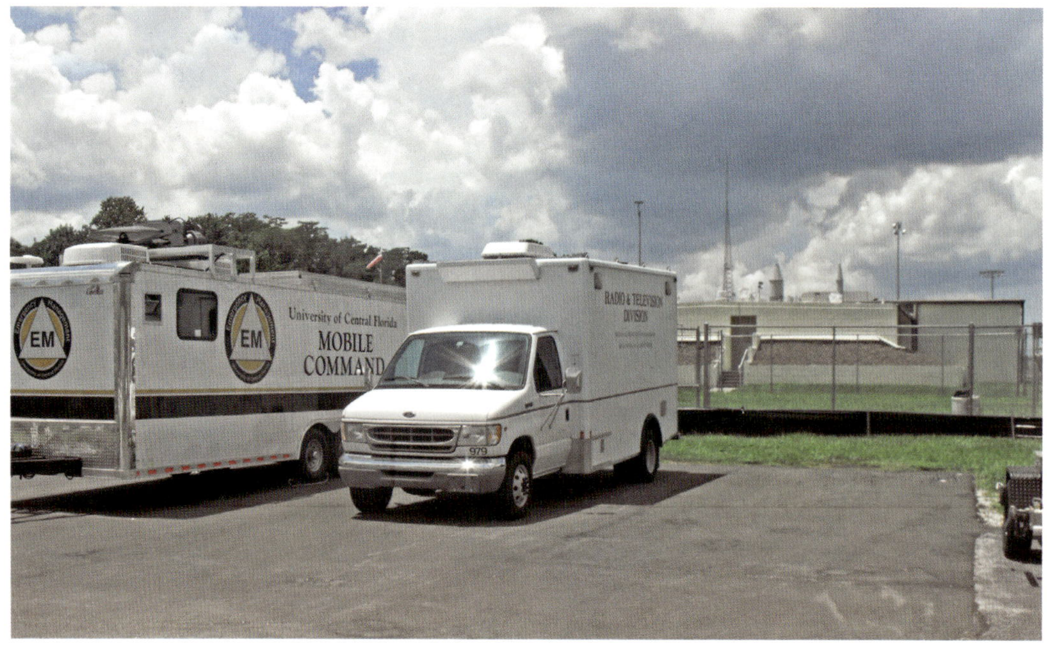

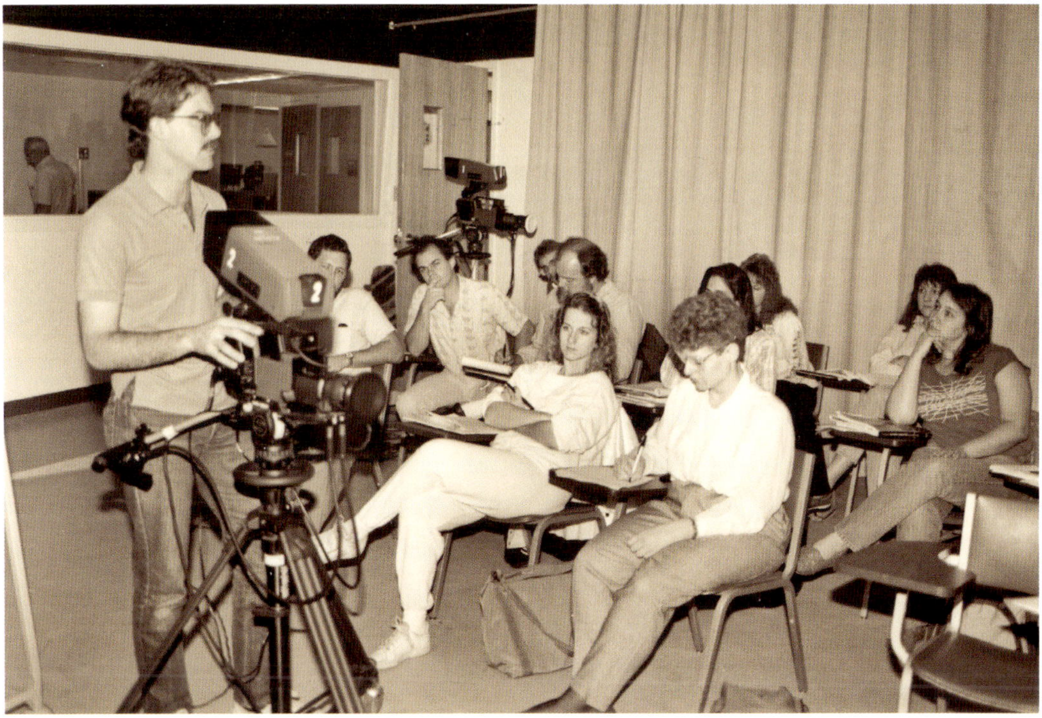

ACQUIRING THE SKILLS: Students work in Studio A, which was housed in the library basement. Even the perspectives walking into the front door of the library can be overwhelming; its five stories offer over 400 computer workstations for student use.

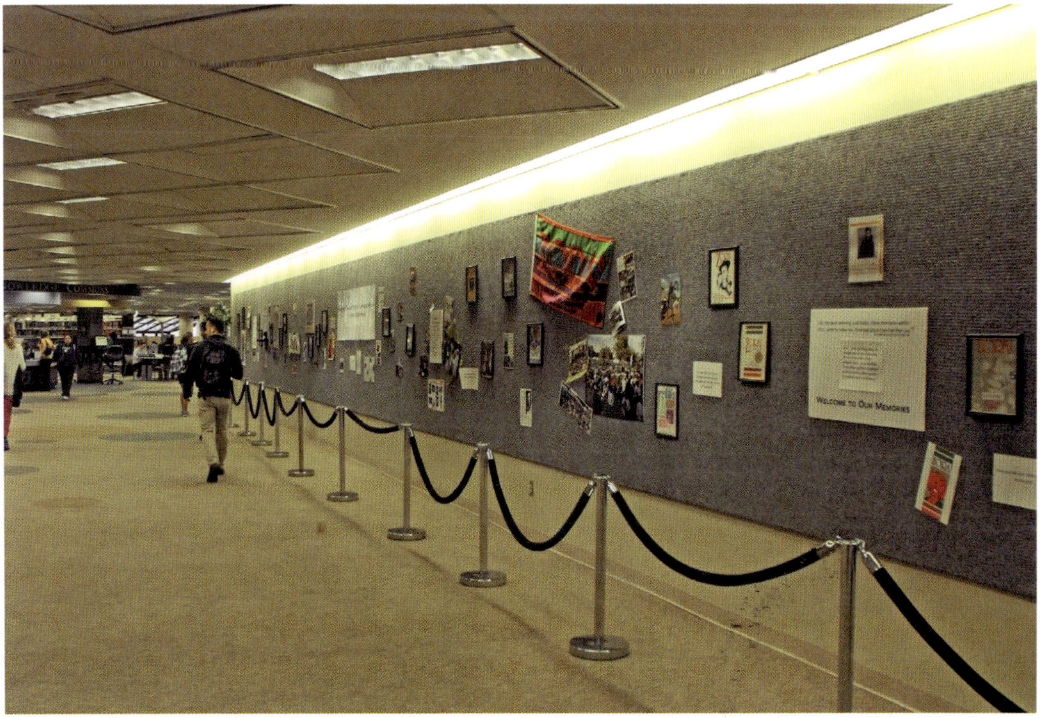

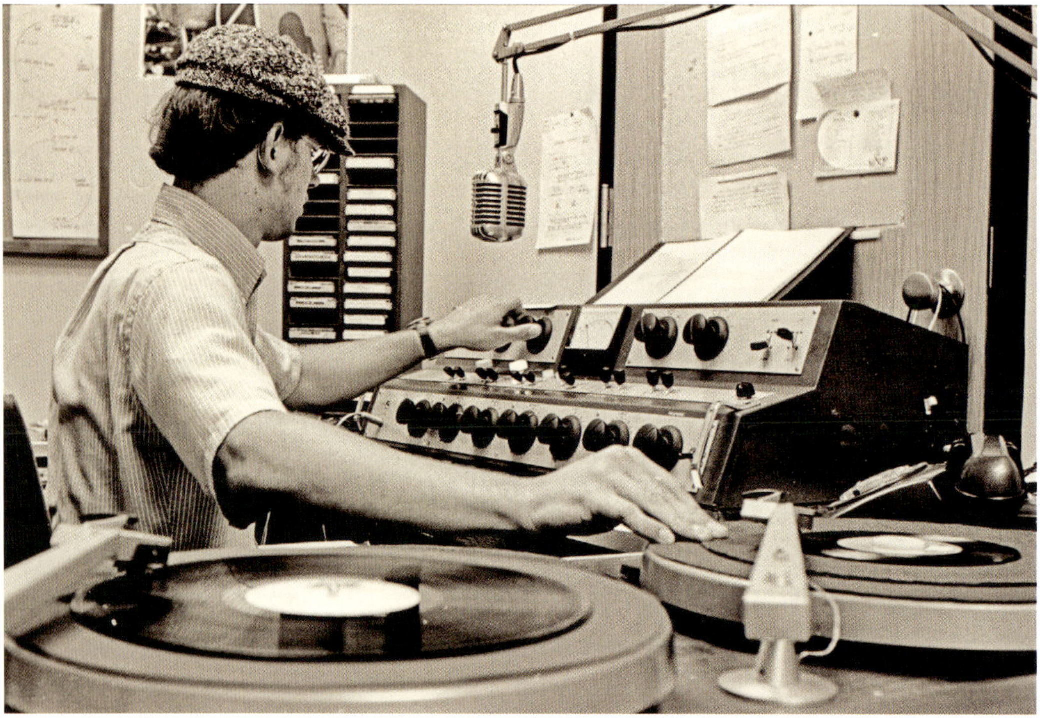

OUT WITH THE OLD: Students, these days, would find the use of a record player unbelievably quaint; CDs have taken the place of albums, earbuds the place of speakers. Students can listen to their favorite tunes right in the middle of the library without disturbing even the person working at the adjacent computer.

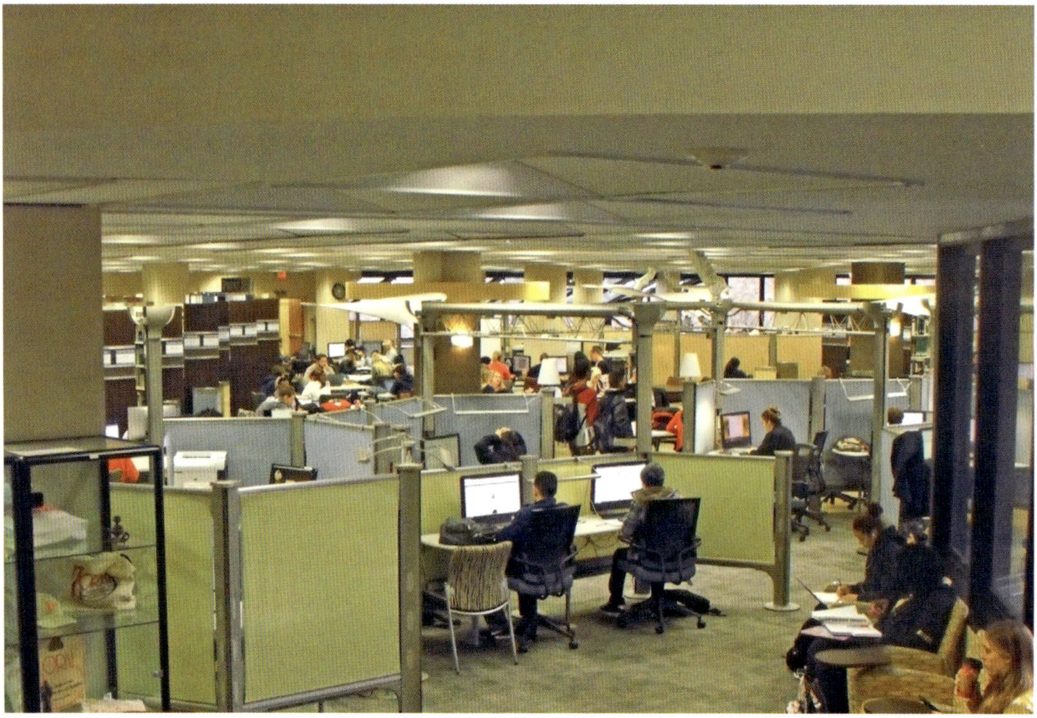

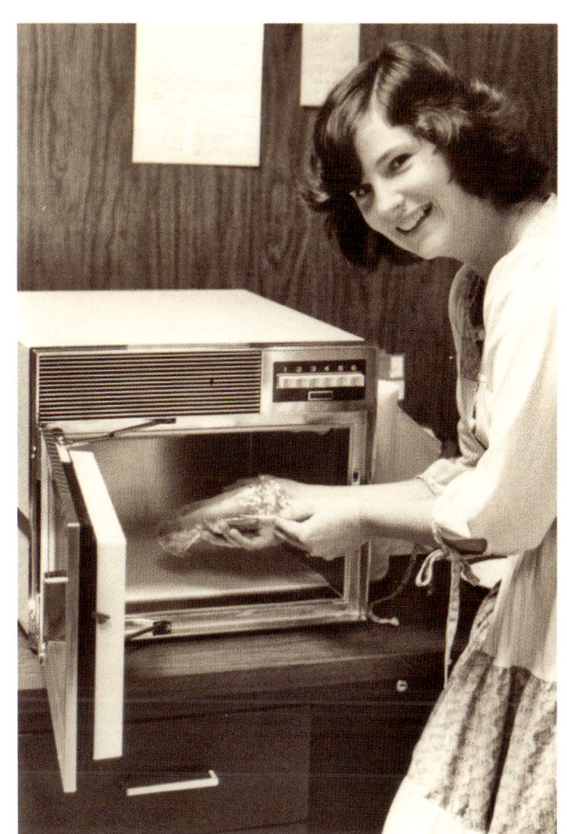

THE TEST OF TIME: While the microwave oven is an innovation which remains useful today, the huge satellite dishes pictured below have been rendered nearly obsolete.

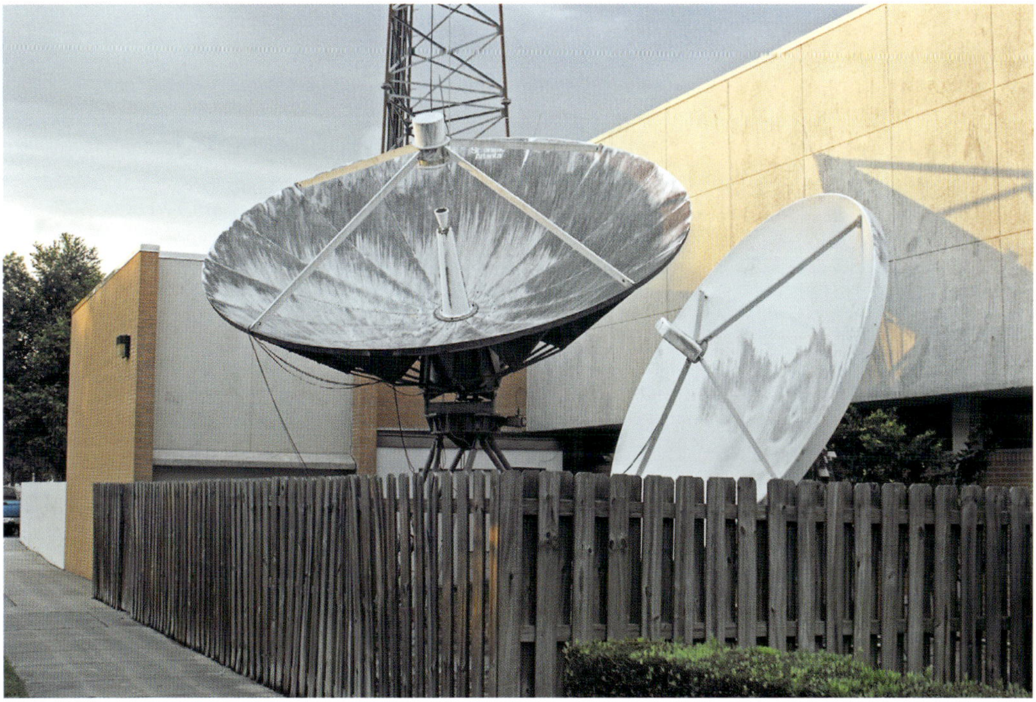

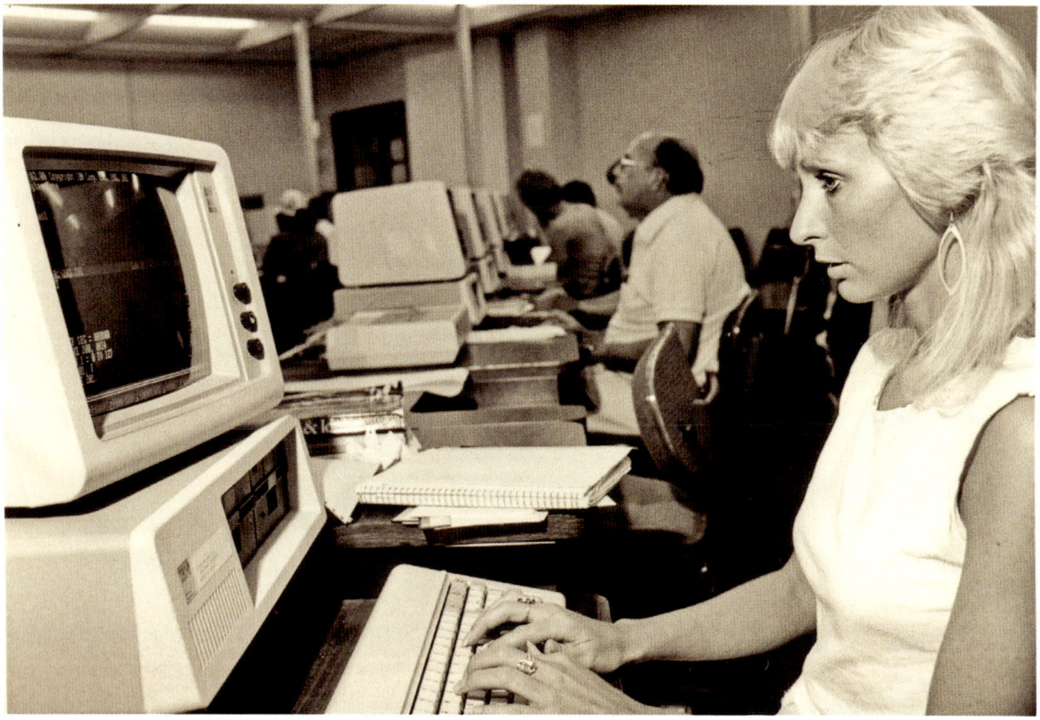

MOD OR MODERN? The archival picture features obsolete tools and a mod hairstyle. In the modern one, student Michelle Underwood uses the latest equipment to design materials to facilitate communicate for persons with Autism Spectrum Disorder.

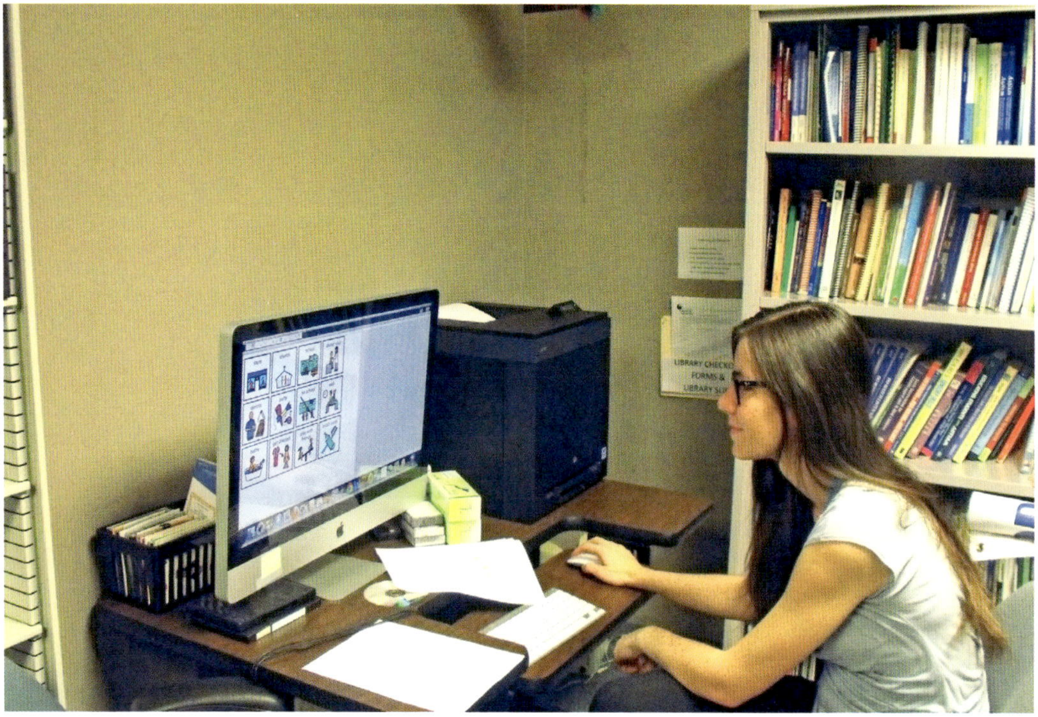

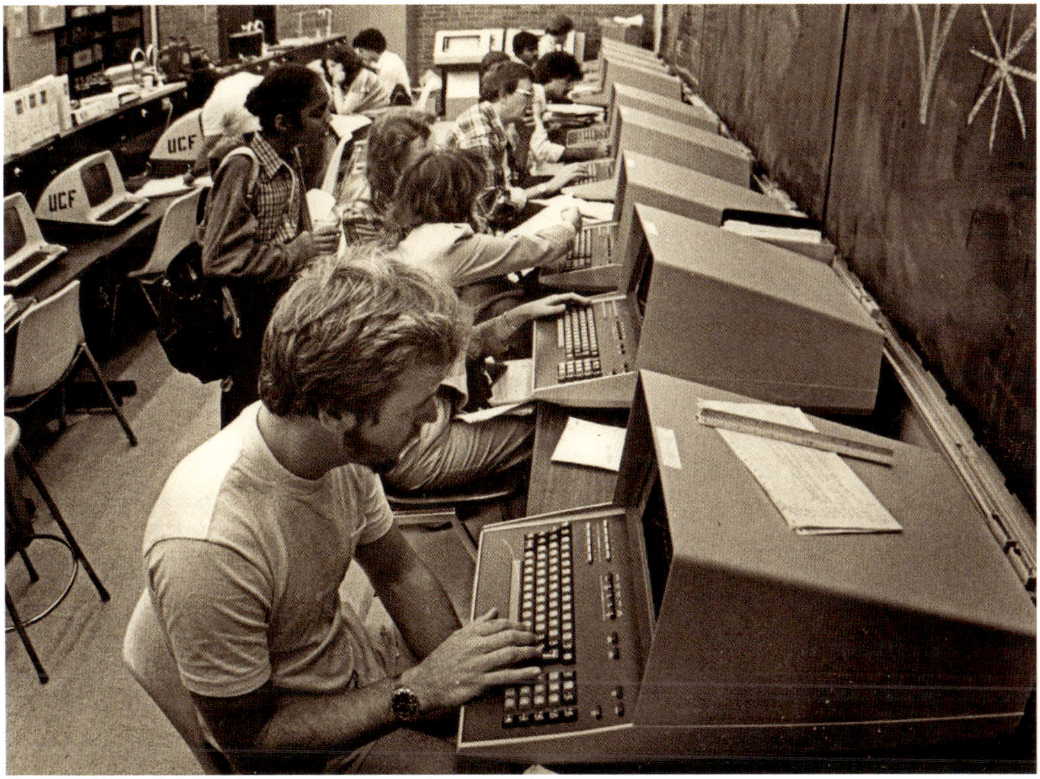

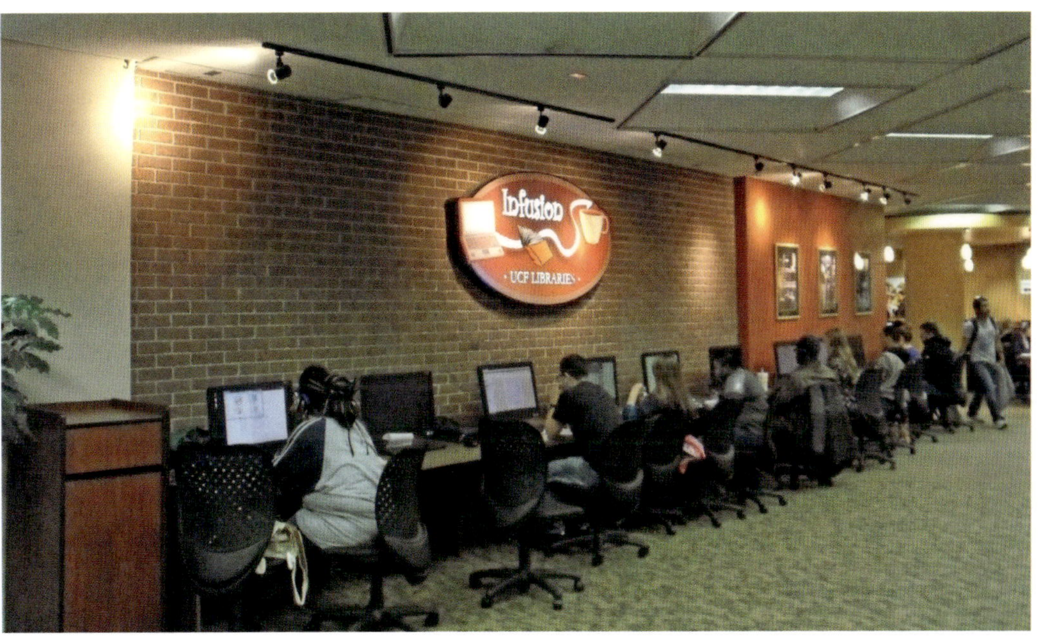

Updated: Students collaborate in a computer lab, and work individually in a coffee shop in the library at the main UCF campus. One of the important skills acquired or enhanced in any college program is the ability to team in order to complete a project or assignment. For some, particularly in the modern world of highly individualized instruction, entertainment, and education, this can be quite a challenge.

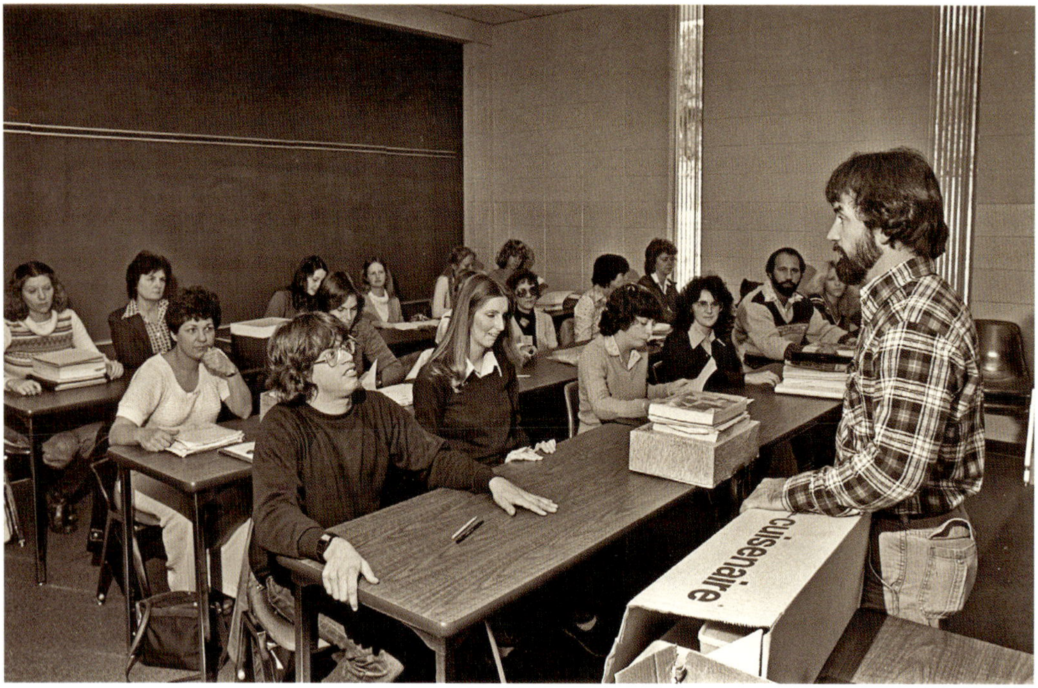

The ultimate equipage: Most modern classrooms at UCF are equipped with modern technology, including high-speed internet access for faculty and students and full projection equipment driven by the latest computers.

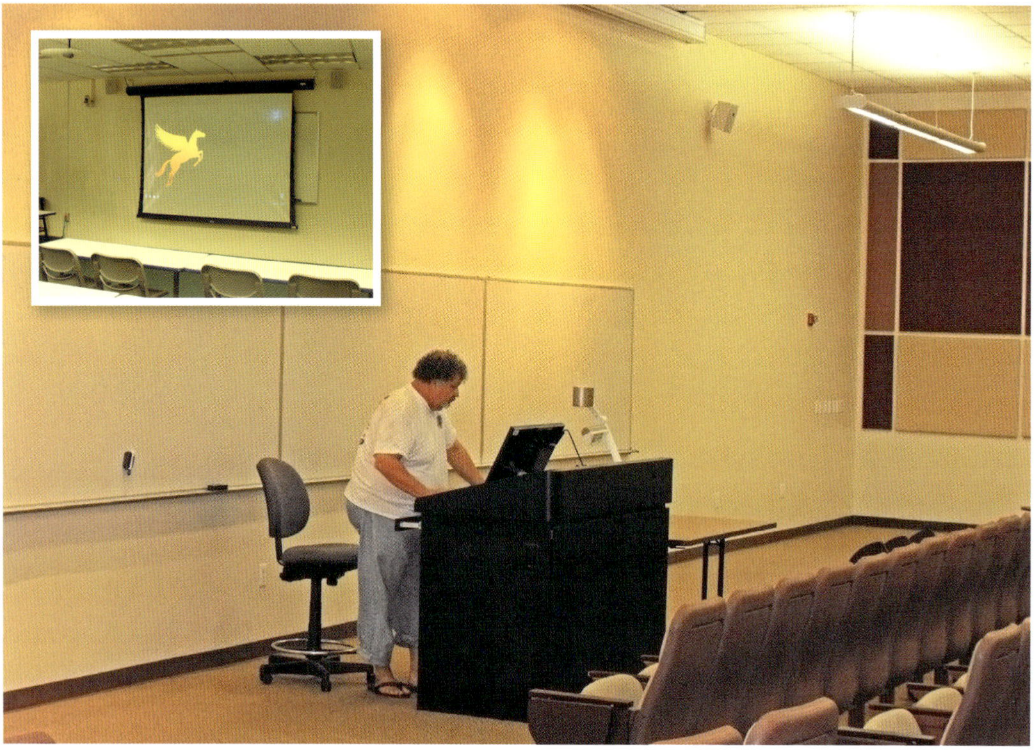

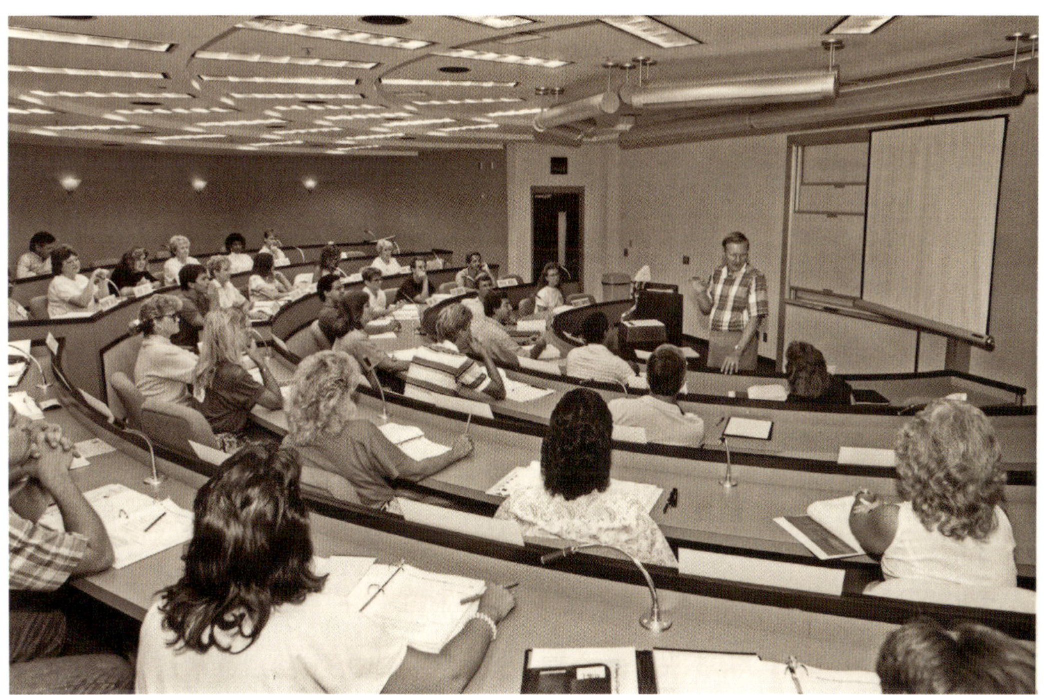

EDUCATIONAL EXPANSION: On 28 June 1989, Professor Bill Callerman taught the first class in the new College of Engineering and Business Administration building. While at that time the classroom in the upper photograph would have been considered large, auditoriums filled with students for one class are now common. This is due to the increase in student enrollment as well as the university's ability to meet the needs of that population through technology. Many classes, even degrees, are offered entirely online.

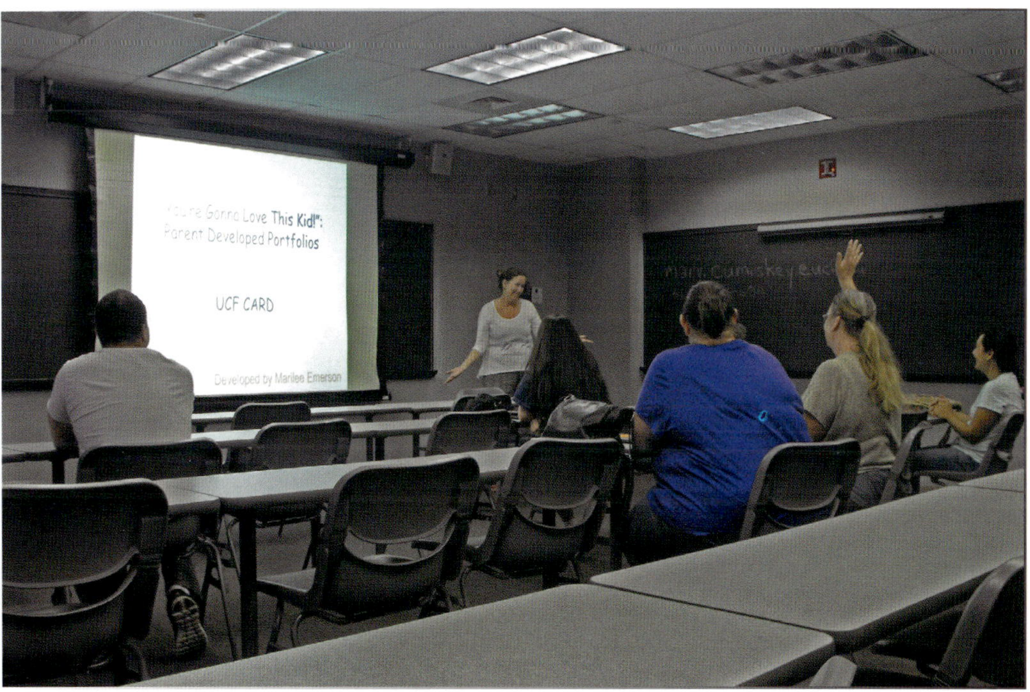

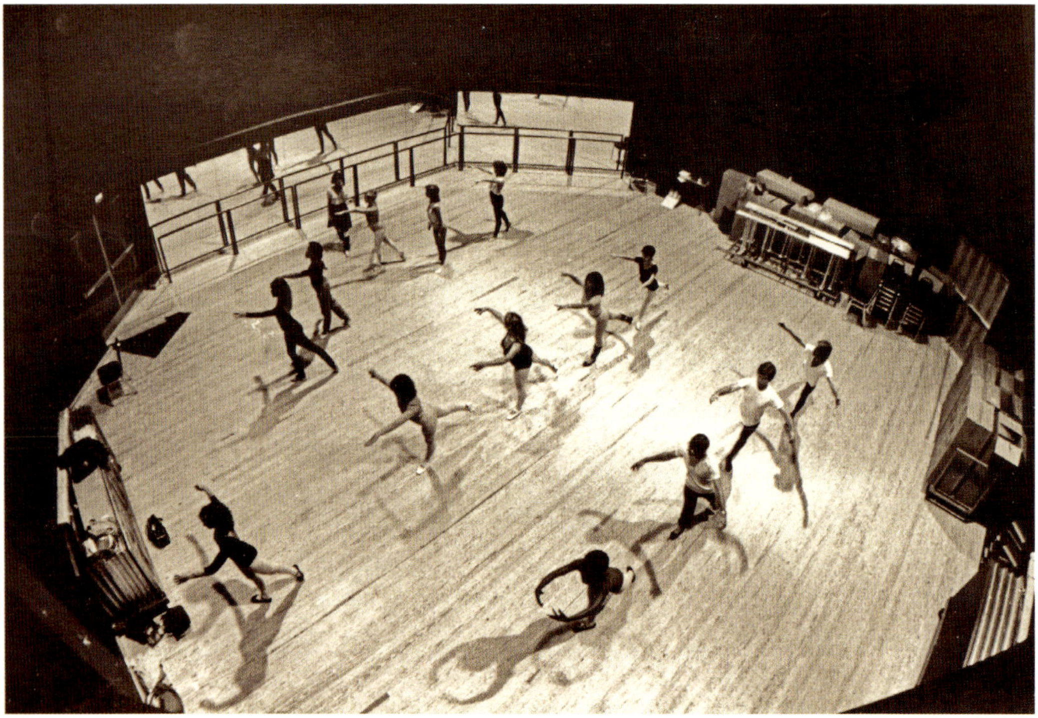

 A beginning ballet class meets in a studio on campus. The College of Arts and Humanities offers a minor in dance through the Theater Department, but many students take a dance class to fulfill elective requirements. Visual arts students use modern equipment in real time during class.

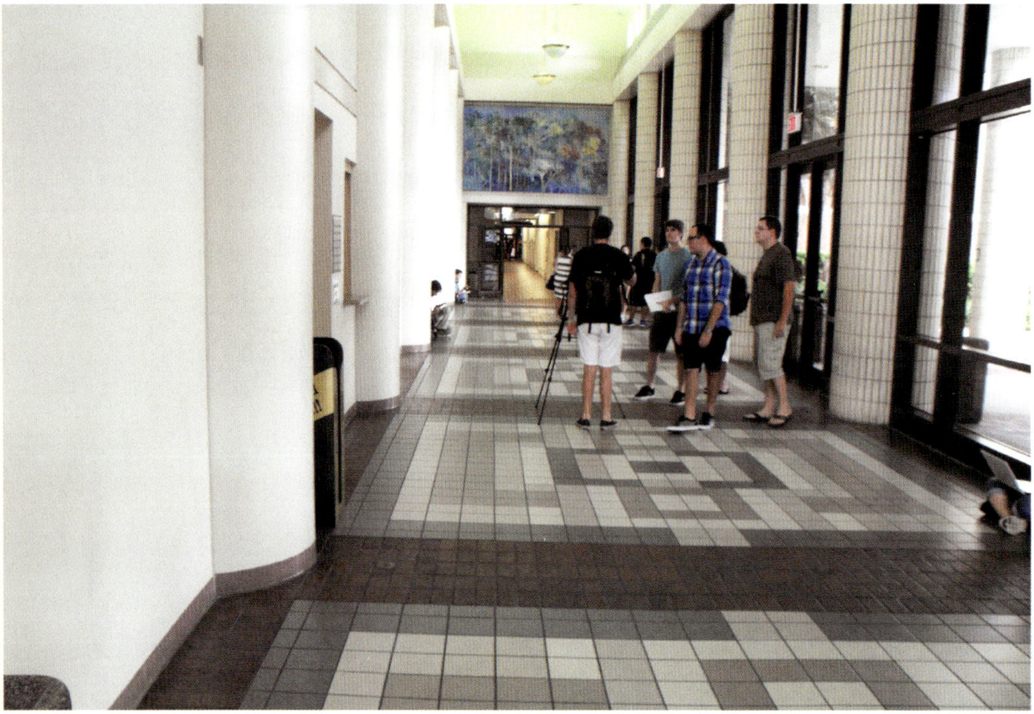

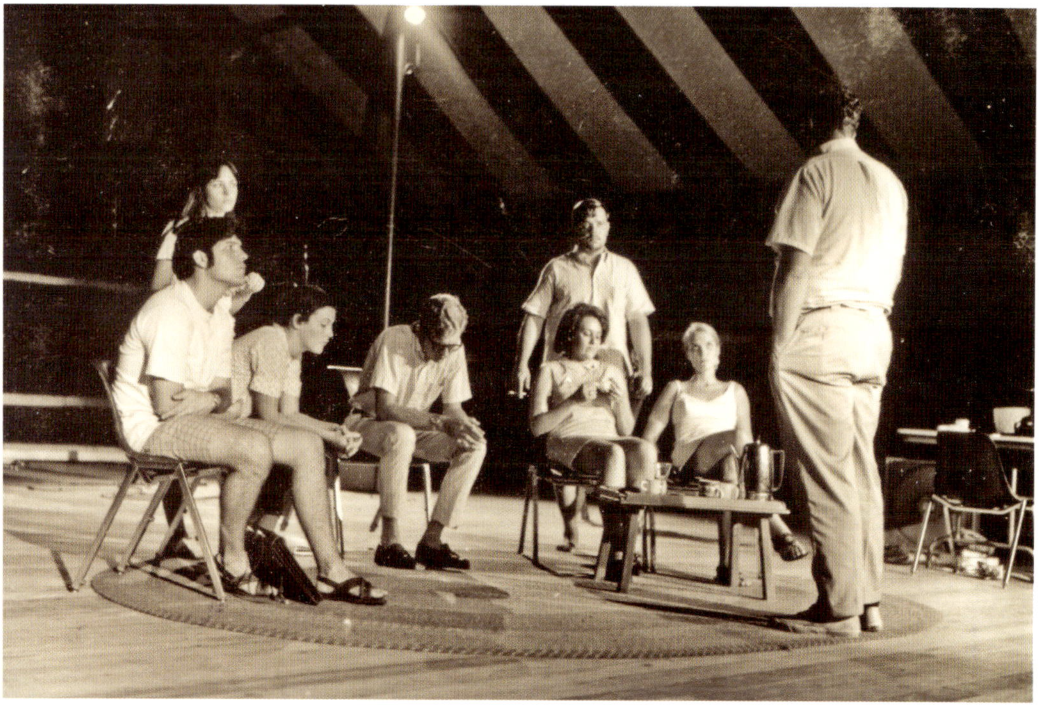

THE OLD BY THE NEW: Theatre UCF now offers five undergraduate degrees, four graduate degrees, and two minors. While state-of-the-art facilities exist on the main campus, performances in the satellite communities offered through relationships with state colleges offer students interested in theatre the opportunity to stay involved while not driving long distances for practices or performances.

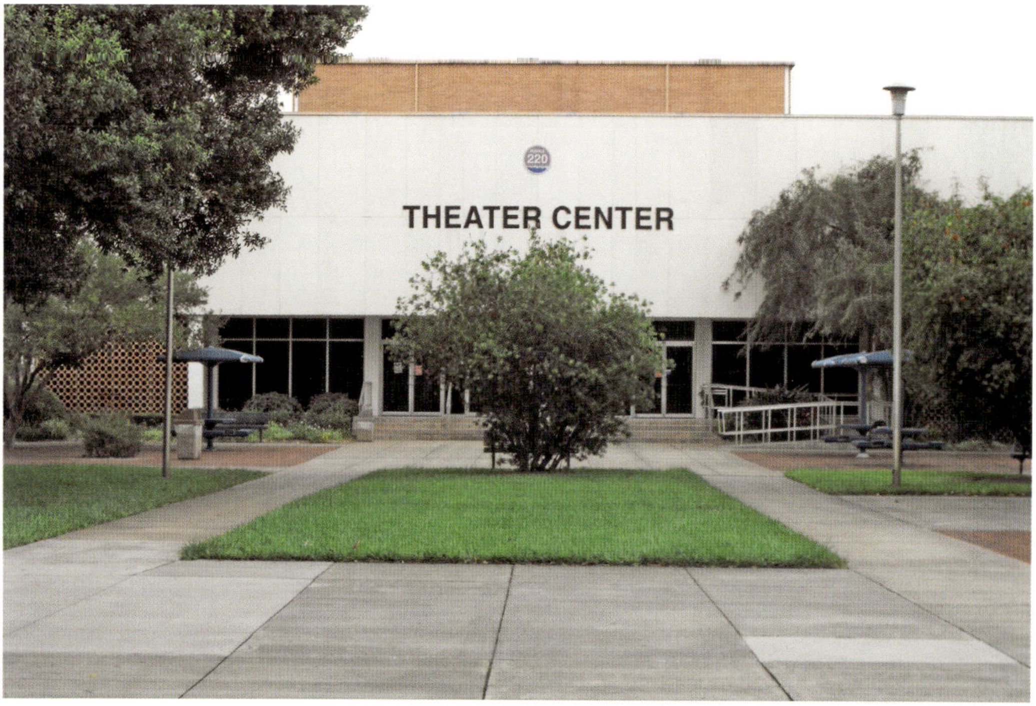

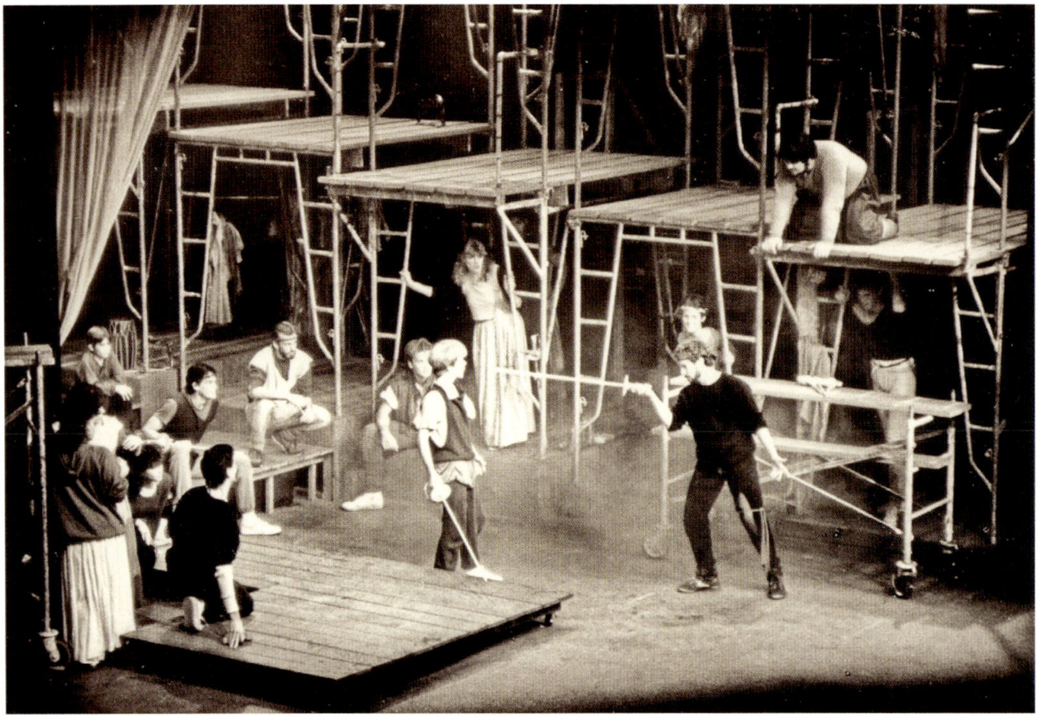

PERFORMANCE READY: Students at FTU rehearse. All along the walls of the current performing arts complex buildings are framed posters depicting past performances. UCF has grown faster than any other public university in the United States.

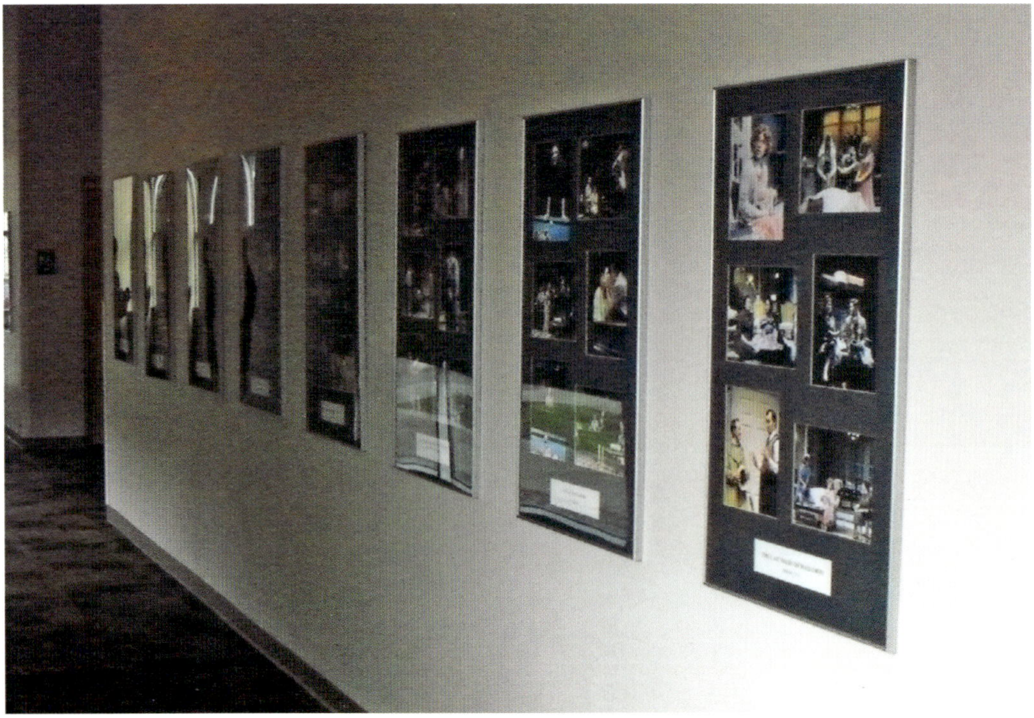

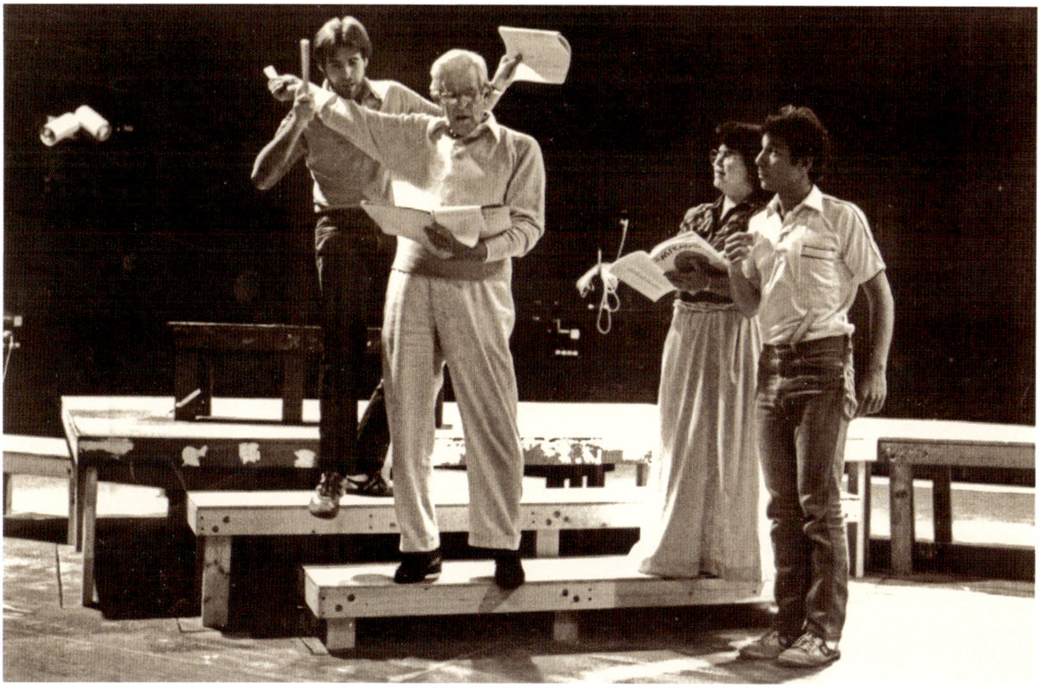

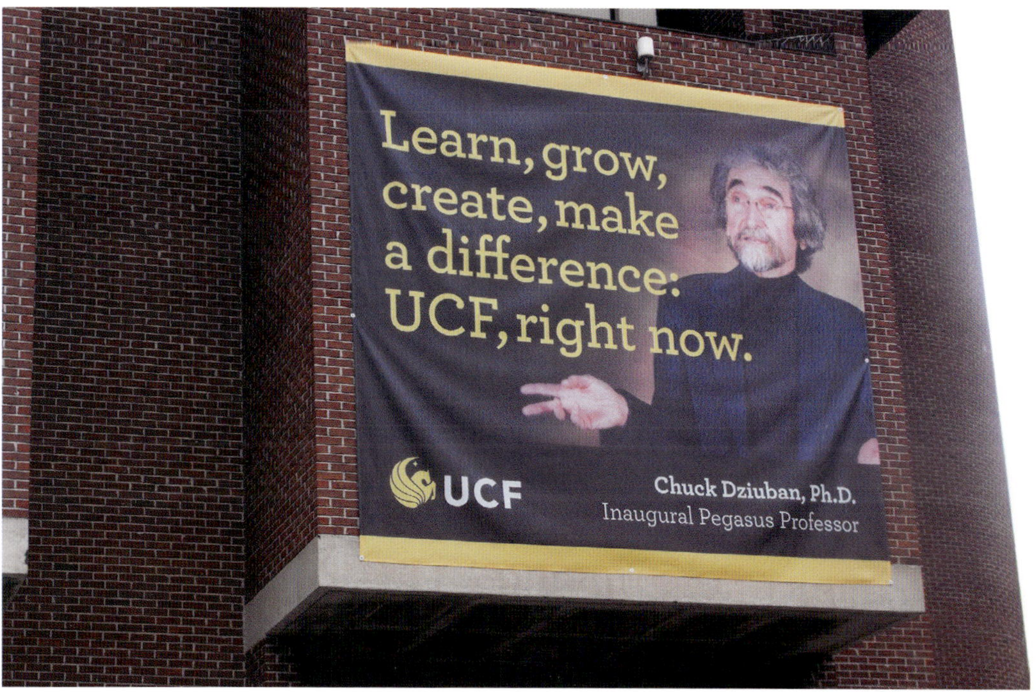

TEACHING BY DOING: By the time students reach college level, an expected skill is to be ready and open to taking instruction and counsel from teachers. Whether face-to-face or on a giant banner, students should pay attention. Dr. Dziuban is an innovative teacher who has been at the university since 1970; he is Director of the Research Initiative for Teaching Effectiveness and excited about the world of opportunities open to students and faculty.

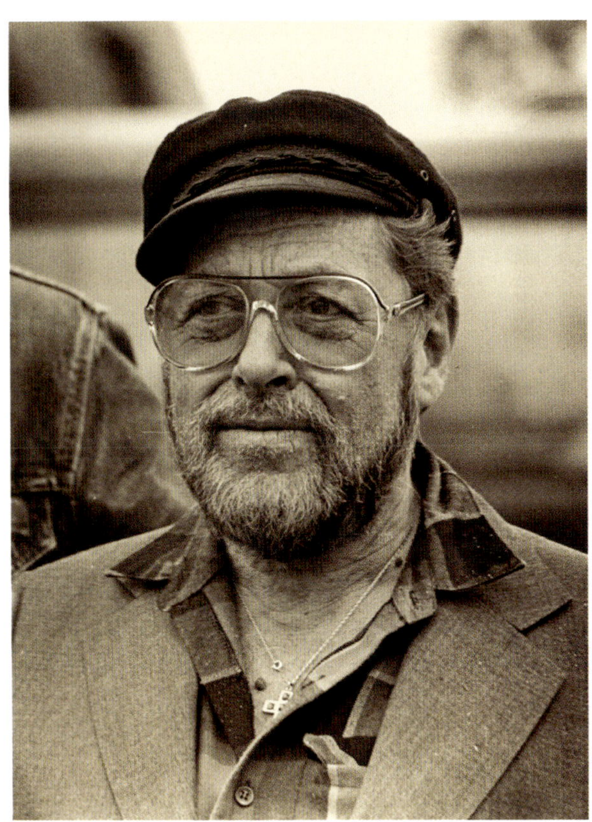

CURRICULAR AND EXTRA:
Playwright Tennessee Williams on
a visit to UCF. The arts complex at
UCF involves not only classrooms,
studios, offices, and auditoriums,
but galleries and practice rooms.
A student works in the art gallery in
the Visual Arts building.

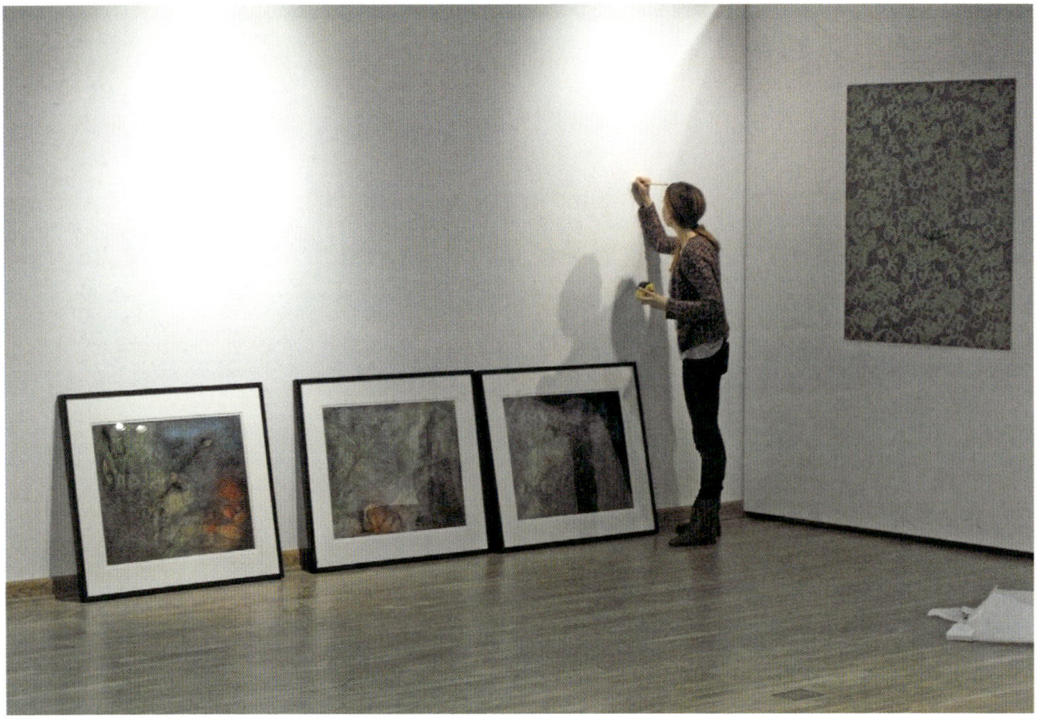

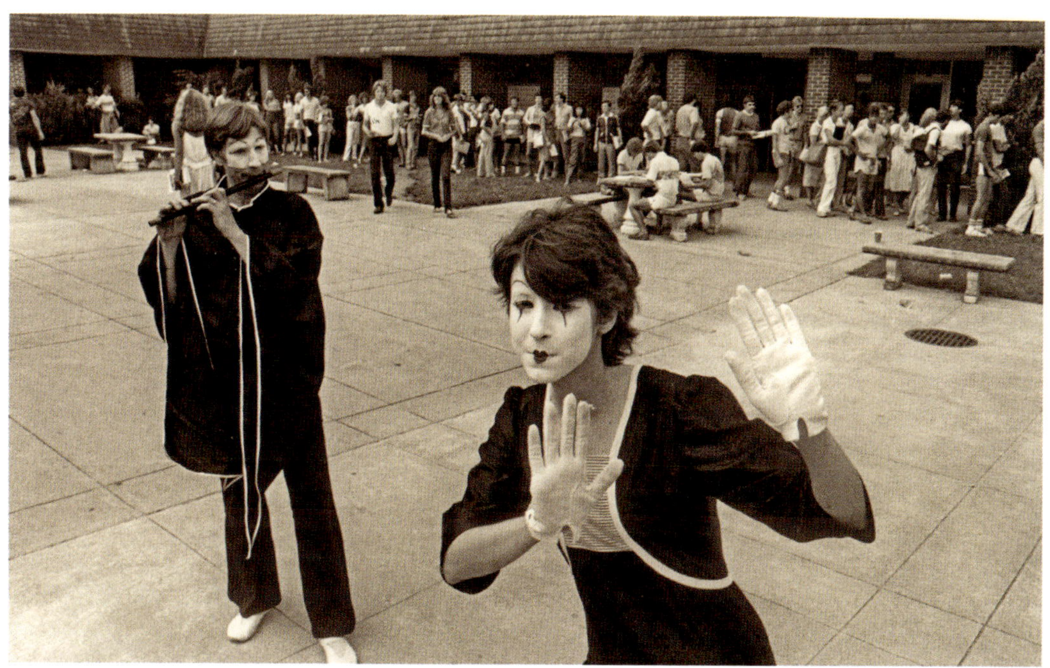

INTERDISCIPLINARY: A mime and accompanist entertain during drop/add, decades ago. These days, drop/add is handled exclusively online, eliminating not only waiting lines but paper and pencil. This leaves time for other pursuits, including collaboration. Two communication disorders students discuss an upcoming community event.

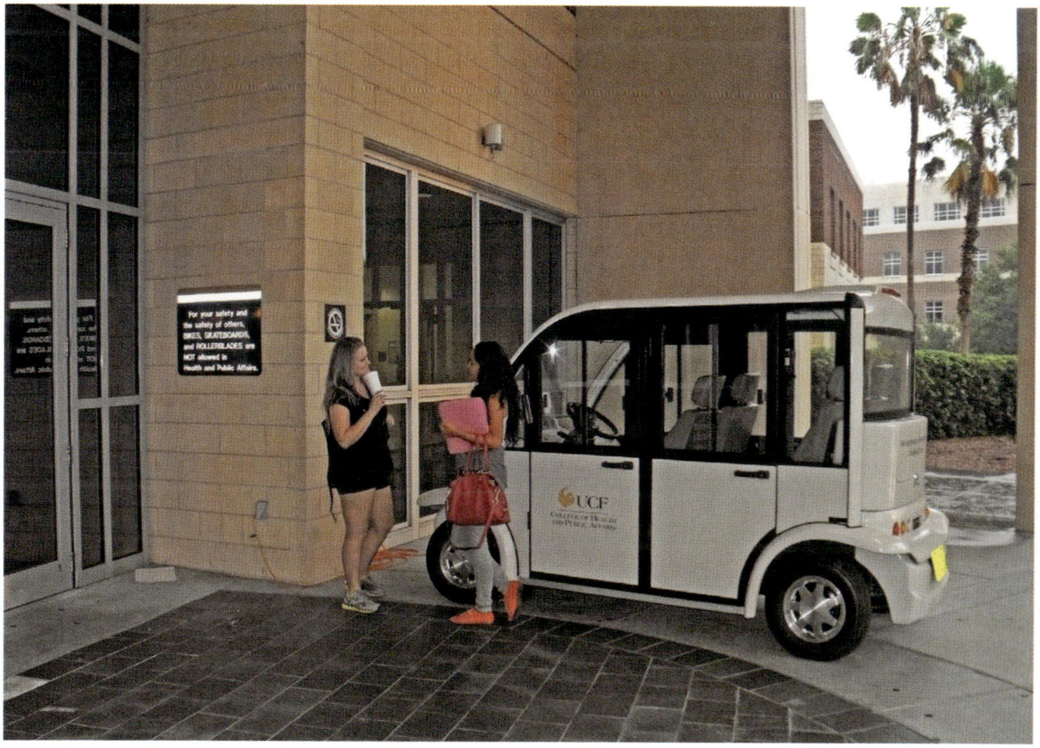

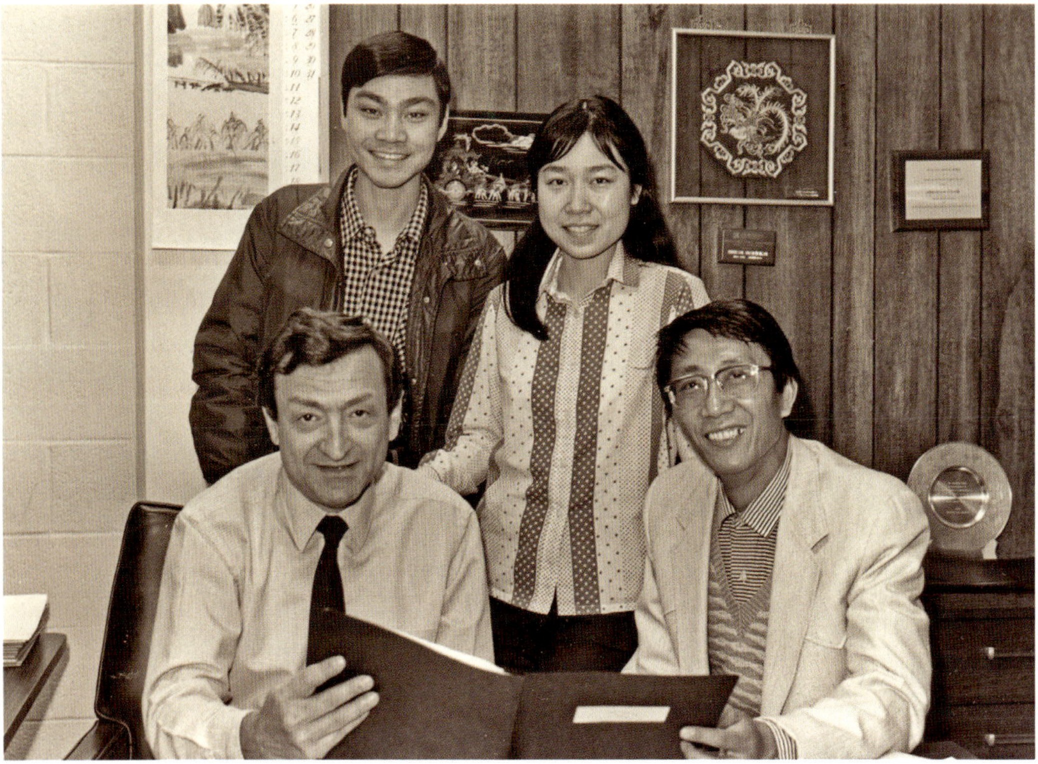

 Dr. Pizam, Director of the Hospitality Management program, is pictured in this 1987 shot with visiting Chinese students. University of Central Florida is an extremely diverse place, reflecting not only the diversity of the nation, but of the state of Florida. Faculty members keep regular office hours and meeting one-to-one with students is still an honored tradition in academia.

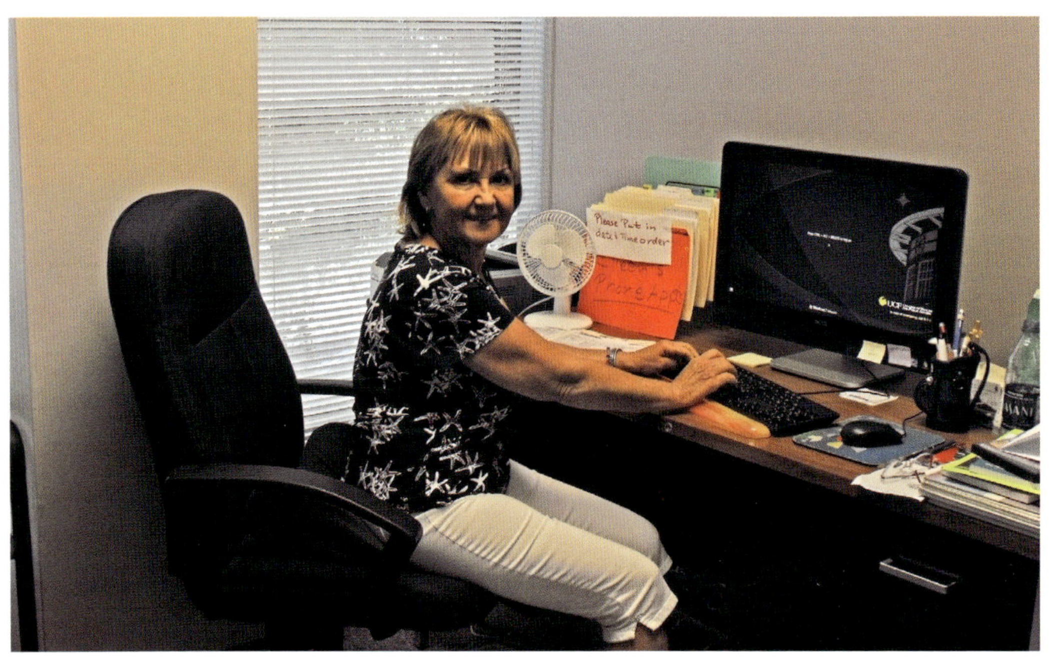

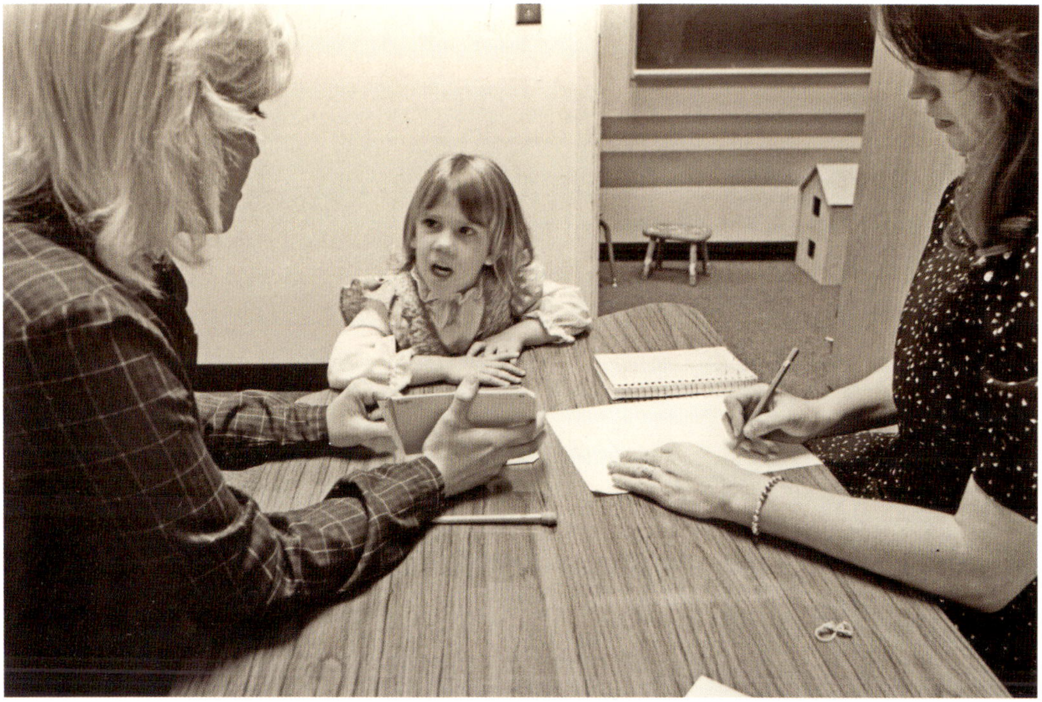

LITTLE INSTRUCTORS: The Department of Communication Sciences and Disorders is part of the College of Health and Public Affairs. It offers bachelor's, master's, and doctoral programs in speech-language pathology. UCF is a research institution, and there are ample opportunities for students to share what they are learning.

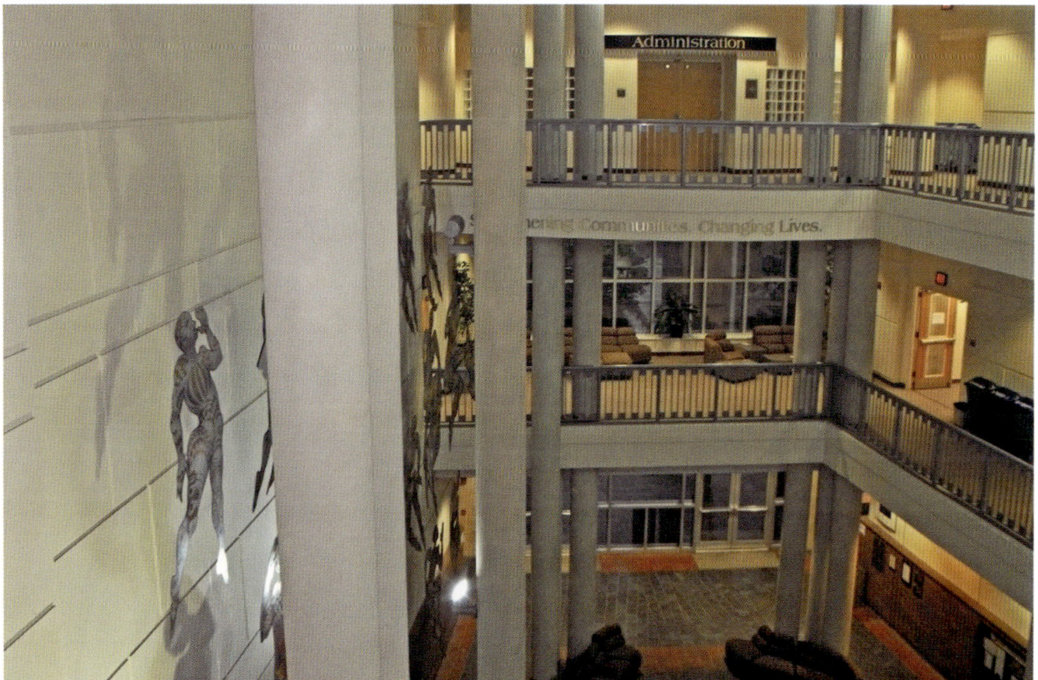

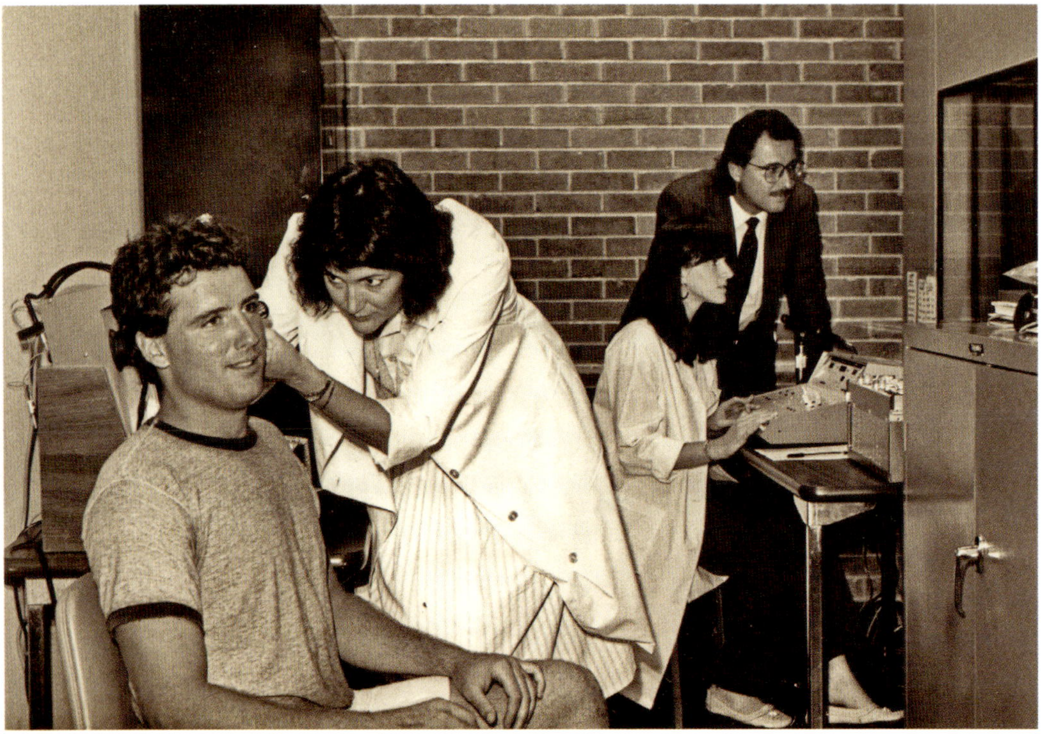

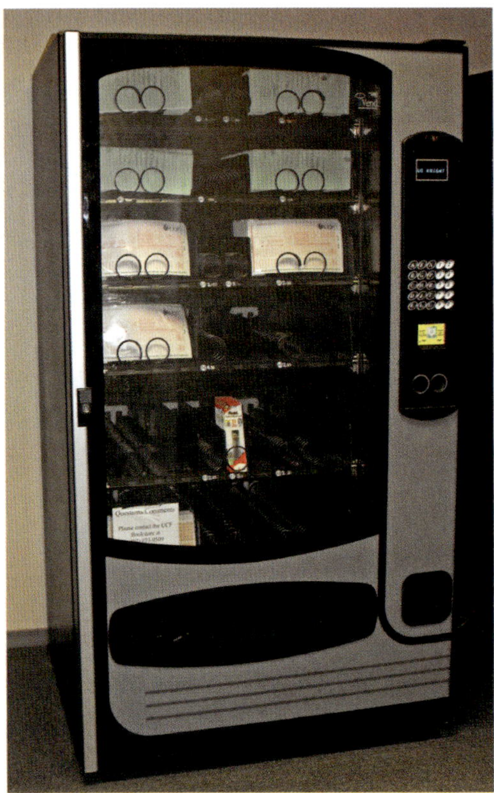

DOUBLE DUTY: Baseball player Brian Shaughnessy has his hearing tested by instructor Michele James-Trychel on 17 September 1987 while John Tetnowski works with student Kim Glodek. The equipment in the Department of Communication Sciences and Disorders in this photograph is quite dated, as contrasted with a modern vending machine which dispenses scantrons, calculators, and flash drives.

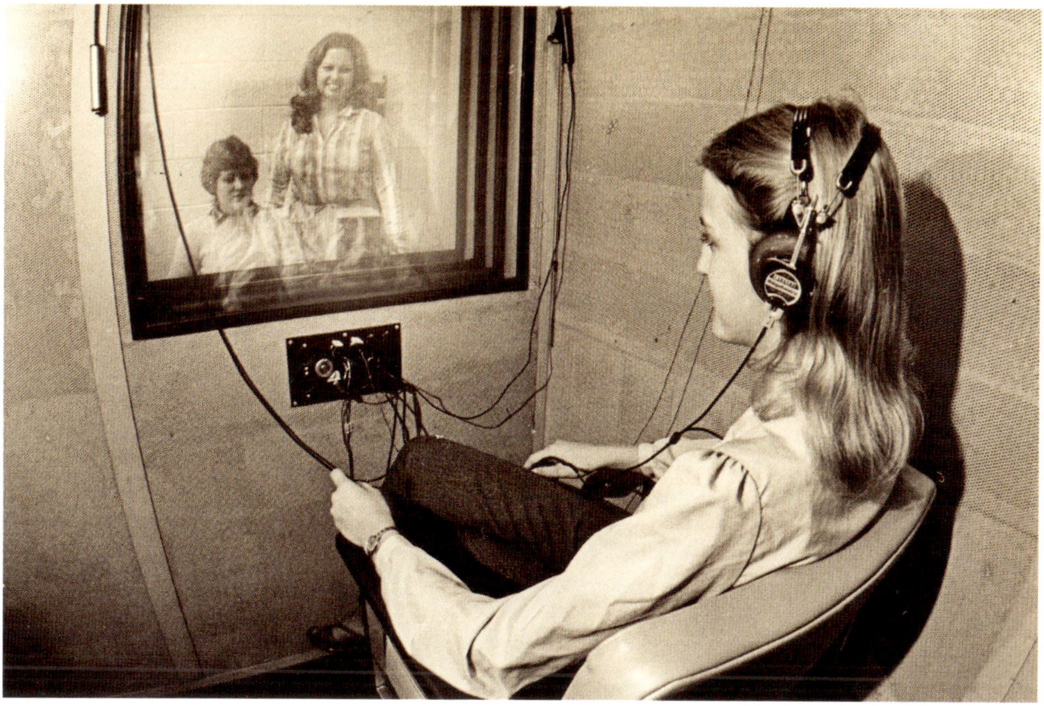

COHPA: The College of Health and Public Affairs occupies several large buildings on campus and is comprised of seven departments, but although classrooms and public spaces may be vast, actual work is often done one-to-one in controlled settings. Modern students can also take classes at one of several satellite campuses.

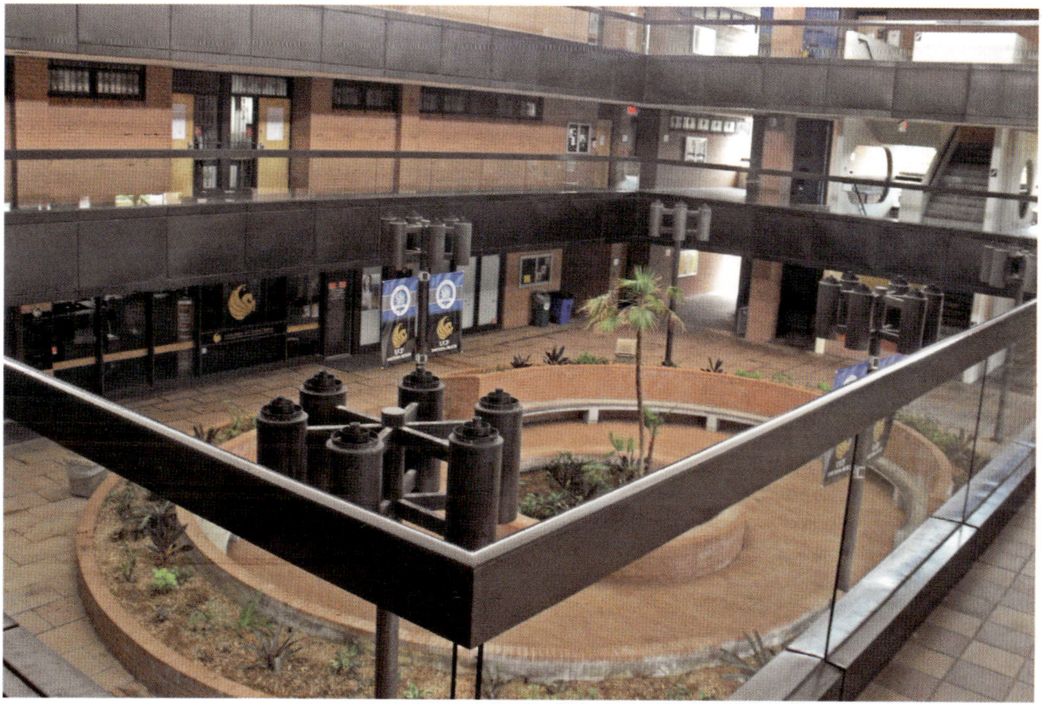

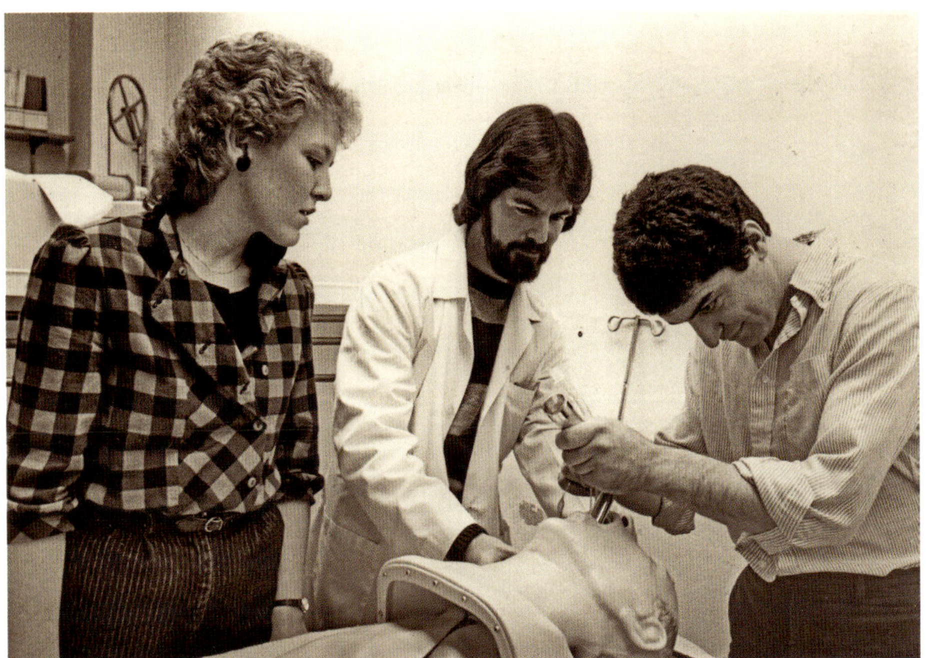

IN THE CLASSROOM, IN THE WORLD: Mr. Tim Worrell, then Associate Professor and Director of Clinical Education in the Cardiopulmonary Sciences Program, instructs students. UCF is home to many outstanding faculty members, Mr. Worrell among them. Classes are generally filled to capacity, and students sometimes wait a semester or two to take a class with a particular professor, but it is usually worth the wait. In the modern world, a student can register from almost anywhere.

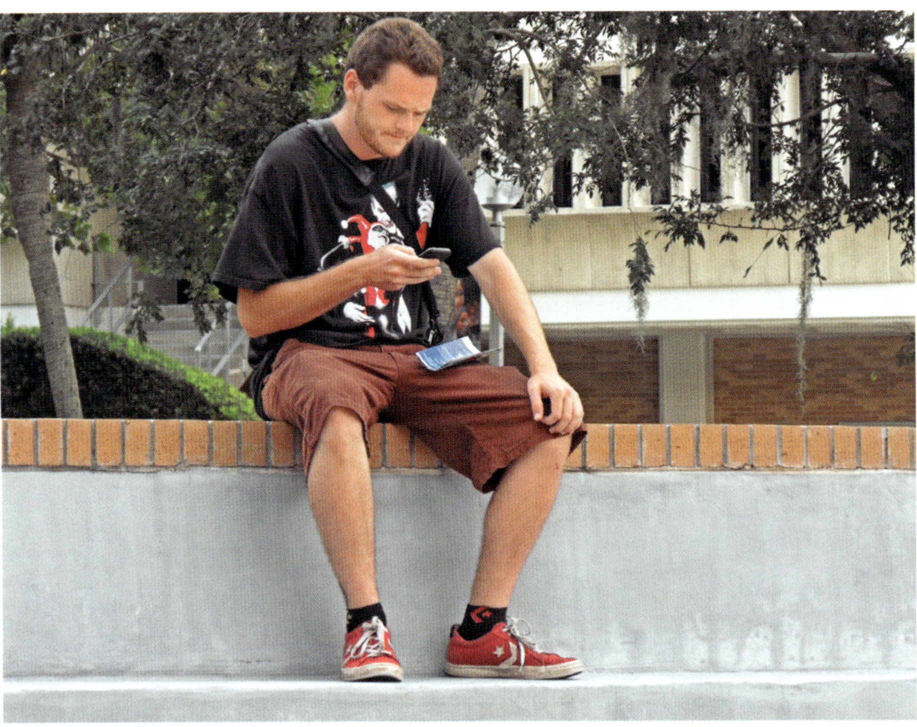

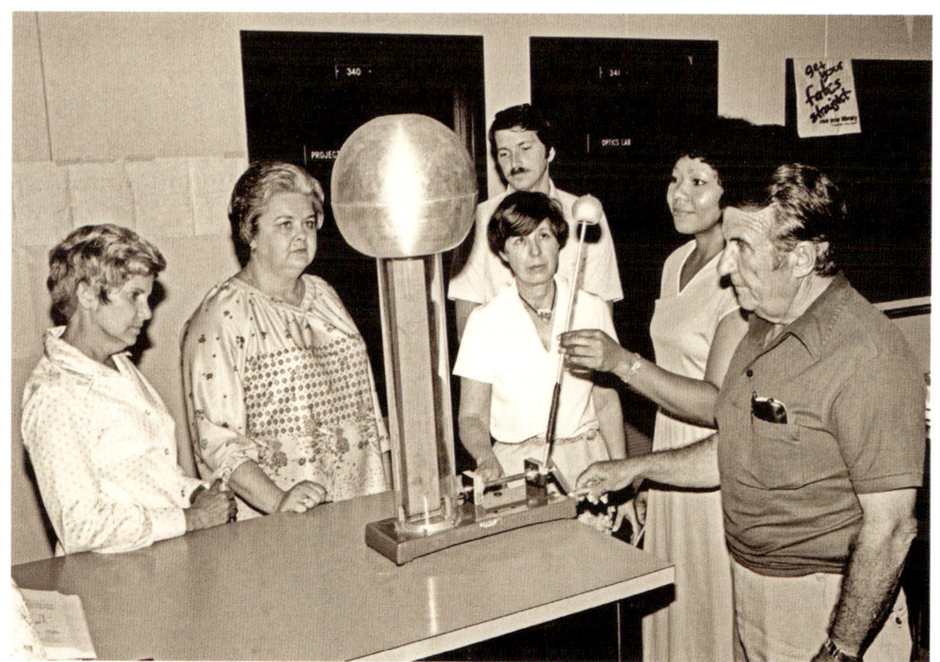

POWERFUL DEMONSTRATIONS: Two demonstration of the laws of physics; one generates electromagnetic fields; the other harnesses the sun's energy to take care of the problems of waste management on the nation's second biggest public university campus. While textbooks and lectures can teach much, hands-on demonstrations often cement concepts in learners' minds.

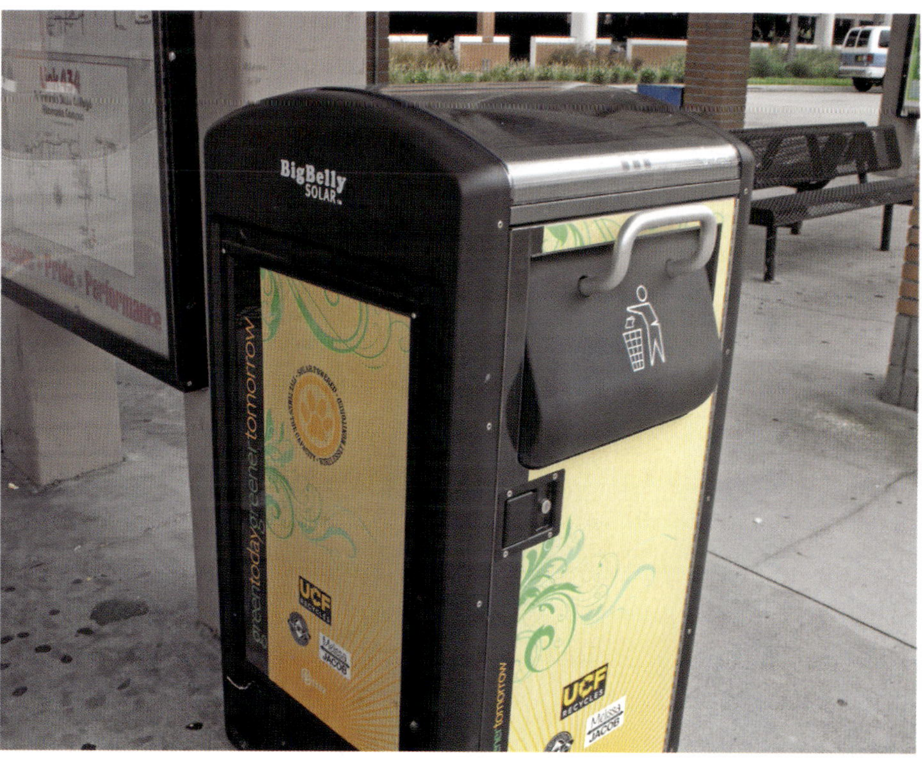

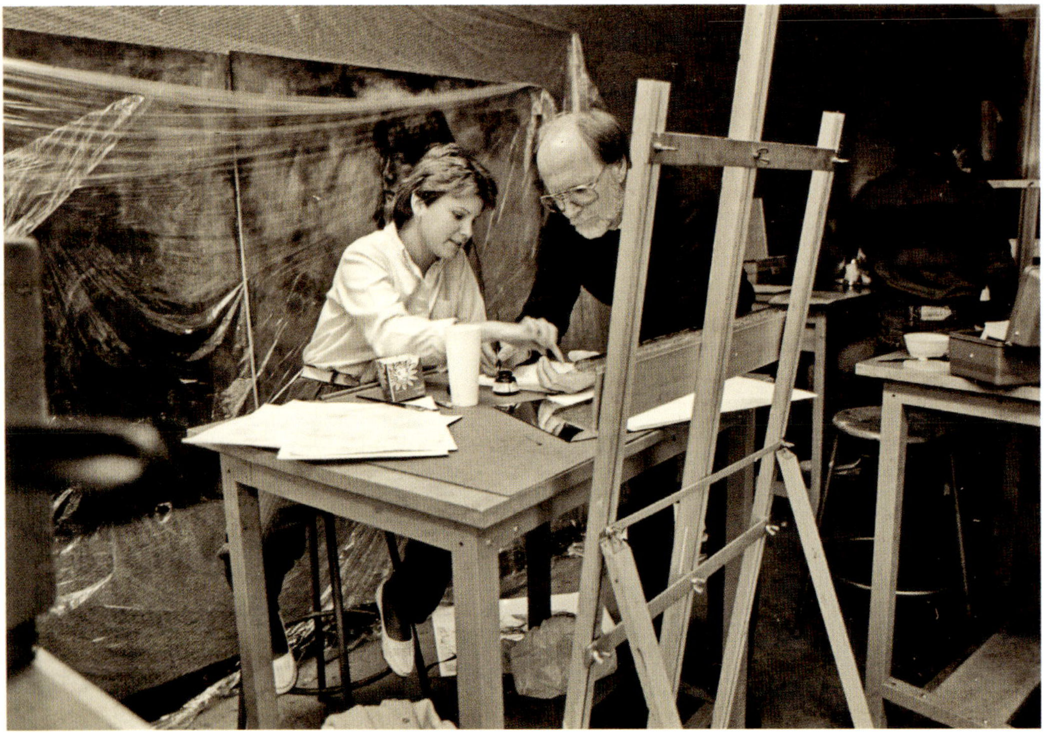

GLOBAL IMPACT: Professor Steven Lotz, founder of the Art Department, works with an art student. While UCF is known for its schools of engineering and other sciences, it is also competitive in the fine arts.

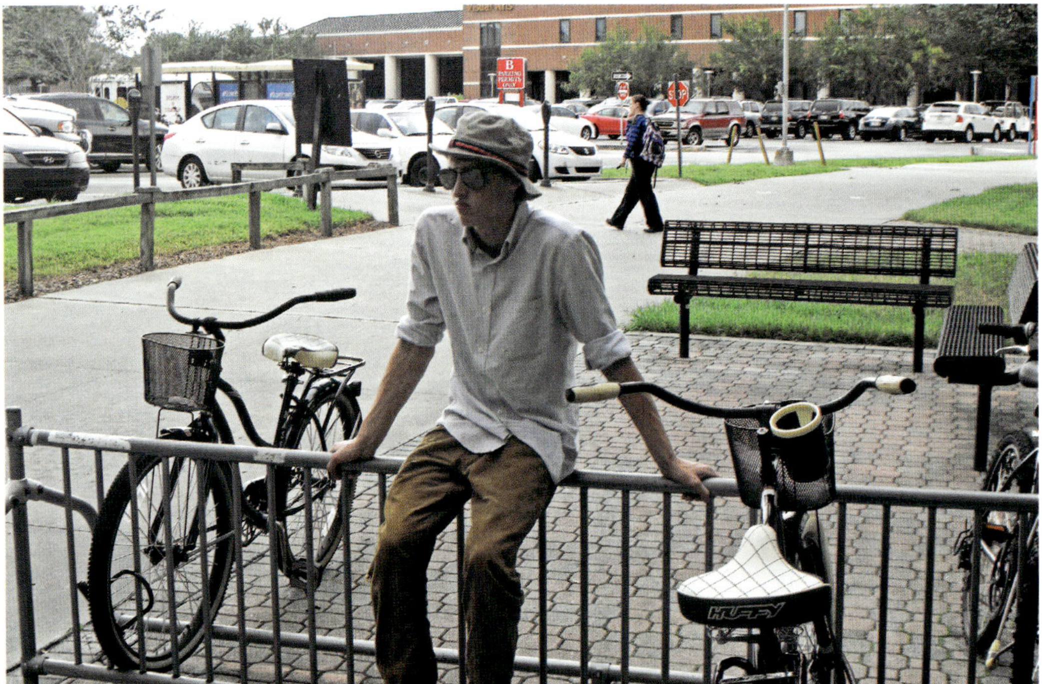

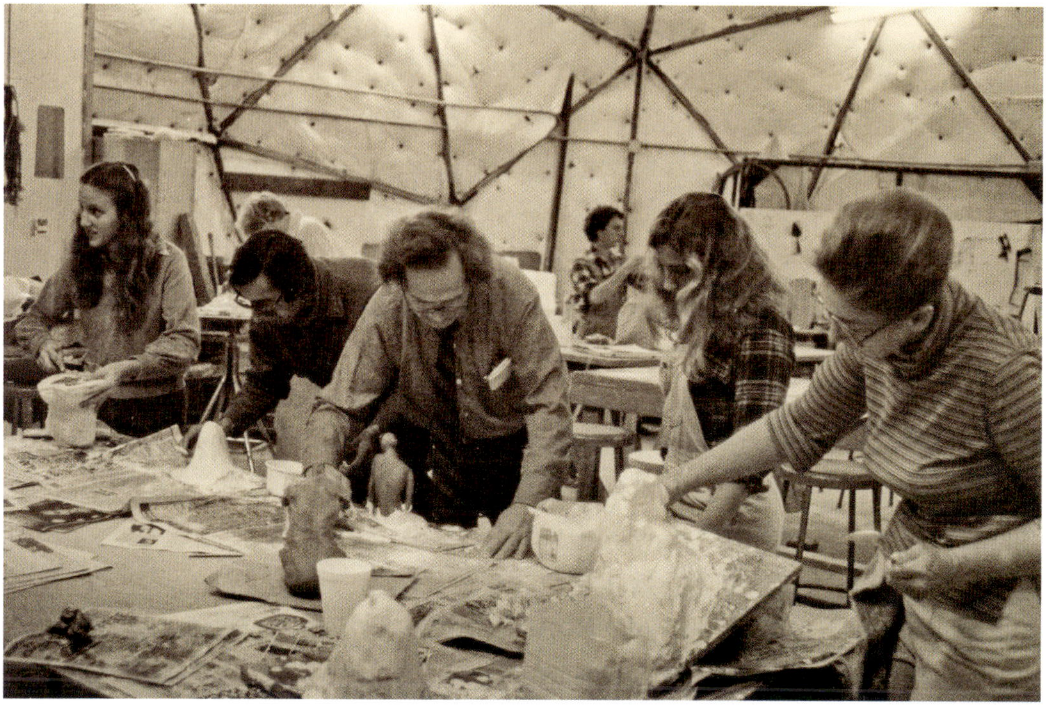

MIXING MEDIUMS: Art can be messy, and expensive. Johann Eyfells, FTU art professor, works with sculpture students. In the visual arts building, student work is prominently and beautifully displayed. Part of being an art student is learning how and where to display your work, sometimes a taxing experience. Students gain practice in displaying work after college along the walls of the school buildings.

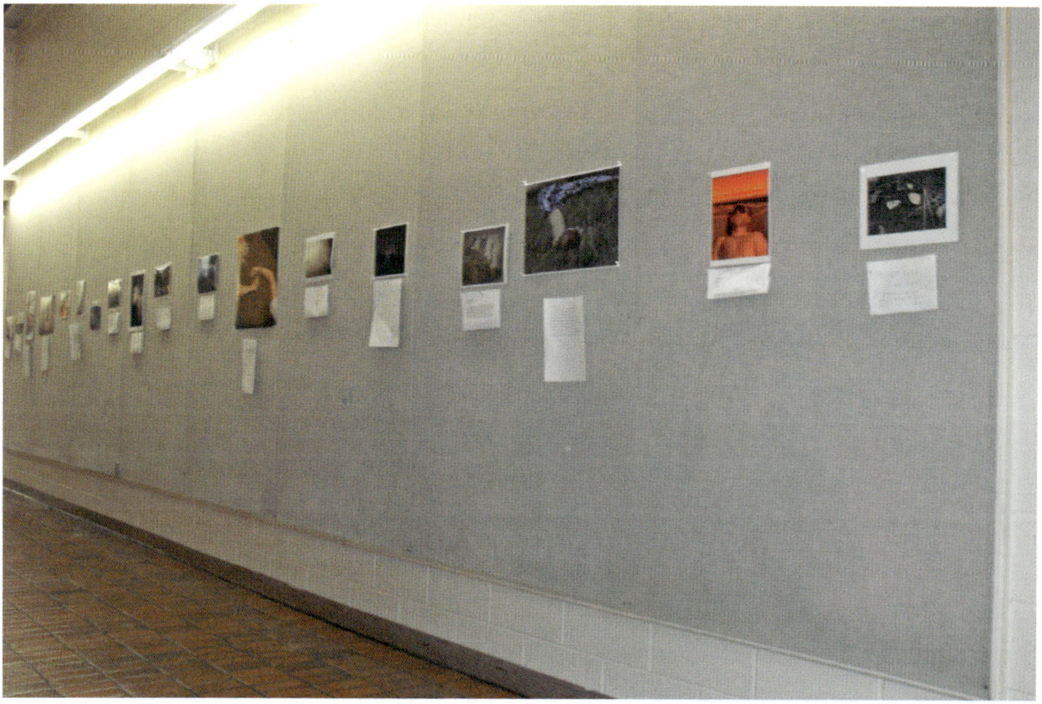

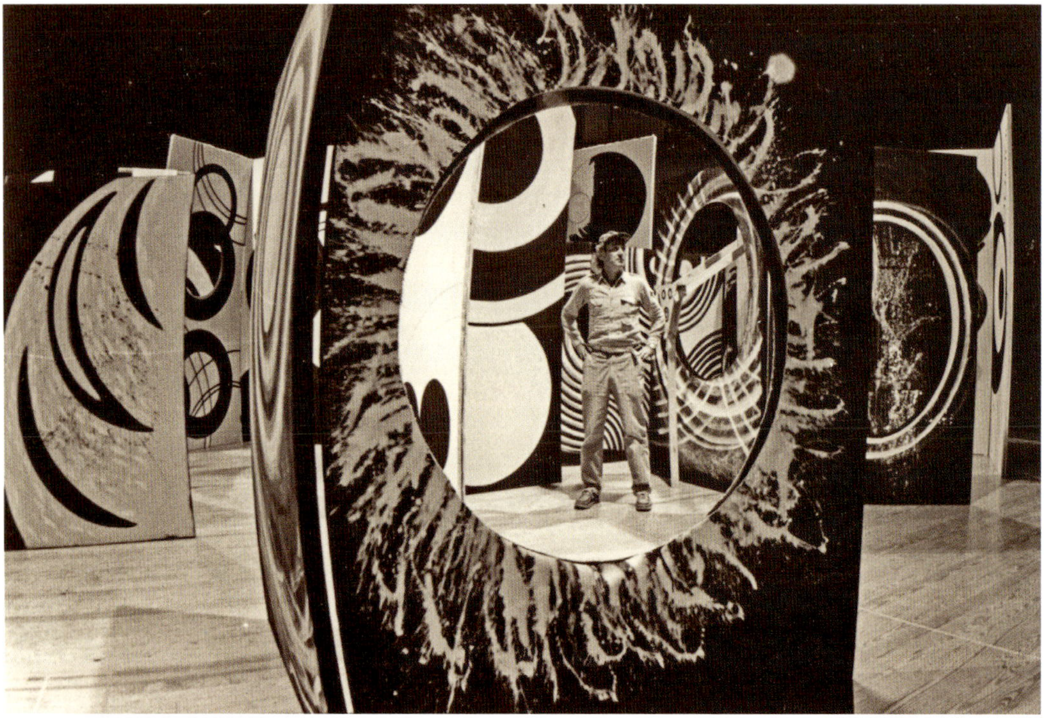

POWERFUL PERSPECTIVES: Dr. Gaudnek, FTU art professor, viewed standing in what was known as his labyrinth. The elements of sculpture, including size, work together to have impact: this sculpture near Colbourn Hall is fondly known as the French fries.

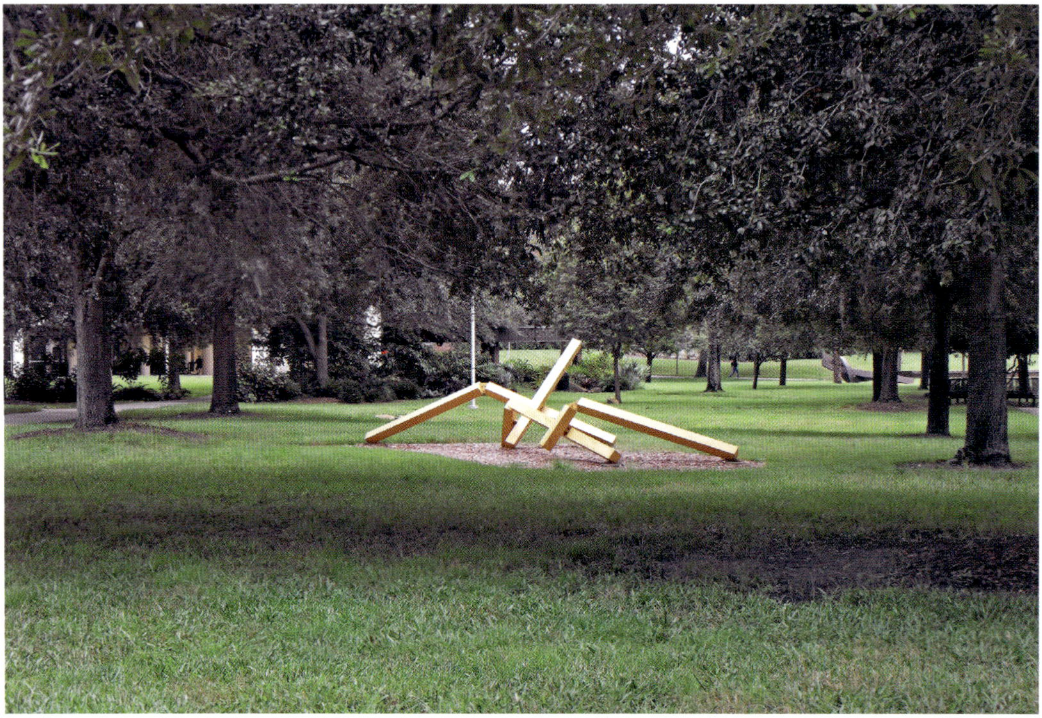

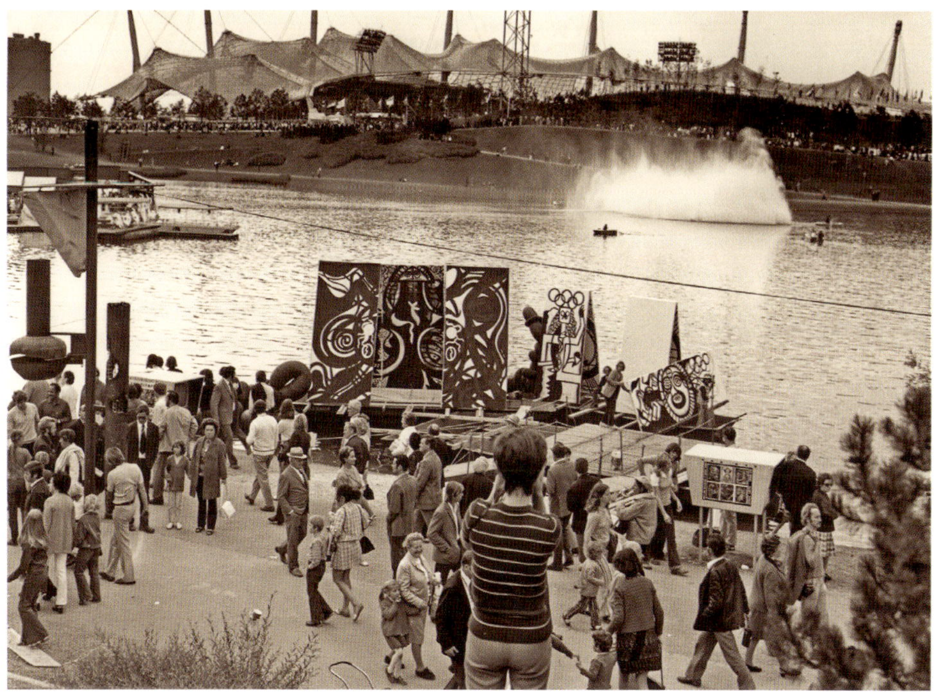

UCF AFAR AND WIDE: In 1972, FTU's art department enjoyed the distinction of being the only United States university invited to participate in the Olympic games in Munich. Dr. Gaudnek and Professor Eyfells led the effort to build giant sails and sculptures to be floated on boats and floats, constructed in full view of the public on the shores of the Olympic Lake. Faculty artists continue the tradition of taking an active role in their communities.

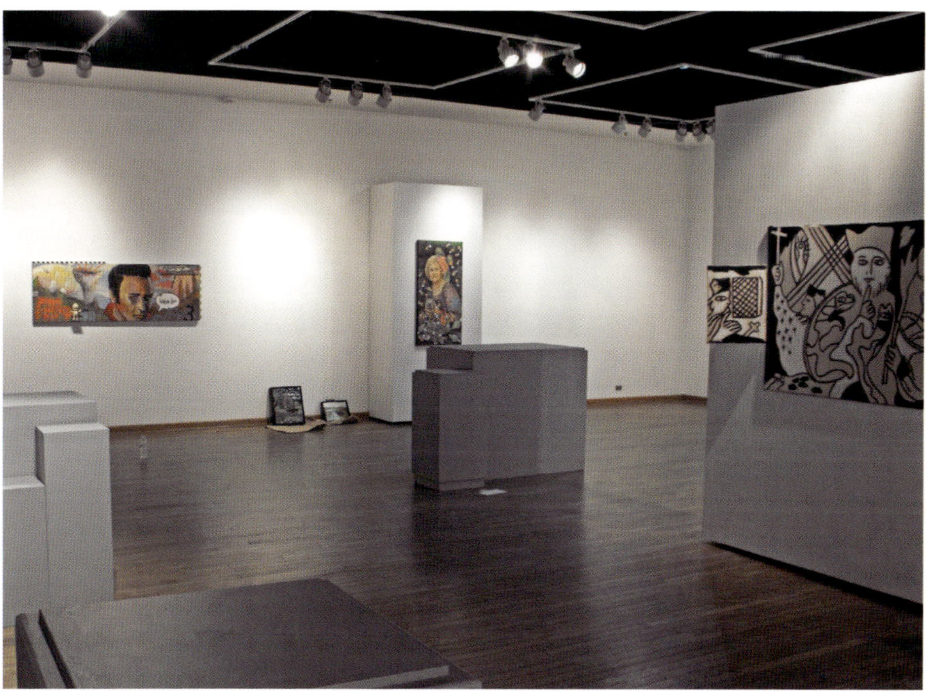

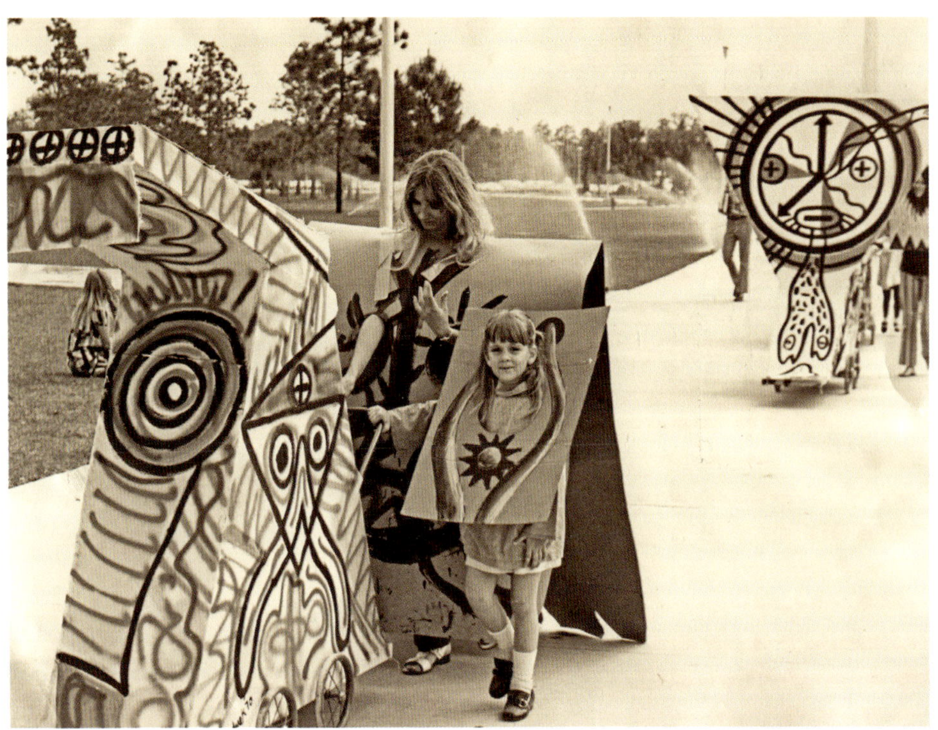

EARLY IMPACT: Never too early for higher education; Dr. Gaudek's wife and young daughter participated in the festivities in Munich. The outdoor sculptures on campuses right here in Central Florida often reflect local flora and fauna and are placed for all citizens to enjoy.

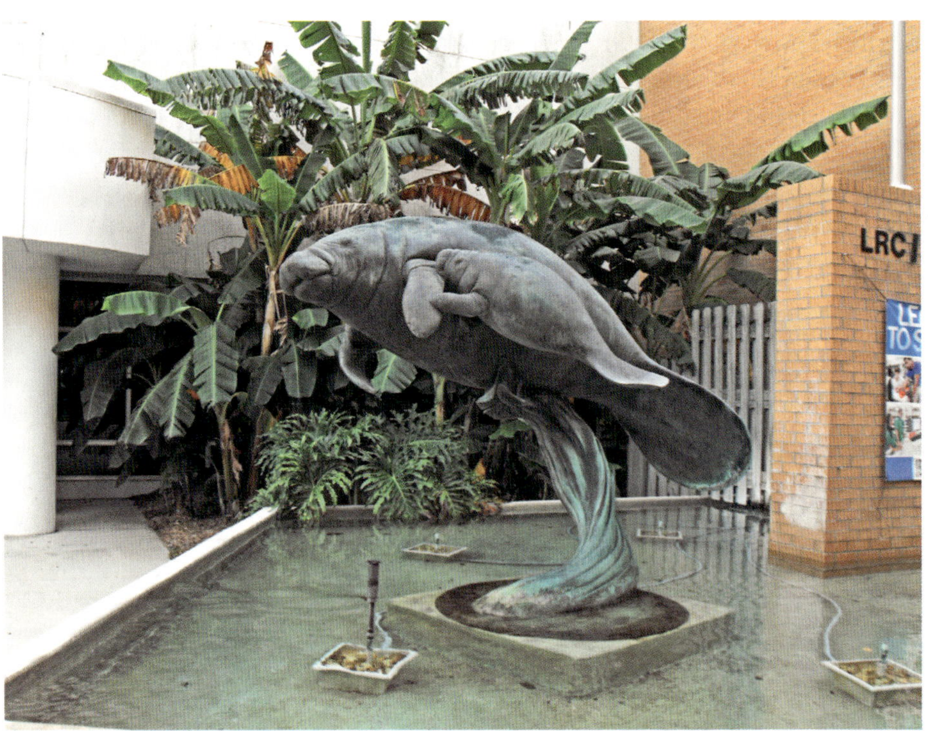

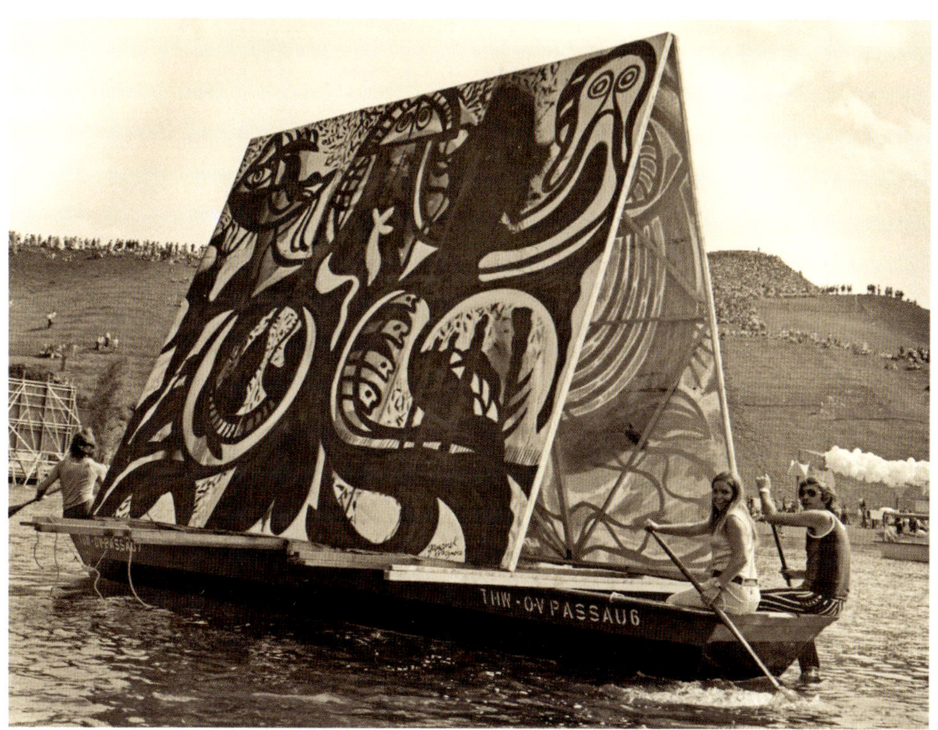

STUDENT EFFORT: Two FTU students pilot a sculpture on the Olympic Lake. At UCF, a student works in the gallery. Not all students work in their major field; wise students often choose jobs outside their field of study to expand perspective and enhance learning and understanding.

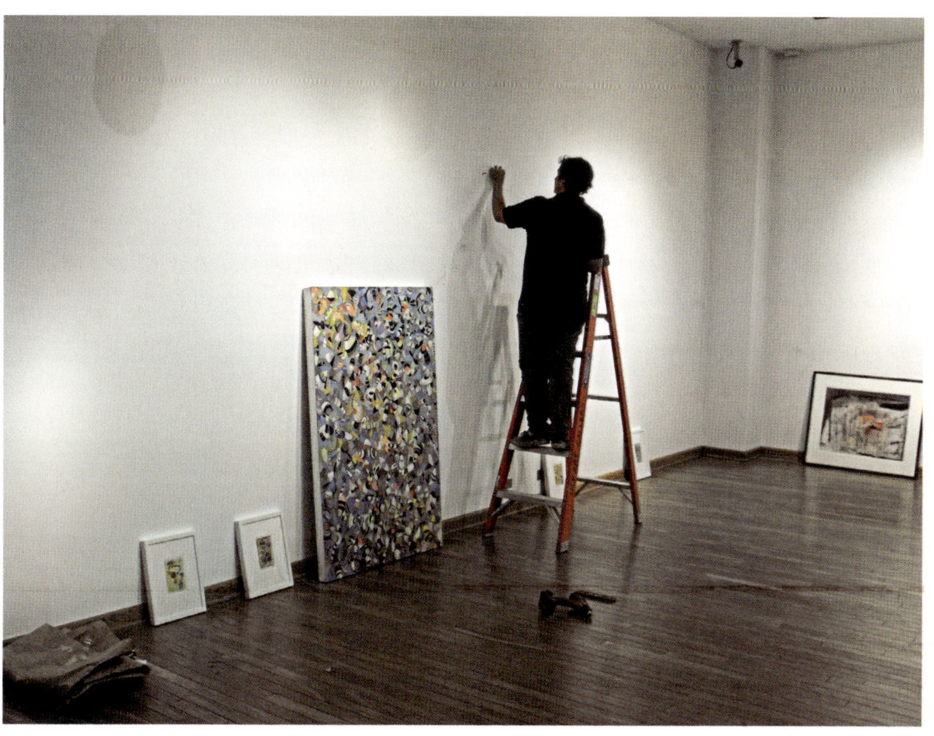

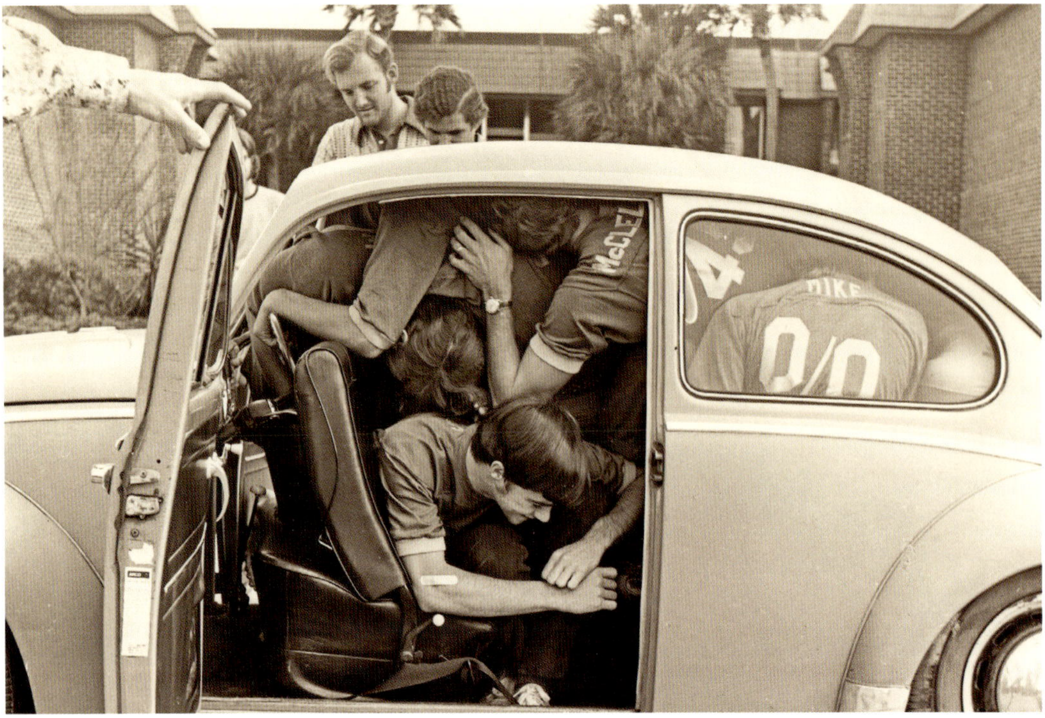

SIGNS OF THE TIMES: A wonderful photograph from the early 1970s captures the fun of Greek Week; a UCF student, today, rushes to class behind Millican Hall on a typical Florida mode of transport, the skateboard.

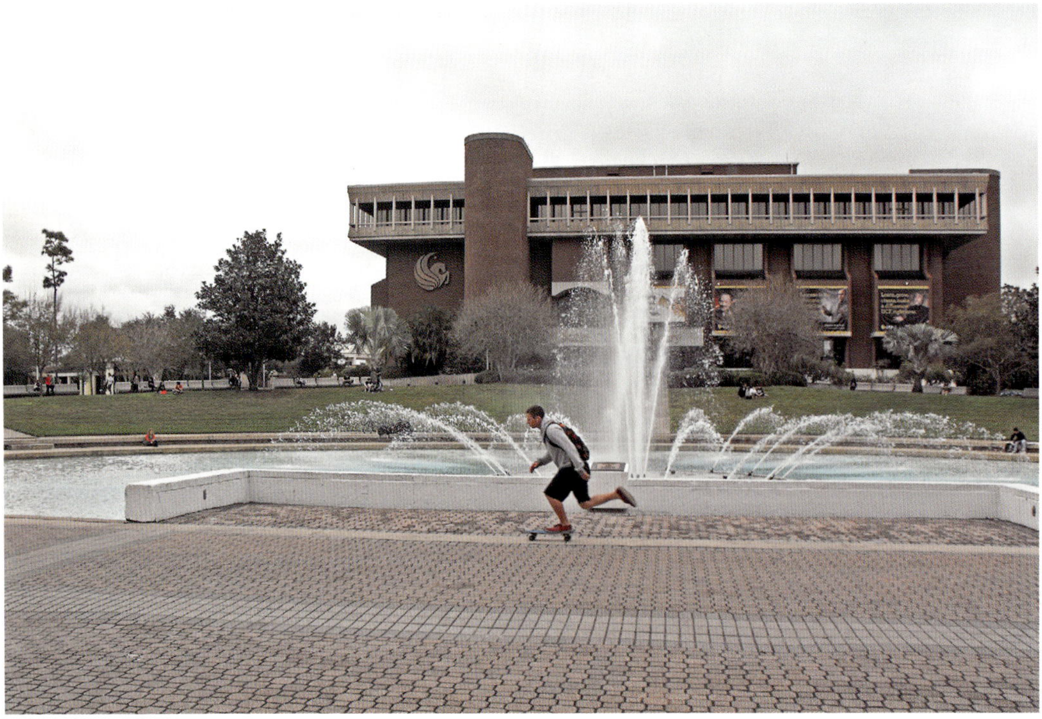

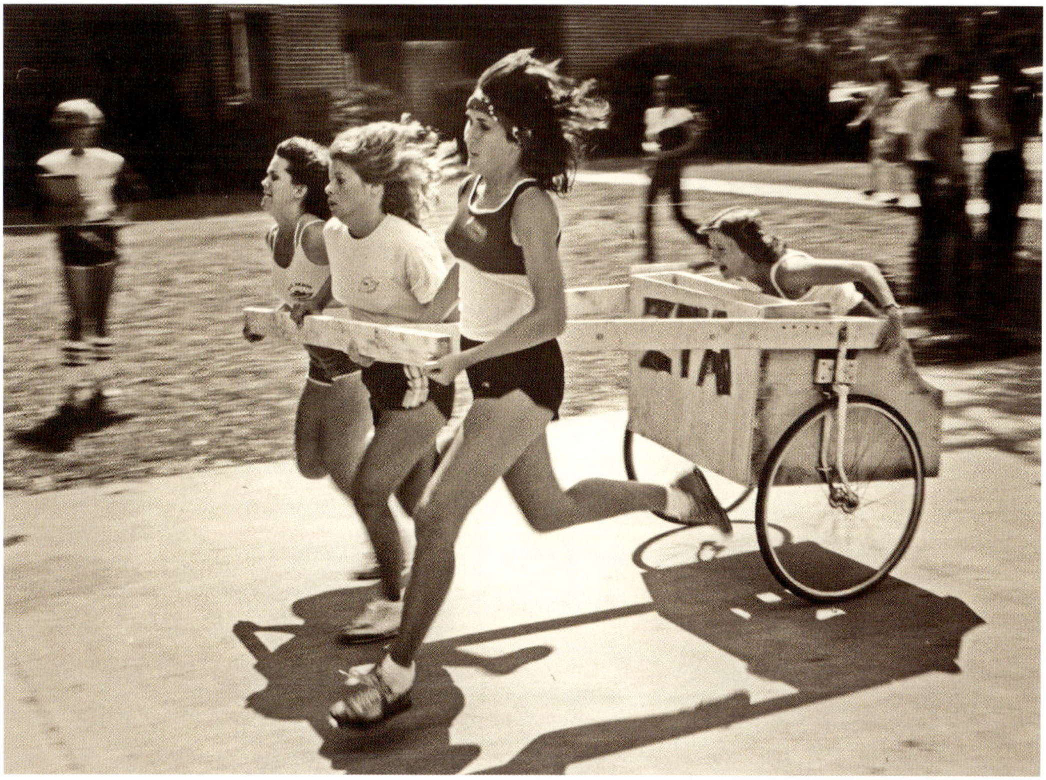

TEAMWORK: Whether for recreation, education, or survival, learning to work together is an important life skill. Knights Helping Knights is a pantry where hungry students can go, daily, for food and toiletries at no cost. The cost of education can be high and some students have very little extra money for provisions.

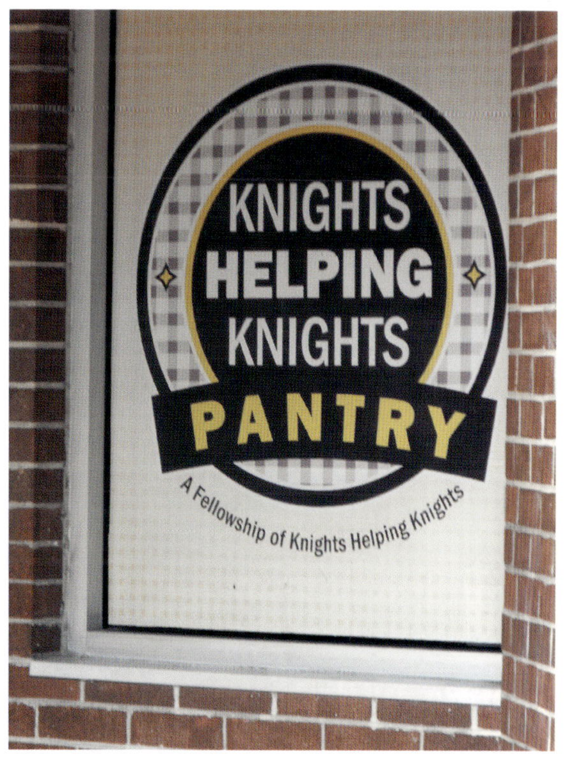

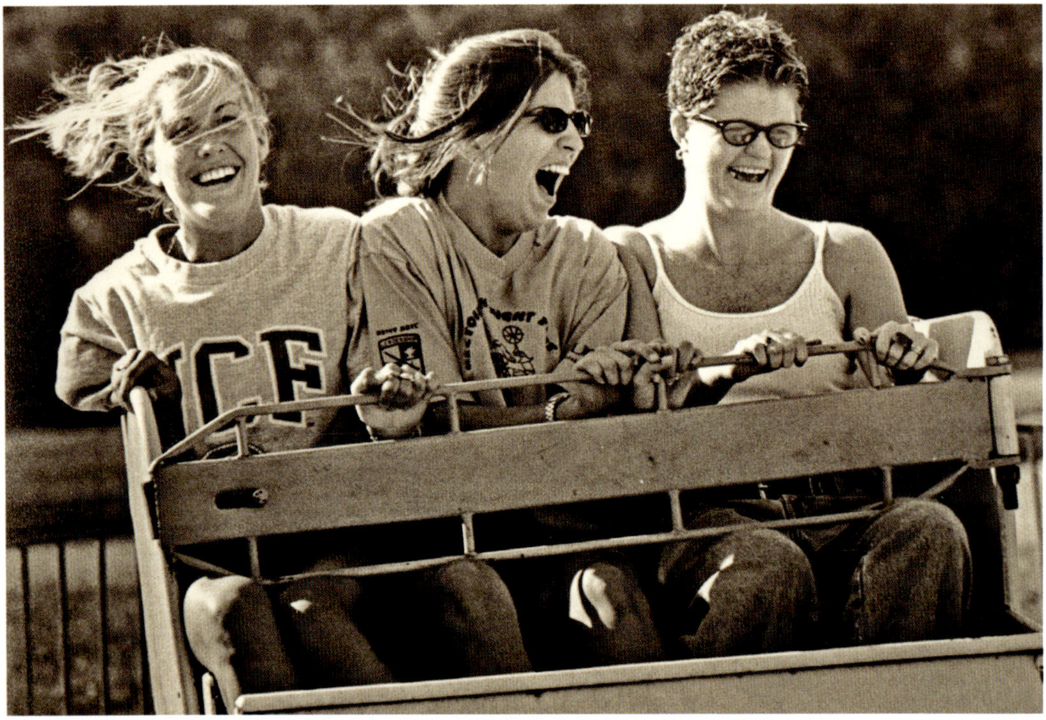

A LITTLE FUN: All work and no play; taking time to laugh, exercise, refresh and recharge is important for faculty and students alike. UCF is close to several world-class beaches and many students, faculty, and staff participate in water sports.

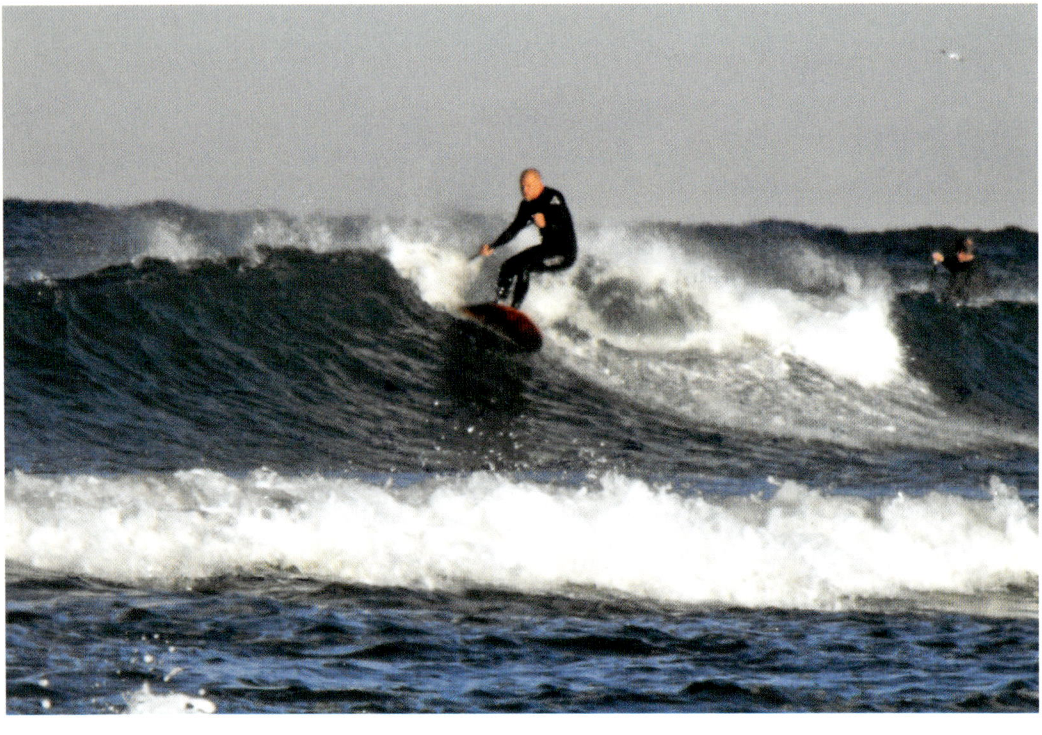

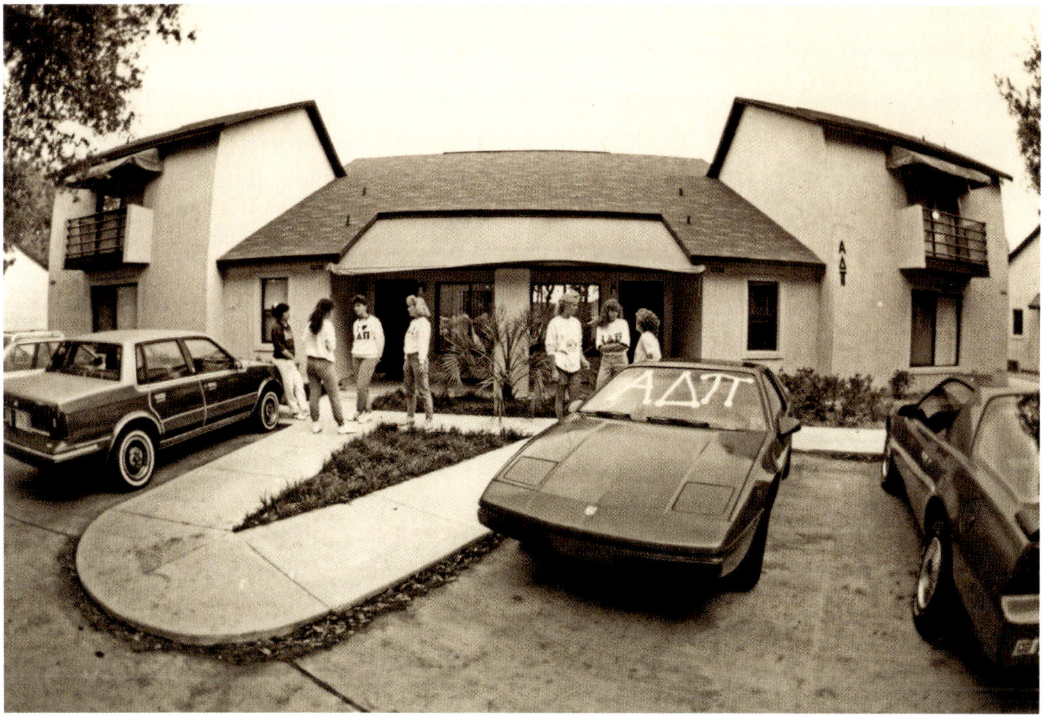

A house away from home: Sororities and fraternities serve an important, even crucial, function for some students in that they provide a home away from home for young people who might otherwise feel lost, alone, and unsupported.

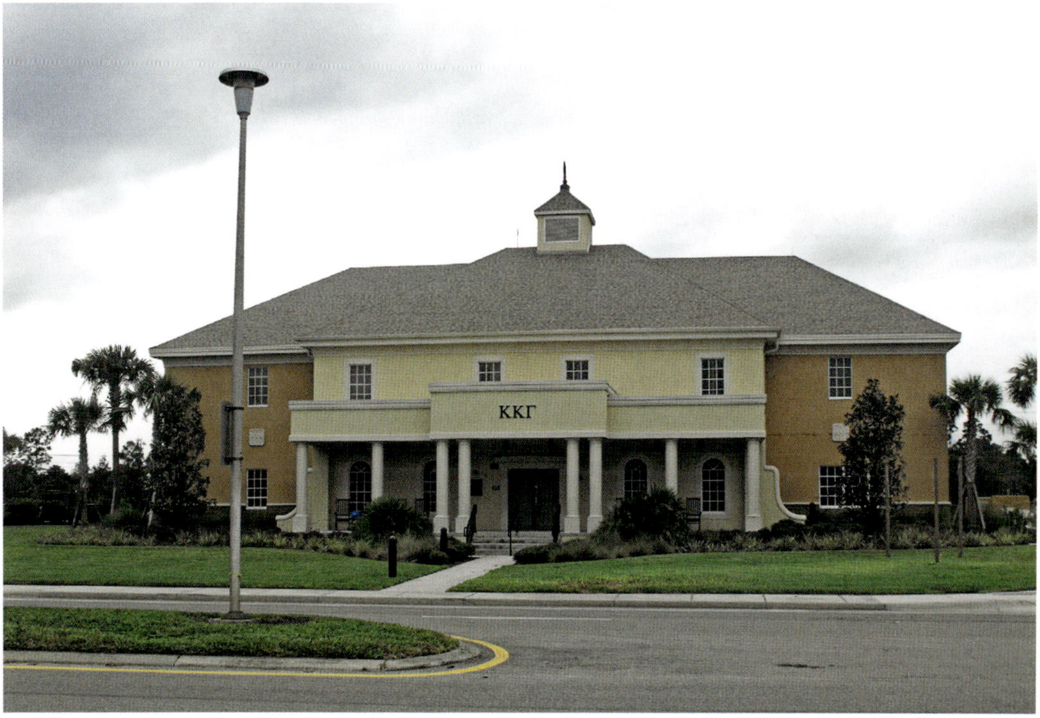

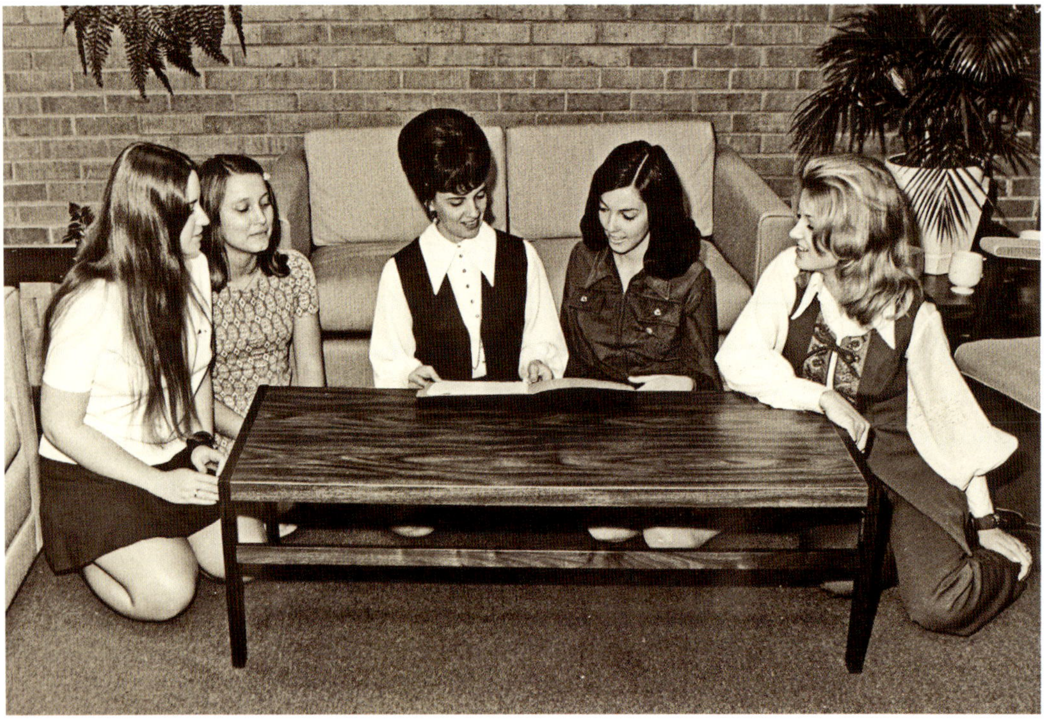

SAFETY NETS: Young people, past and present, work together to provide social and academic support for each other through sororities, fraternities and other campus organizations including religious and political ones.

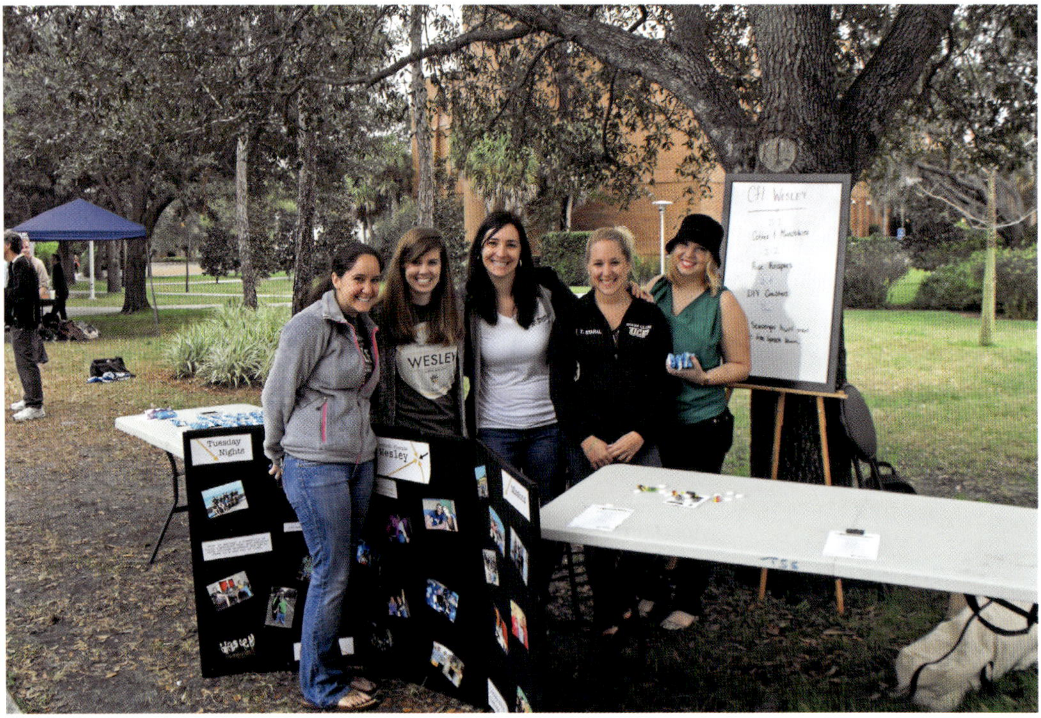

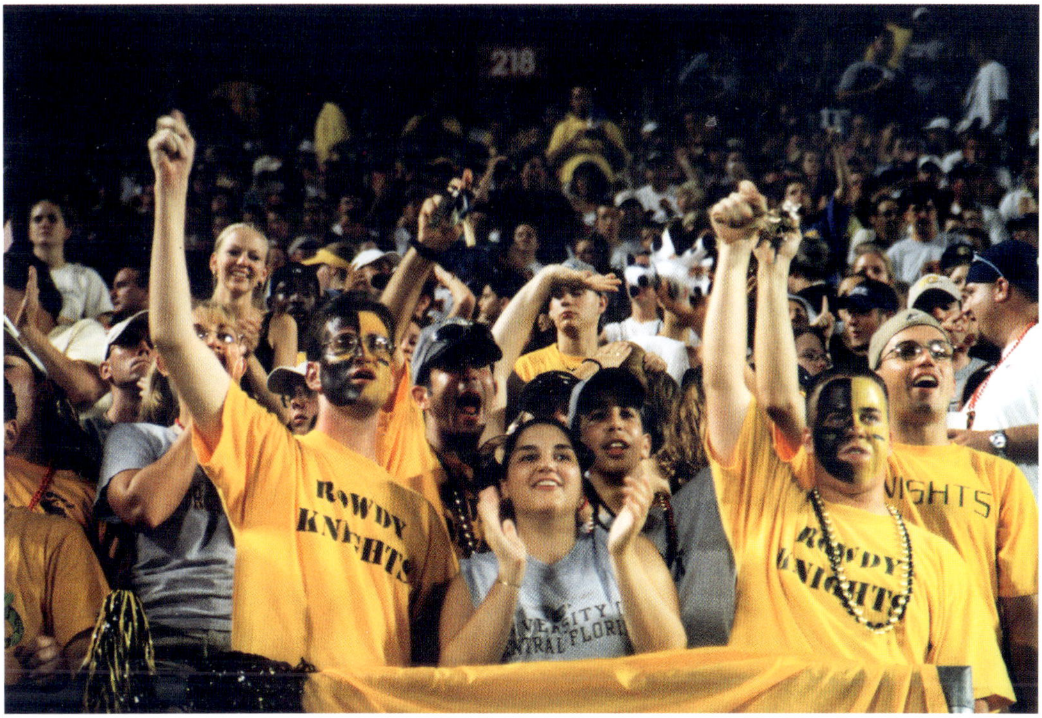

KNIGHTS THROUGH TIME: True to their school; students, faculty, and staff turn out in droves to support their football team, the UCF Knights. The campus is located conveniently close to the neighborhoods of Orlando and many community members come to the games.

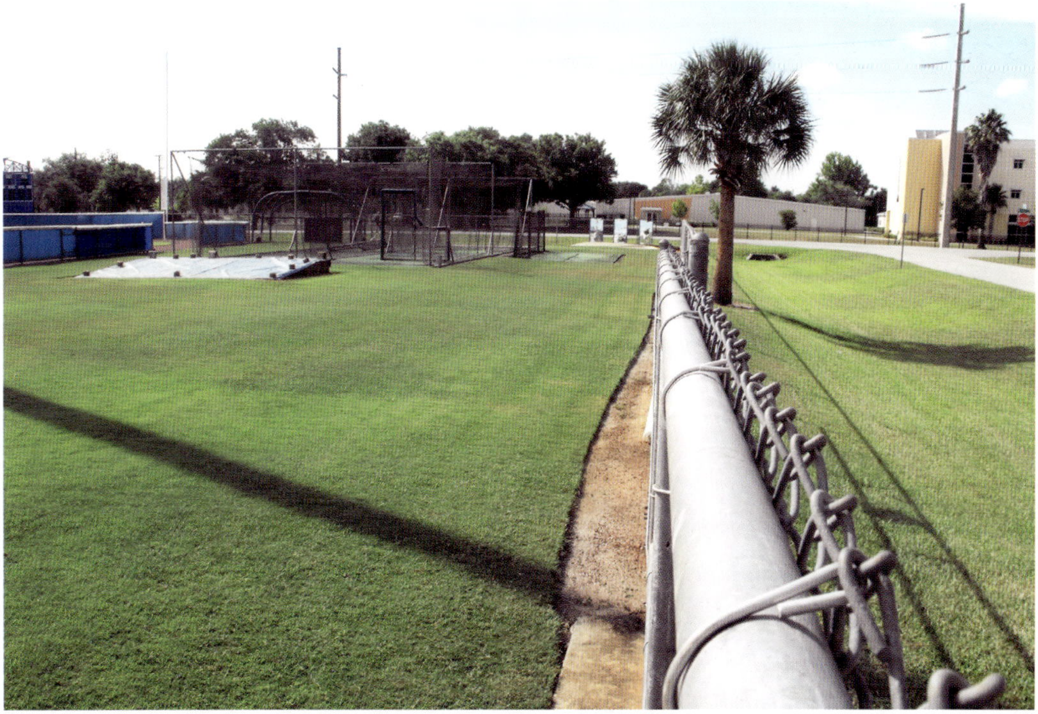

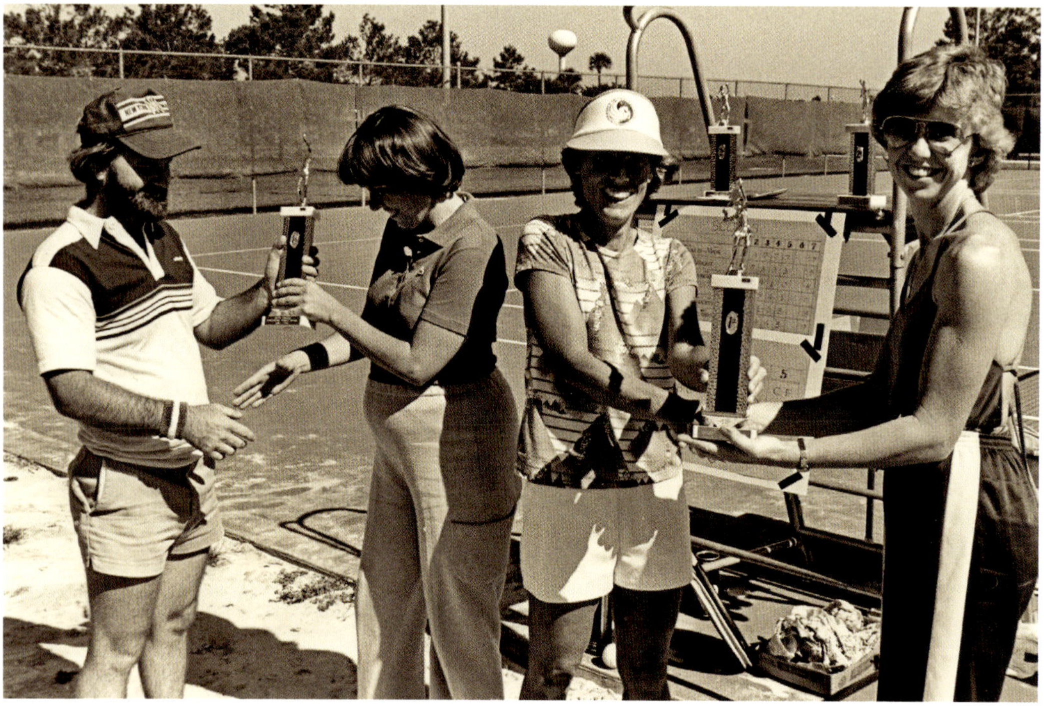

FUN IN THE SUN: Tennis, softball, soccer, baseball, football, surfing, swimming; the list of individual and team sports which can be enjoyed year-round at UCF is a long one. Participation in sports is an important element in not only keeping fit but keeping from becoming overwhelmed with studies.

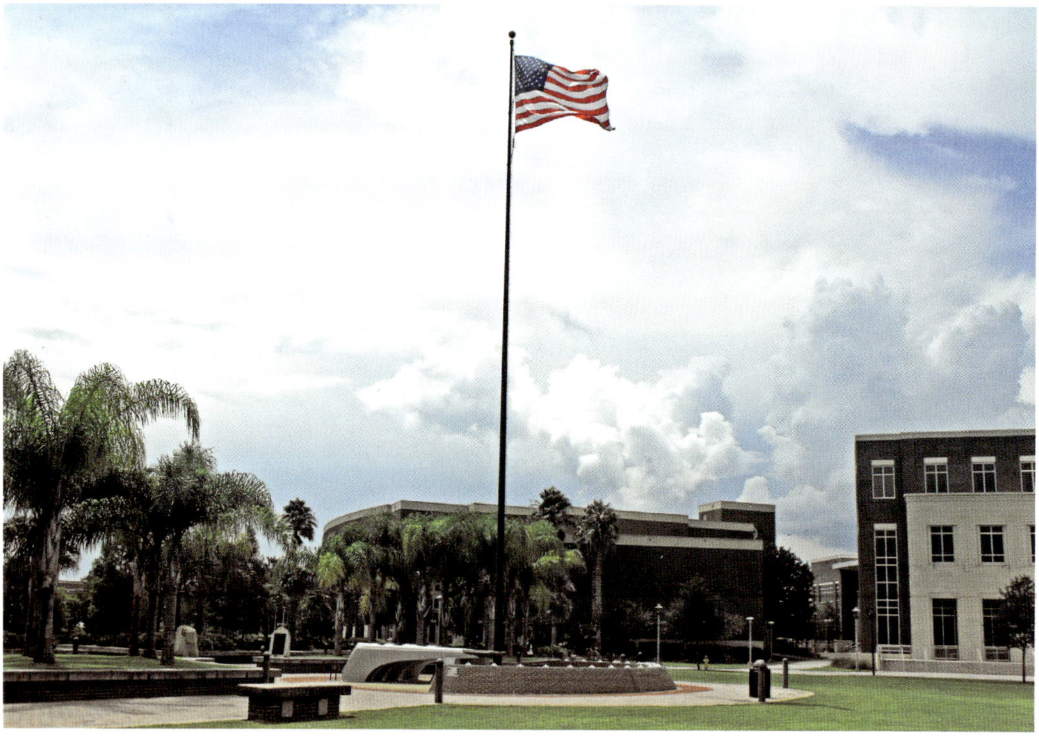

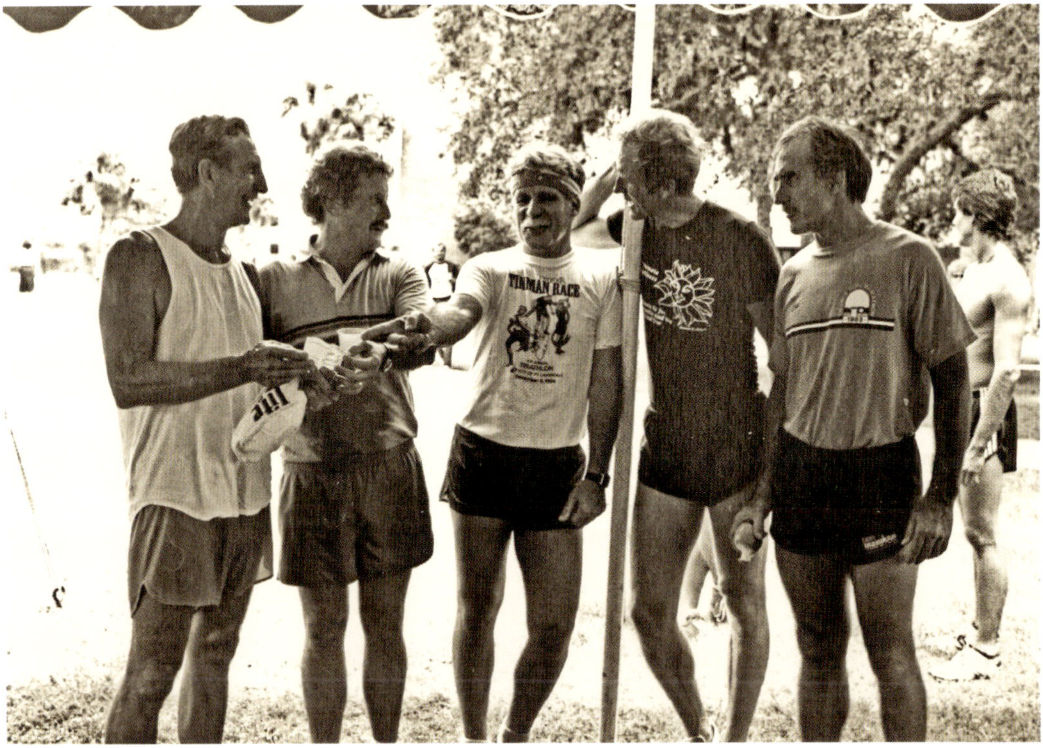

Students and staff who have grown up in the Central Florida area understand the importance of water and shade to daily life in the area. Those who haven't learn it very quickly. While the weather here is mostly a plus, protection from the elements is crucial.

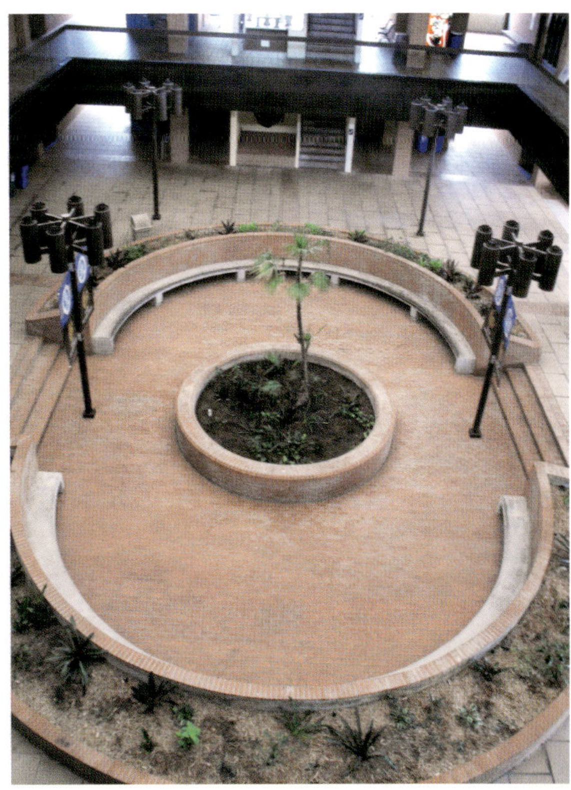

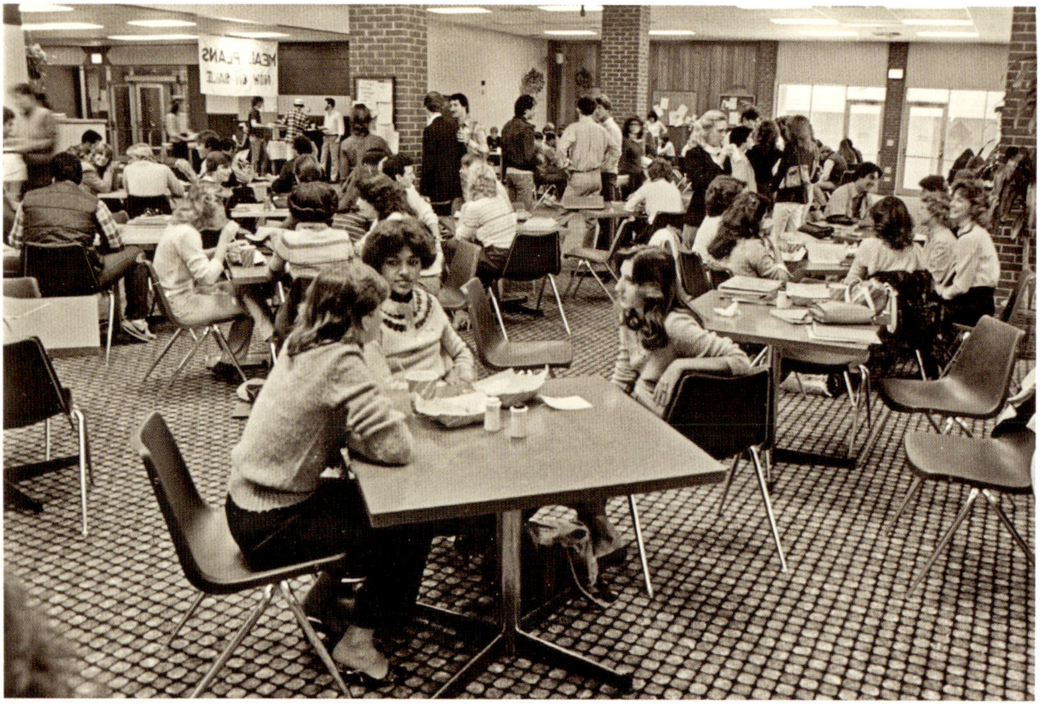

FOOD FOR THOUGHT: As UCF has grown, both in population and geographical area, it has become necessary to expand from the traditional cafeteria-style food plan. Students can now choose to carry cards which work to pay for meals and snacks at dozens of locations throughout campus. Students who commute to campus can easily add money to these cards at one of several locations on campus.

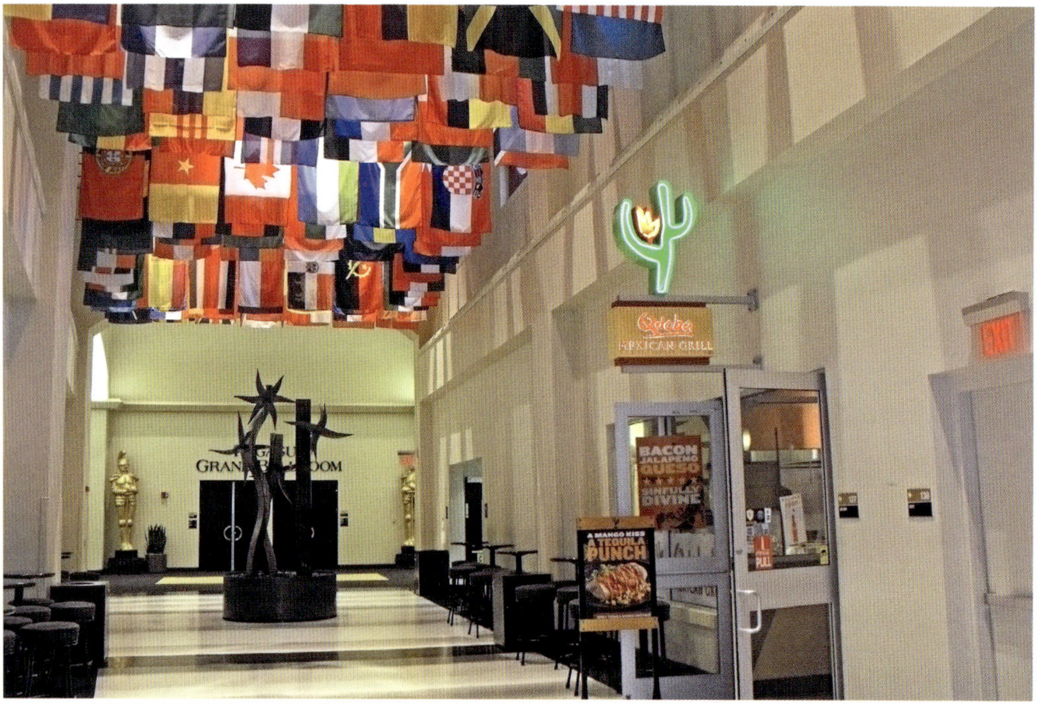

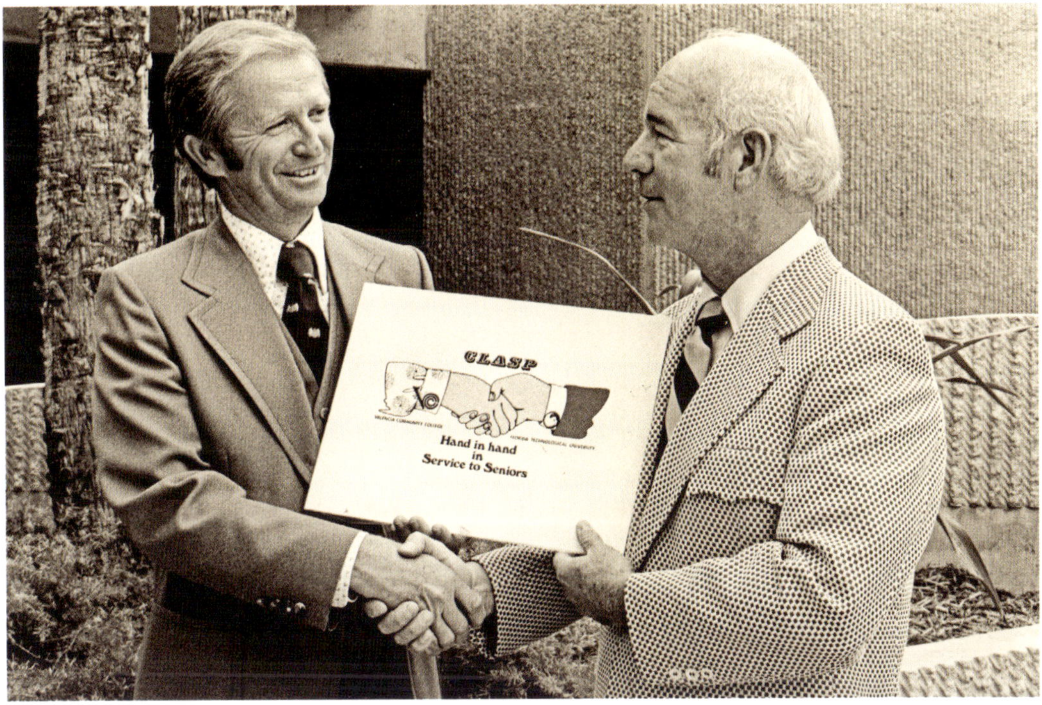

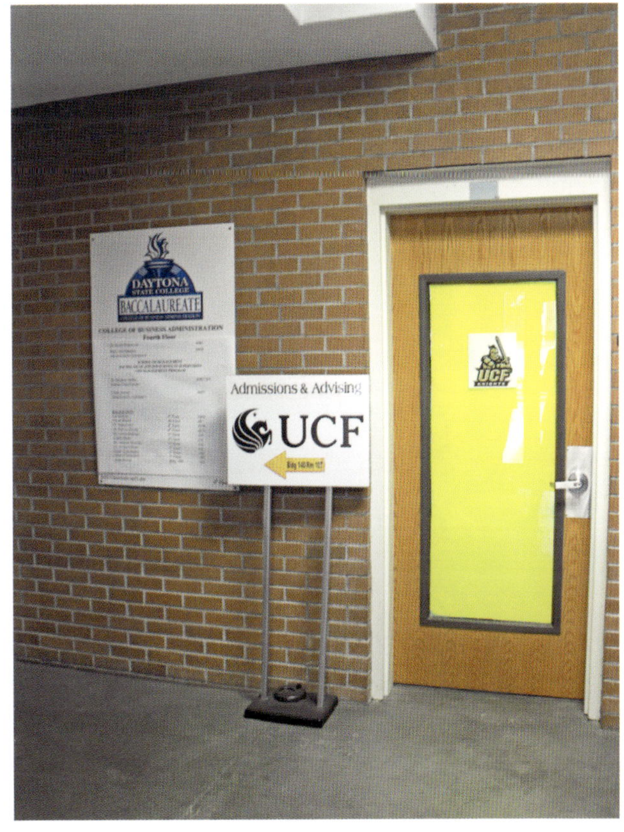

THE LOCAL POPULACE: Liaising with the local community and other educational institutions is crucial to UCFs mission. Dr. Millican shakes hands with Dr. James Collattscheck, then president of Valencia Community College; Daytona State College and UCF share space and services.

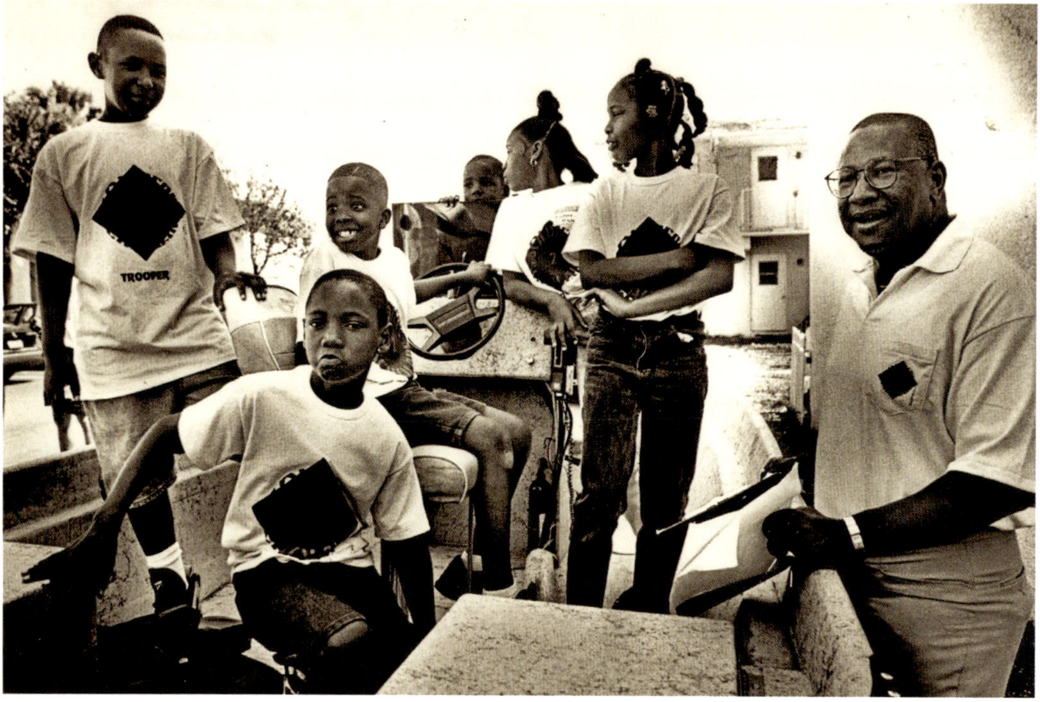

LITTLE LEARNERS: One is never too young to benefit from a trip to UCF! An archival photograph shows local children visiting campus, and a recent one the small library at the Center for Autism and Related Disabilities at UCF where community members can check out all the latest materials on the subject of autism, including children's books.

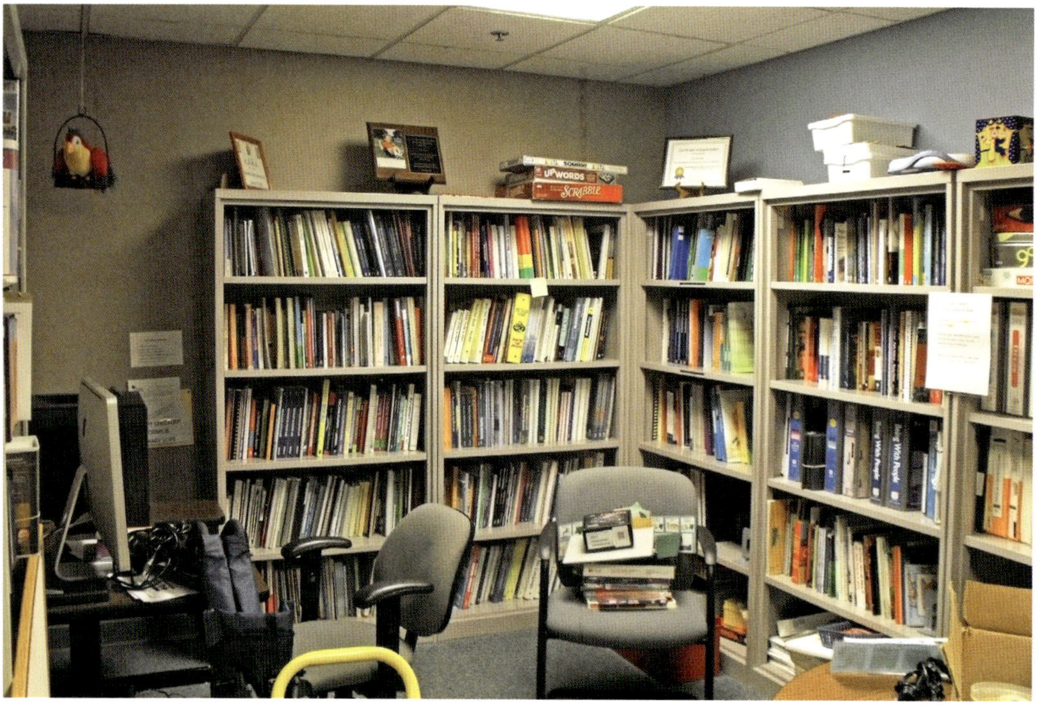

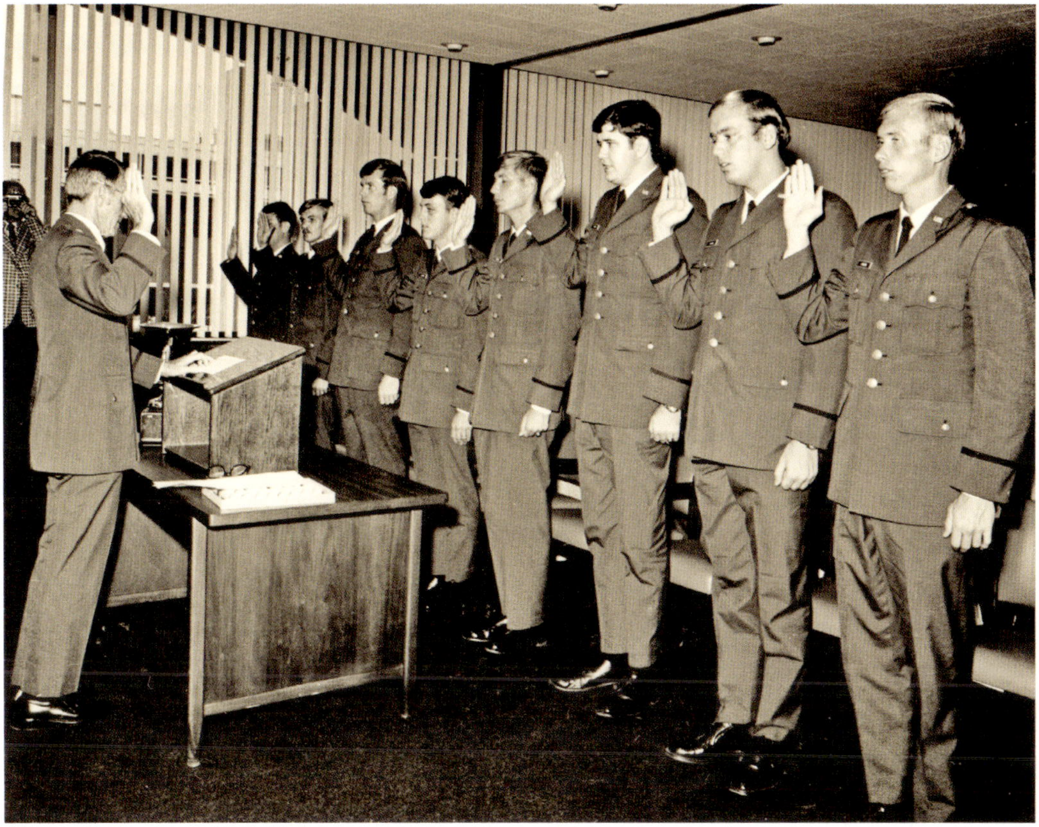

Veterans as well as members of ROTC for various branches of the military are often seen on campus, side by side with other students. This plaque near Ferrell Commons reads, 'This tree is dedicated to those who sacrificed their time, effort, and for some their lives during the Vietnam Conflict. November 9, 1992.'

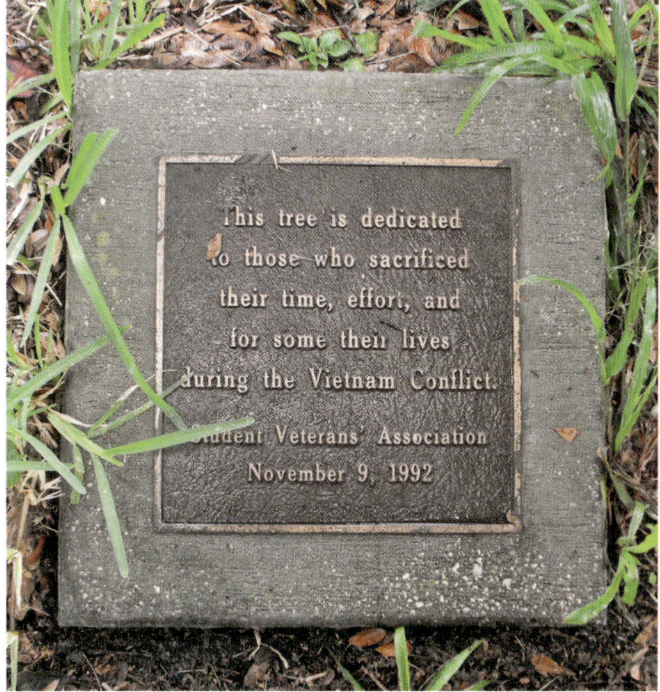

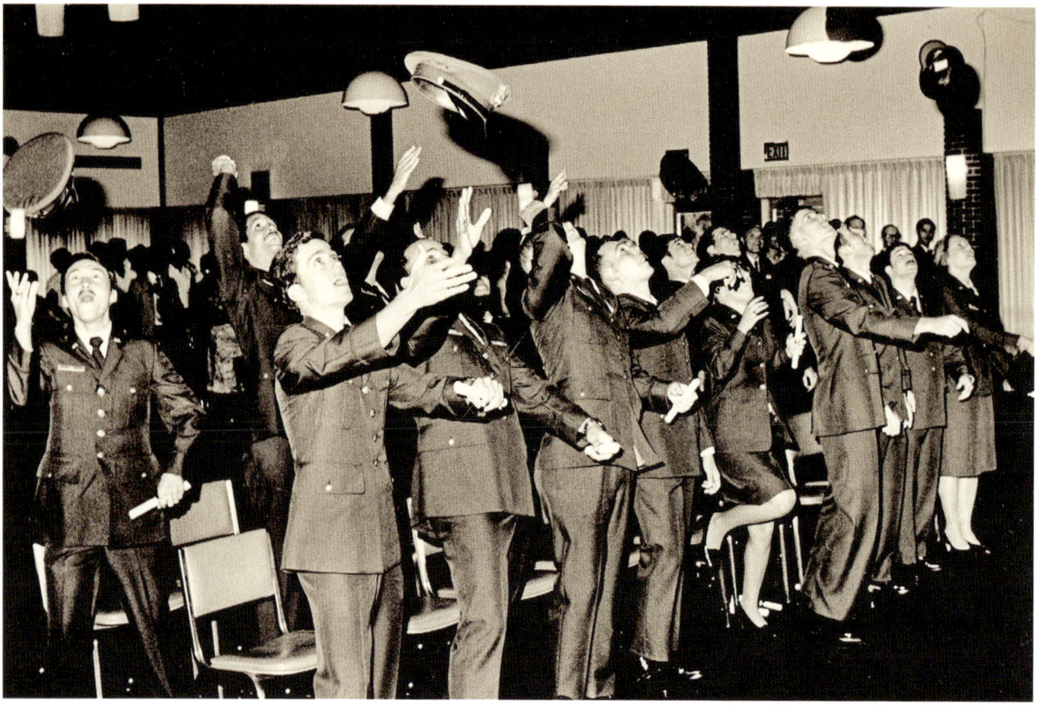

Earned elation: An ROTC graduation ceremony at UCF for students whose mode of transportation will soon transition from the bicycles and personal vehicles which crowd campus to ships, planes, and other military transit. Their lives are about to go from study to active service as they pay the government back for years of education at UCF.

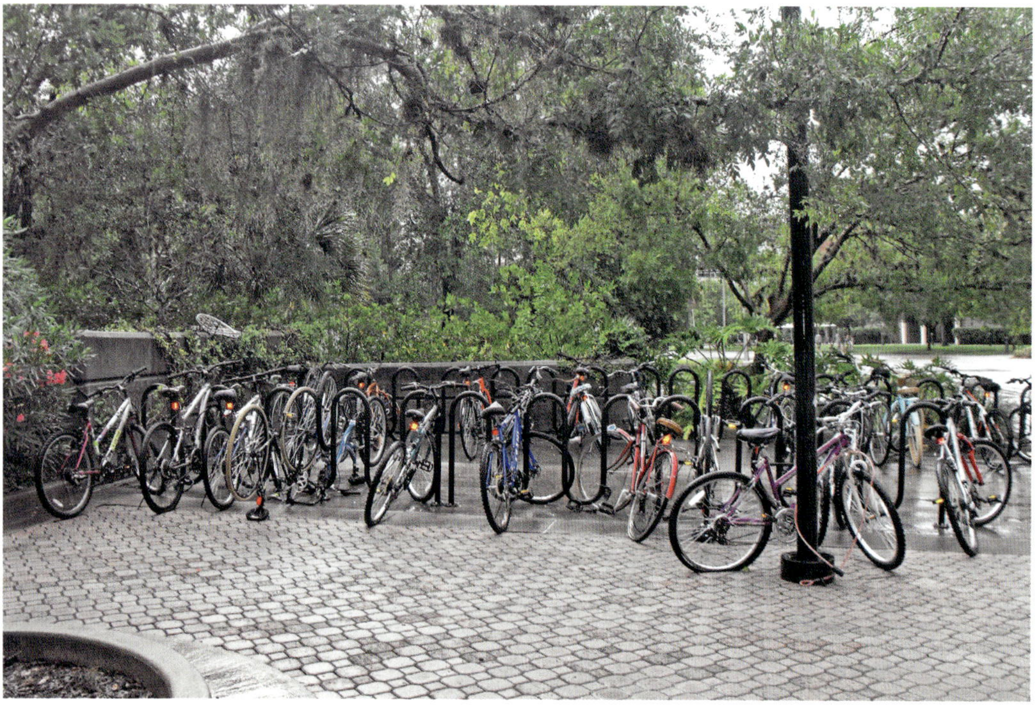

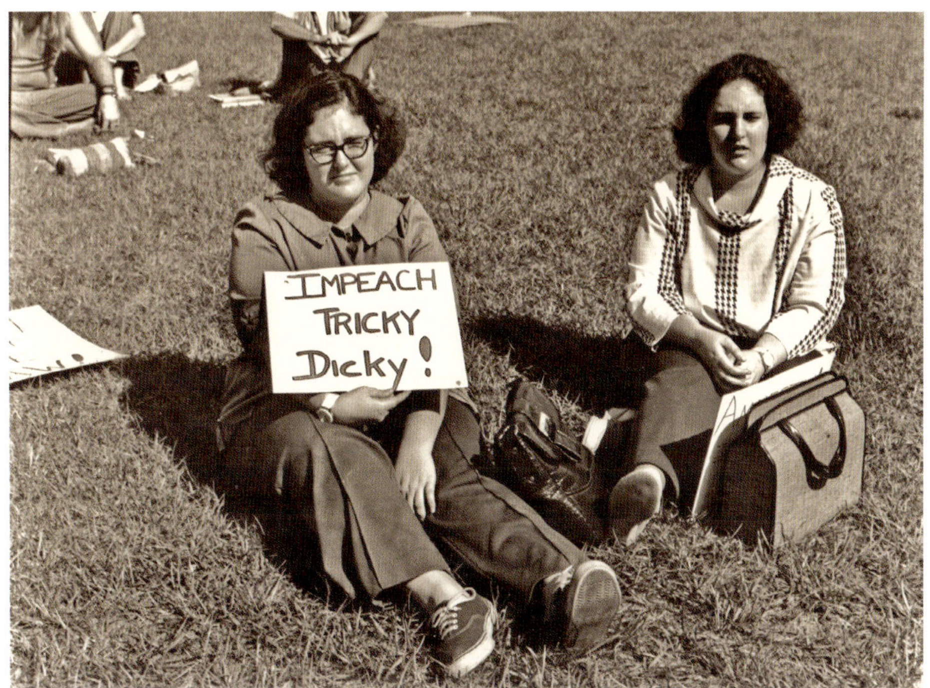

 One of the terrific things about college is learning to express oneself as an adult citizen. Heated debates, inside the classroom and out, are part of higher education. College is one step in turning from the inward focus of adolescence toward participation in the community, country, and world at large and finding an active place in those arenas. At UCF, the mild climate and large open spaces provide ample casual gathering places.

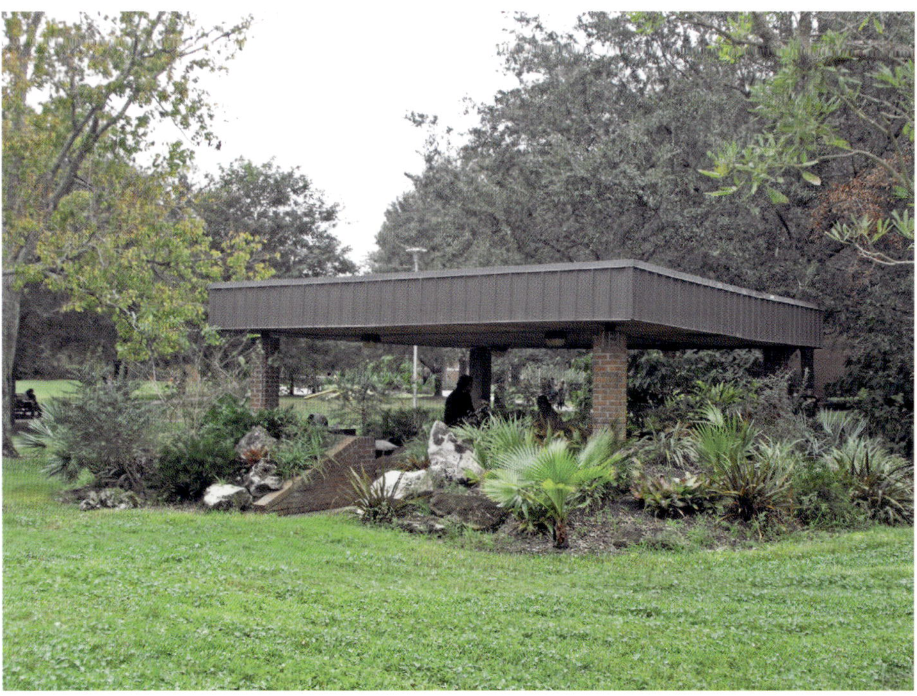

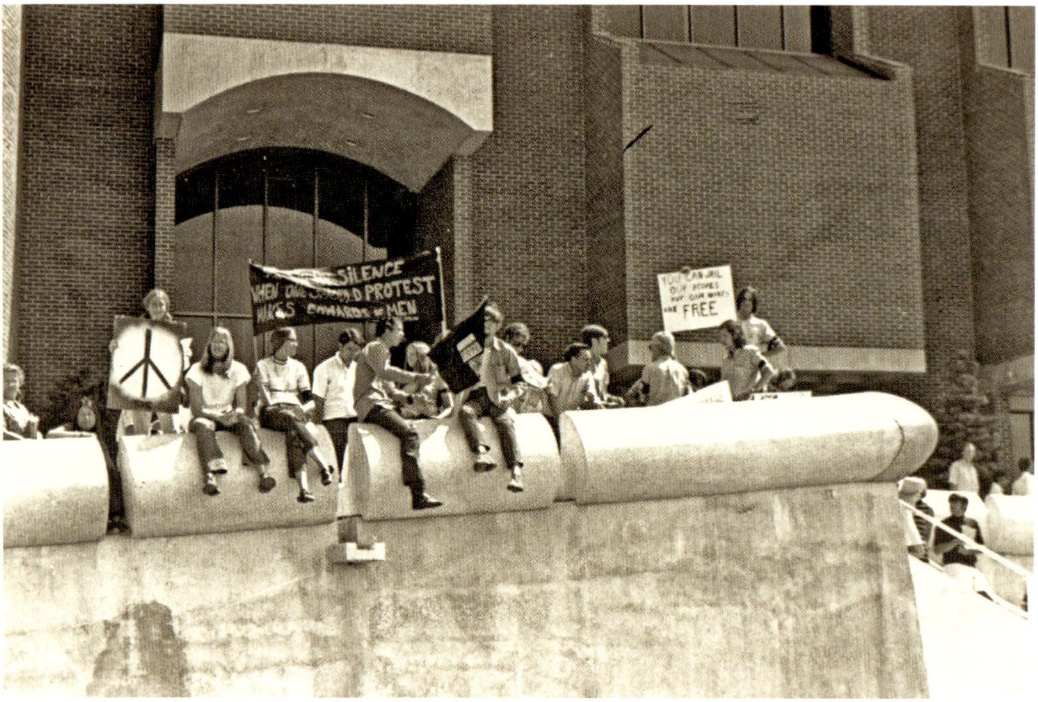

SOCIAL RESPONSIBILITY: Young people on campus across the country took the right of free speech seriously in the 1960s and 1970s and helped change the nation. On the modern UCF campuses, many students set up booths and tables along walkways and in front of the student union to express their beliefs and opinions.

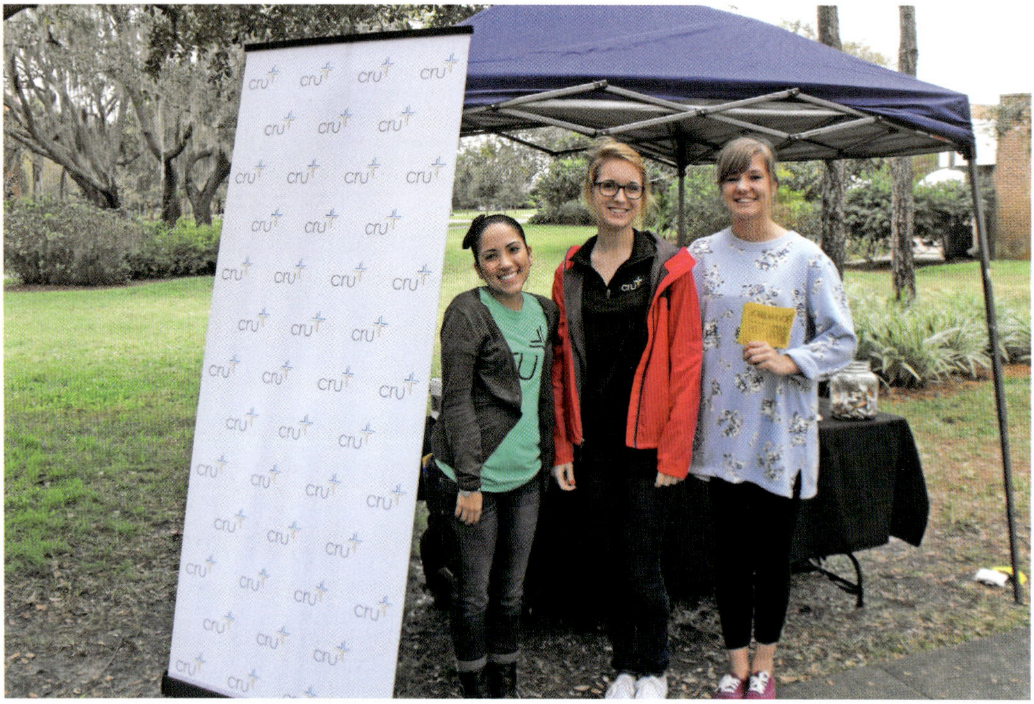

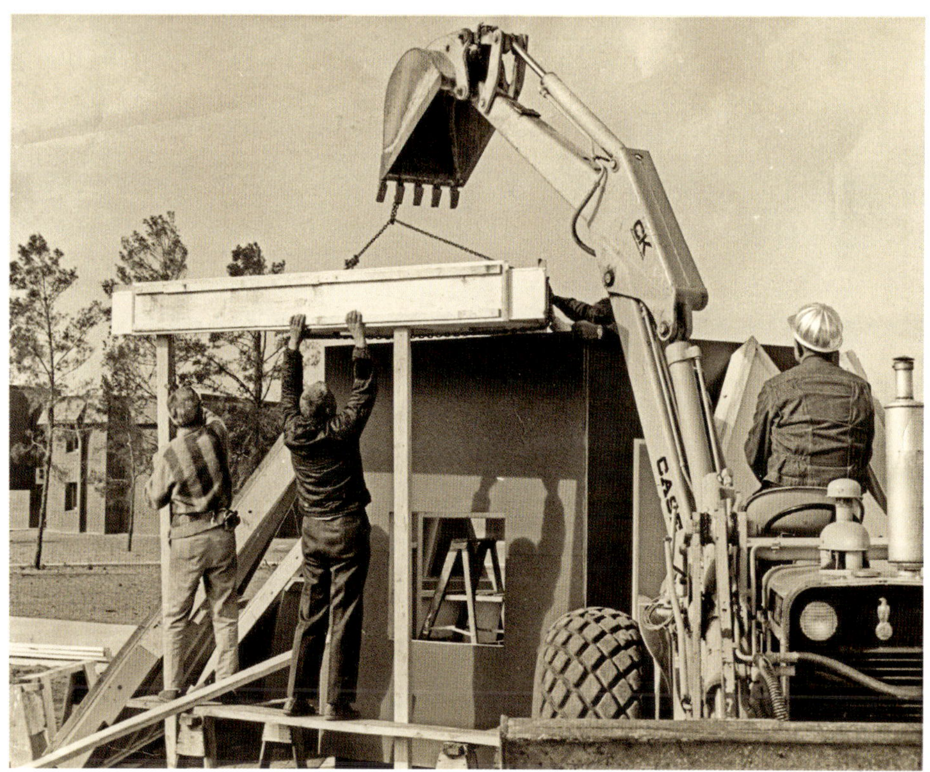

IN THE MEDIA: The original automated post office on the UCF campus was located in an outdoor kiosk. Now, it is in an air-conditioned hallway on the first floor of the student union. As online communication becomes the norm, many students rarely, if ever, send a letter.

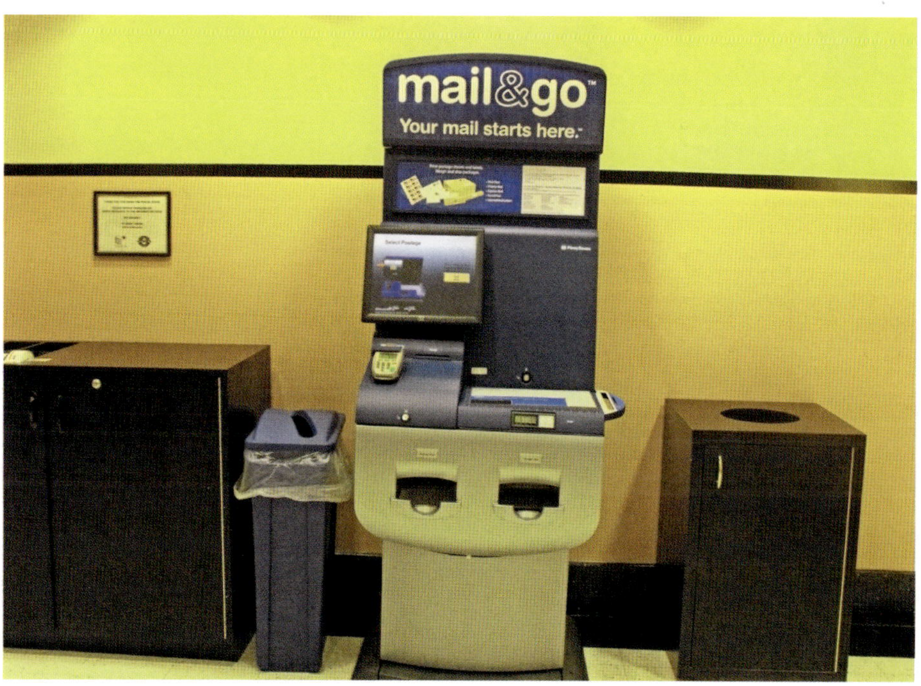

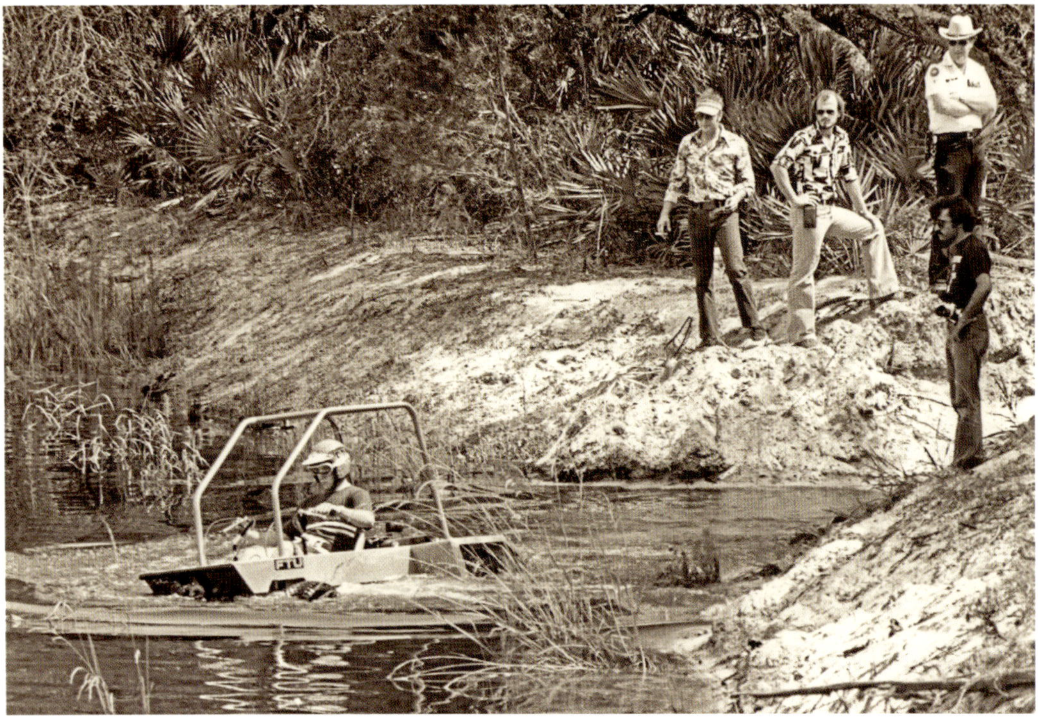

 The natural world in Florida can be dangerous; most inland bodies of water contain snakes and alligators. FTU and UCF have been the sites of several films and caution is always in order. Sandhill cranes are typically seen in pairs all over campus.

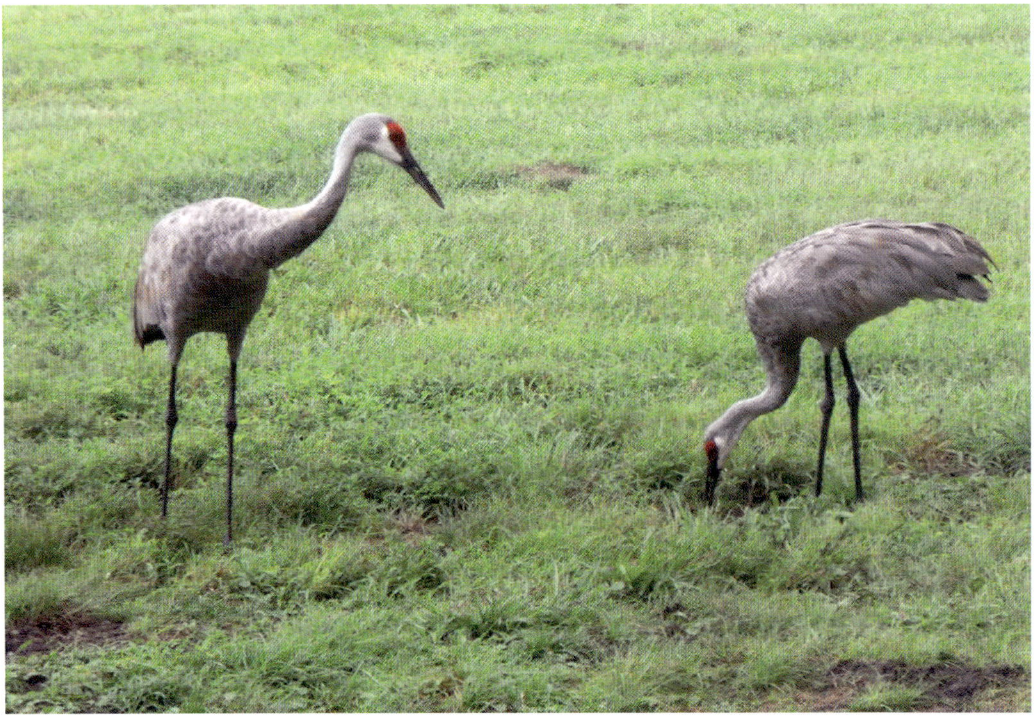

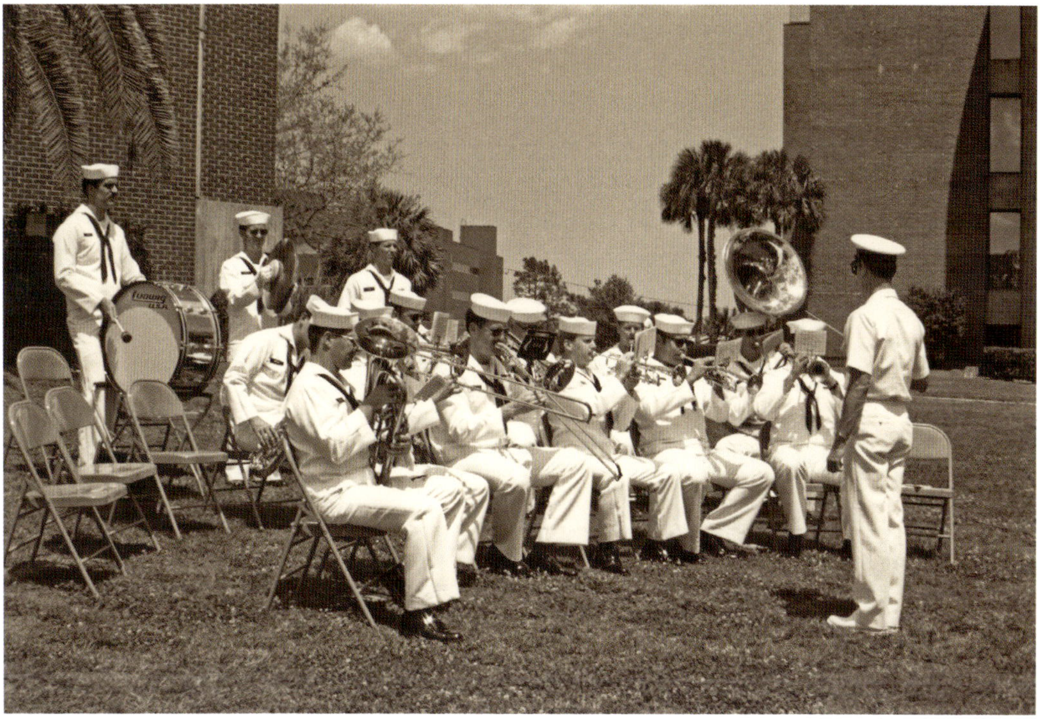

SPACE TO PLAY: The April weather was wonderful for the outdoor festivities; including a Naval band concert, in the 1988 25th anniversary celebrations of the university. It is easy to lose track of time when the weather is beautiful, here, which it often is.

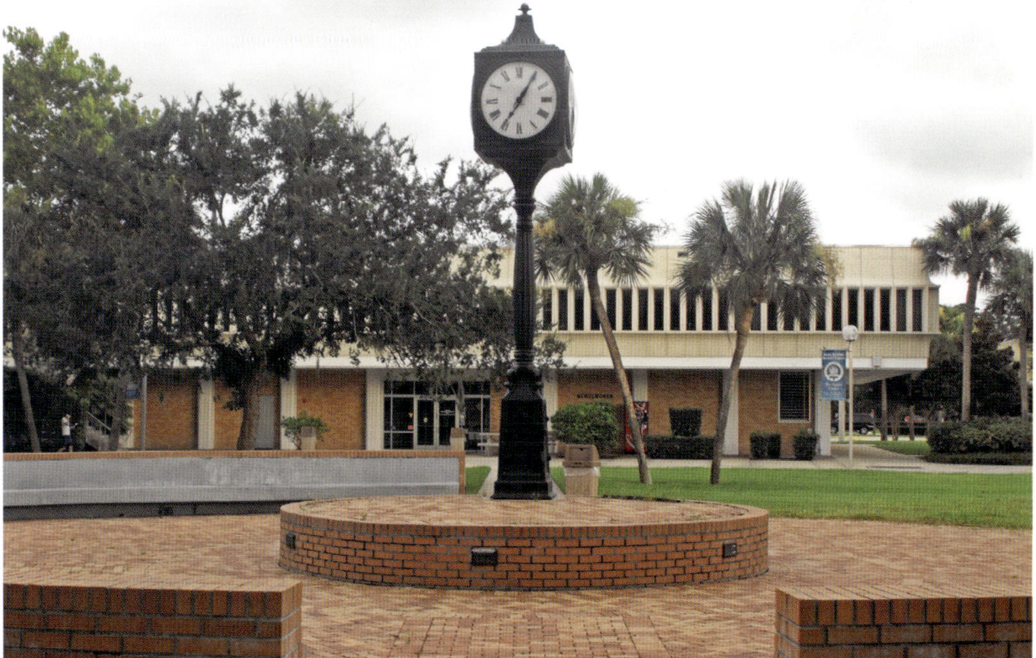

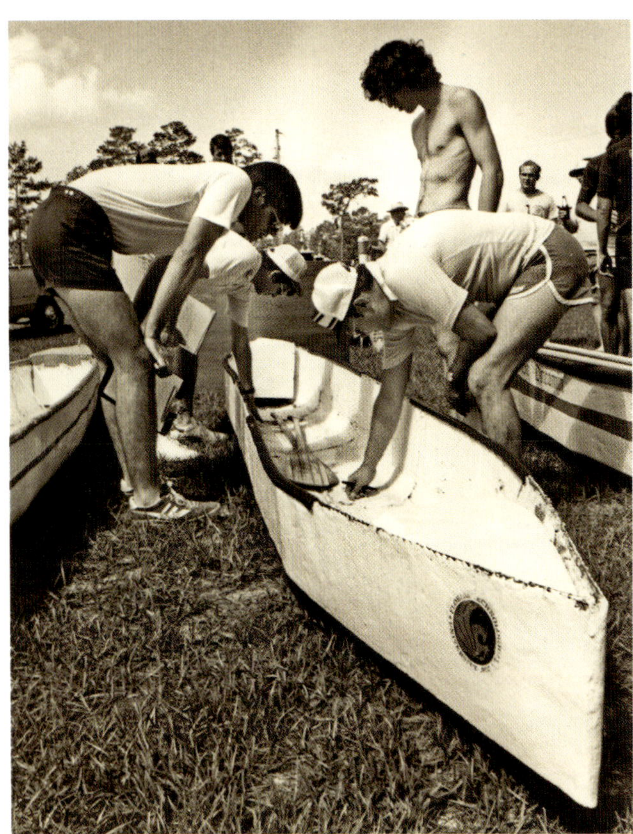

WATER WORLD: A concrete
canoe race at UCF took place on
Lake Claire in 1979. Students
and faculty alike pursue many
water sports, including the
recently popular standup
paddleboarding, on local
lakes, rivers, and even in the
Atlantic Ocean.

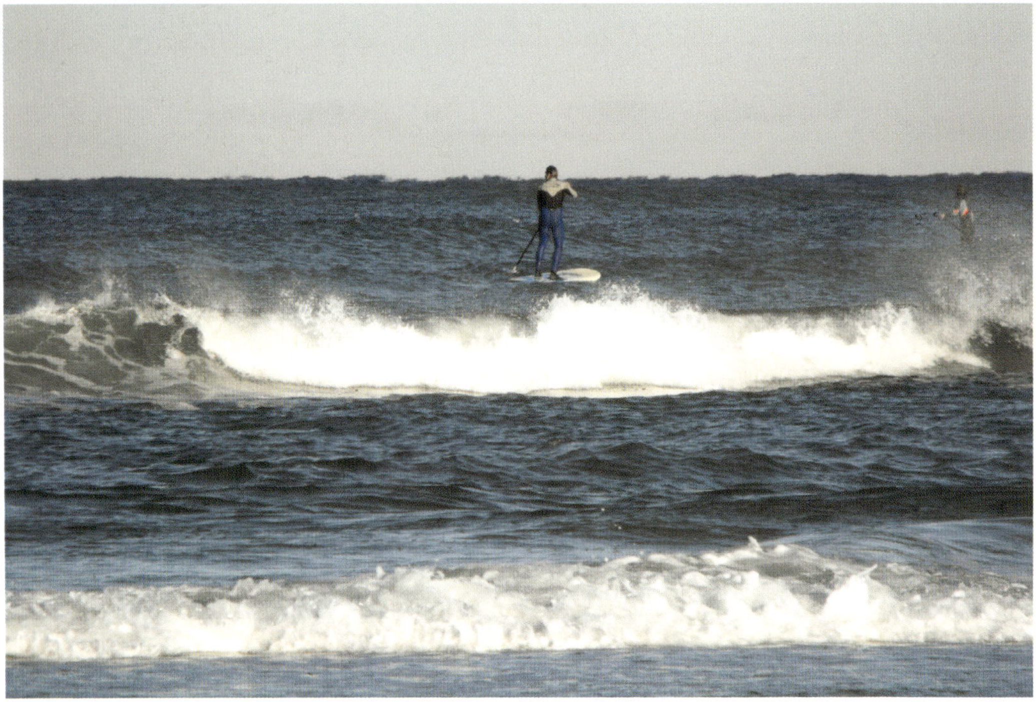

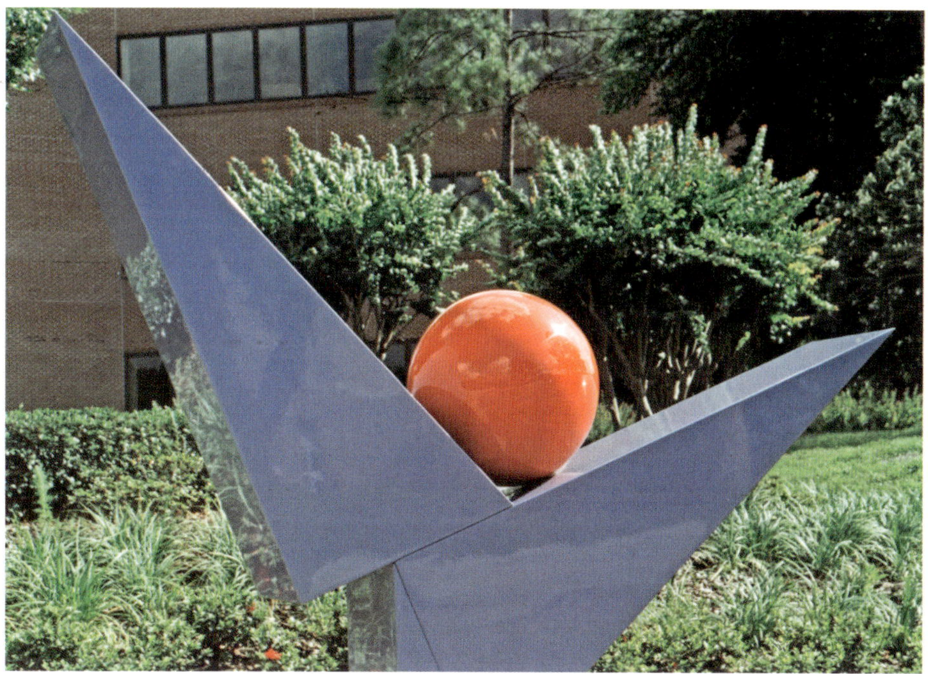

 This modern sculpture by New Smyrna Beach artist and founder of Atlantic Center for the Arts, Doris Leeper, has been moved from UCF to the City Hall in New Smyrna Beach. The winged Pegasus is UCF's mascot; this wonderful rendition stands outside the Honors College.

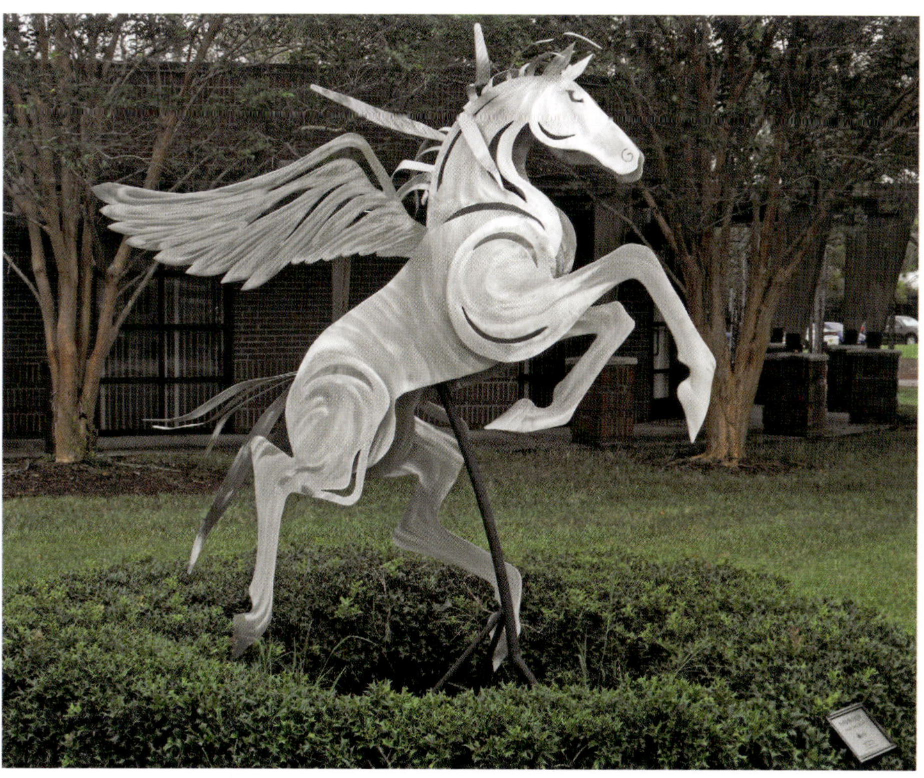

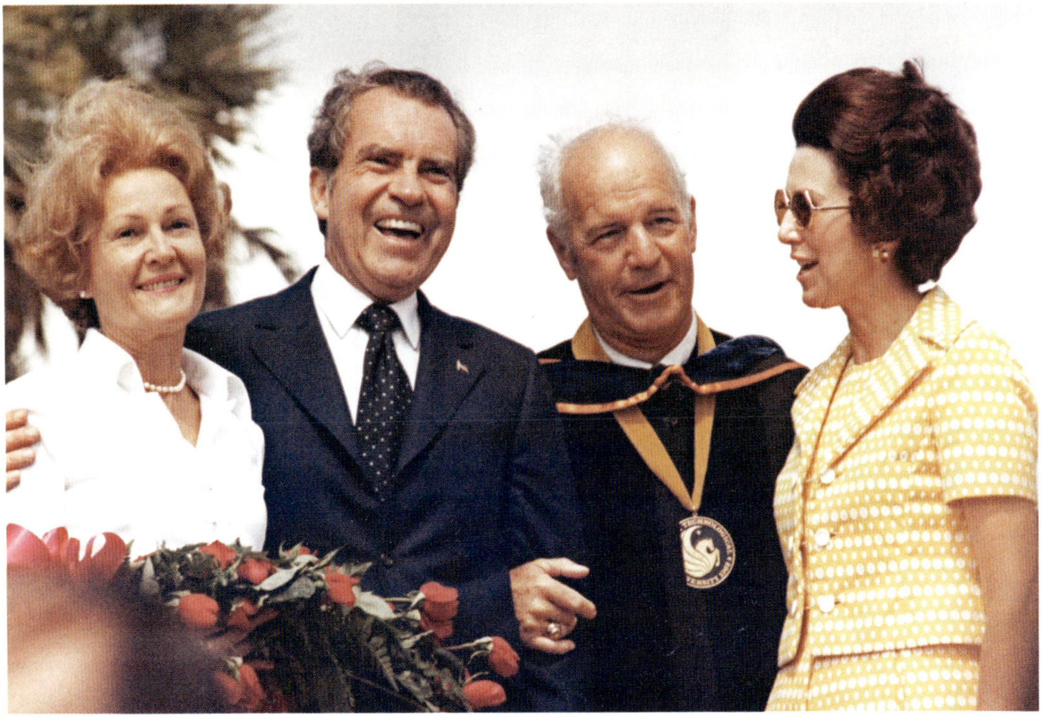

NATIONAL ATTENTION: A year prior to his 1974 resignation, President Richard M. Nixon and his wife Pat visited FTU. The first lady holds dozens of long-stem red roses. There aren't currently rose gardens on UCF's campus, but many strange and wonderful plants can be found.

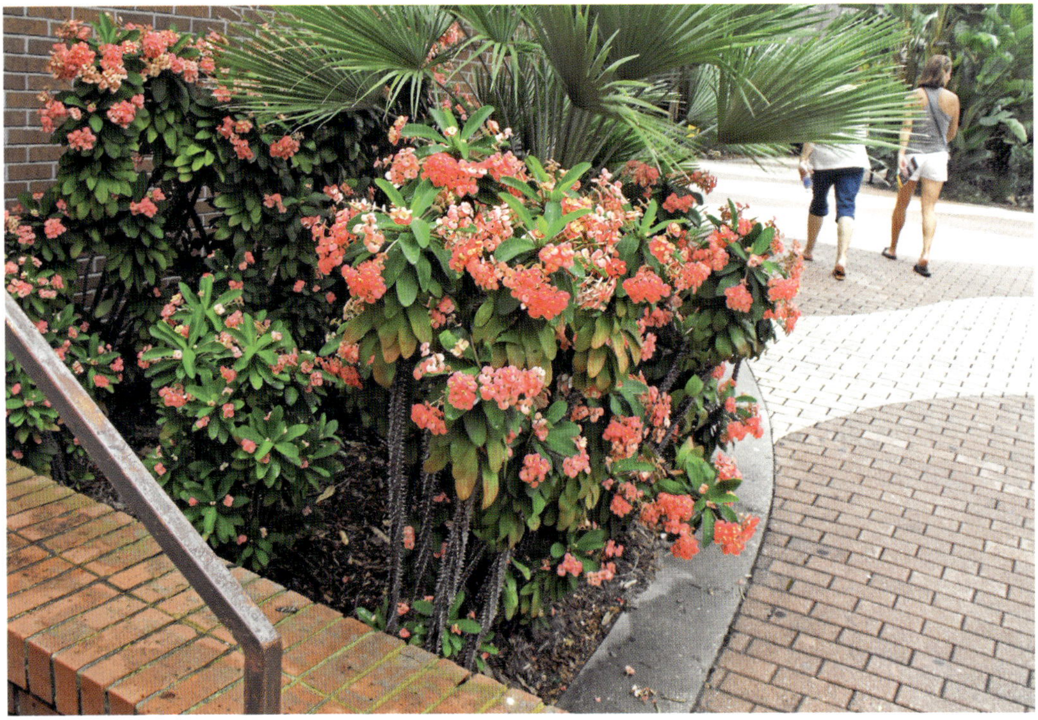

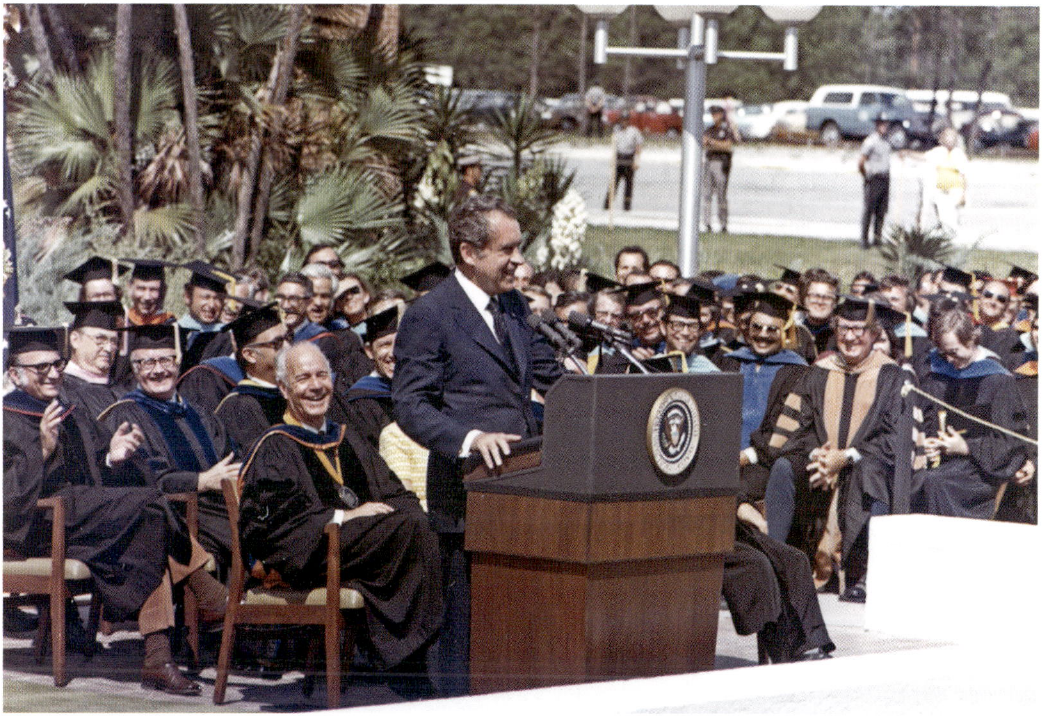

LOCAL ATTIRE: Faculty assembled behind the President smile and clap, adorned in academic regalia. A modern faculty meeting sees staff attired in their casual workday garb. Casual is the norm, here; it is sometimes hard to tell teachers from students.

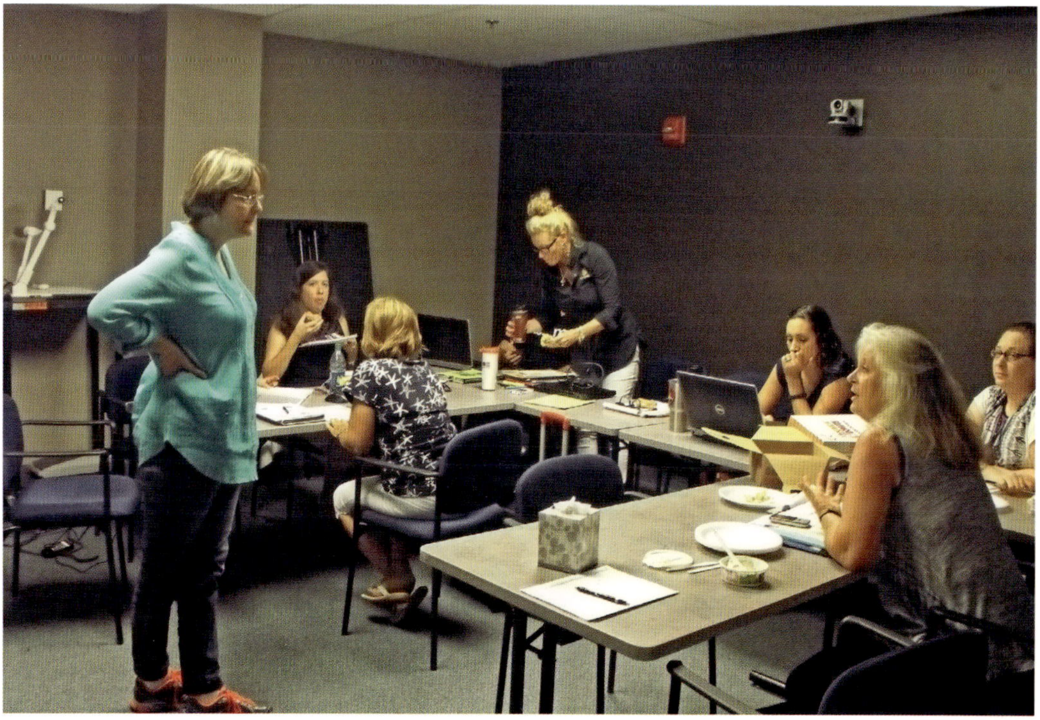

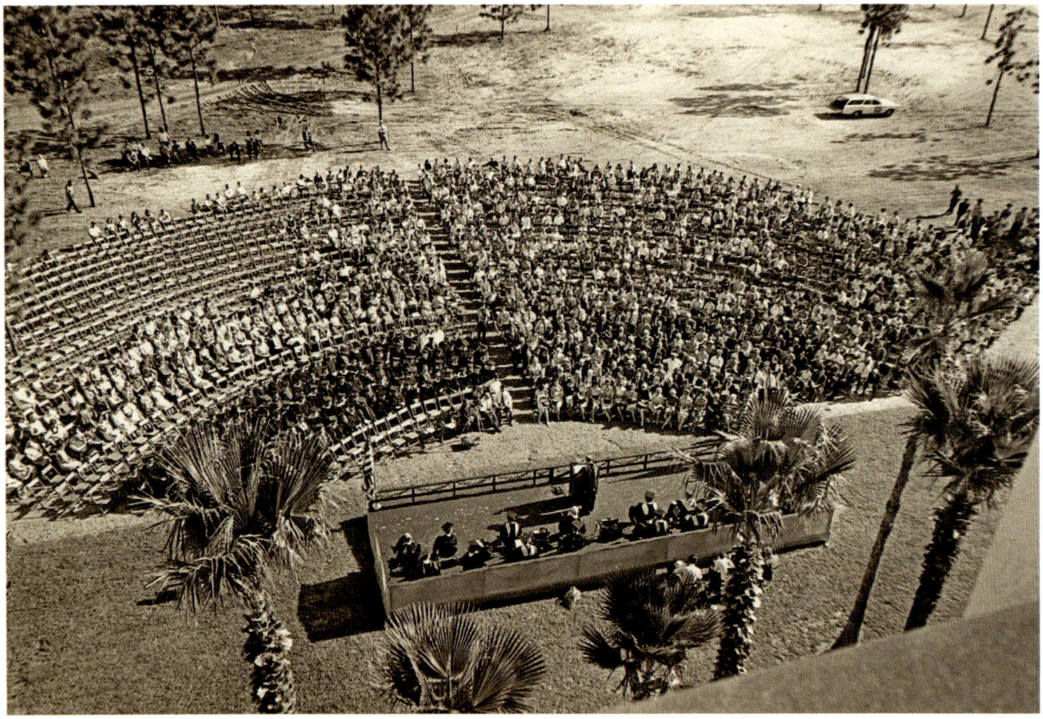

 The first FTU commencement took place on what is now the reflecting pond. The pond is a focal point of the university which has hosted many events, including the annual spirit splash. The concrete on the floor of the pond was painted blue some years ago to hide algae and give a clean look.

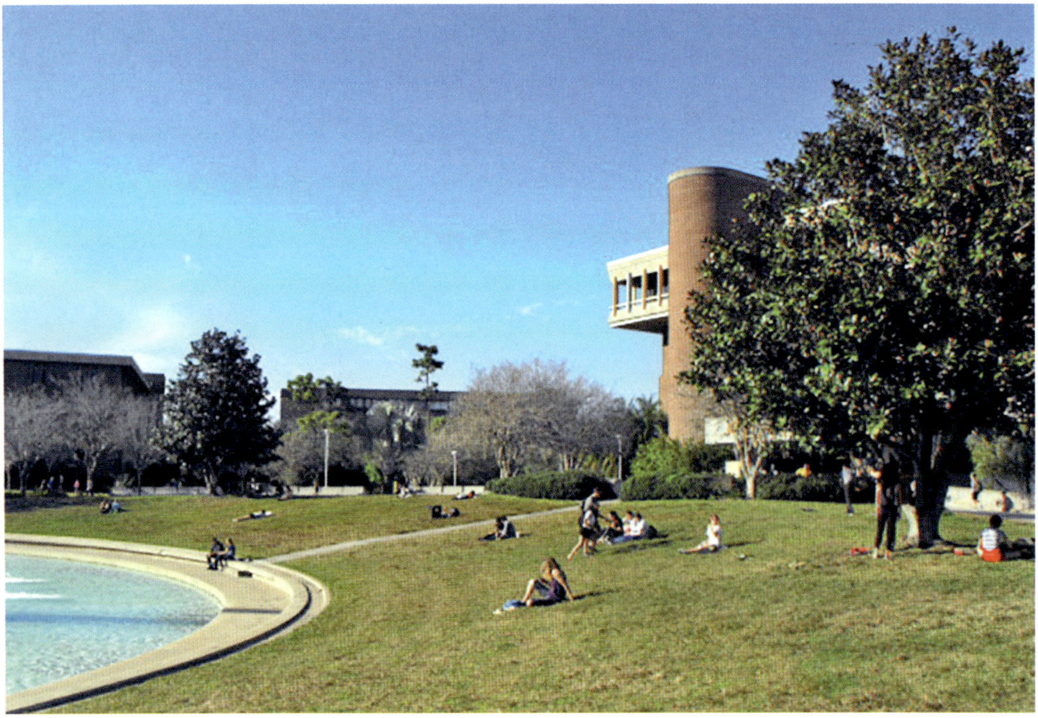

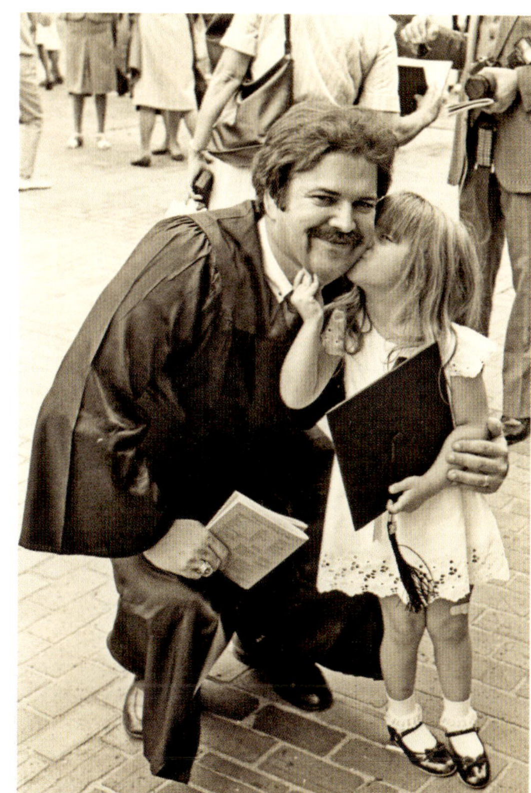

PRIORITIES: Many students, past and present, have families. While some young people right out of high school may need an adjustment period to being on their own in college, adults returning to their educational pursuits after becoming parents naturally have different priorities. They tend to make excellent students and there is nothing quite like your children watching you graduate.

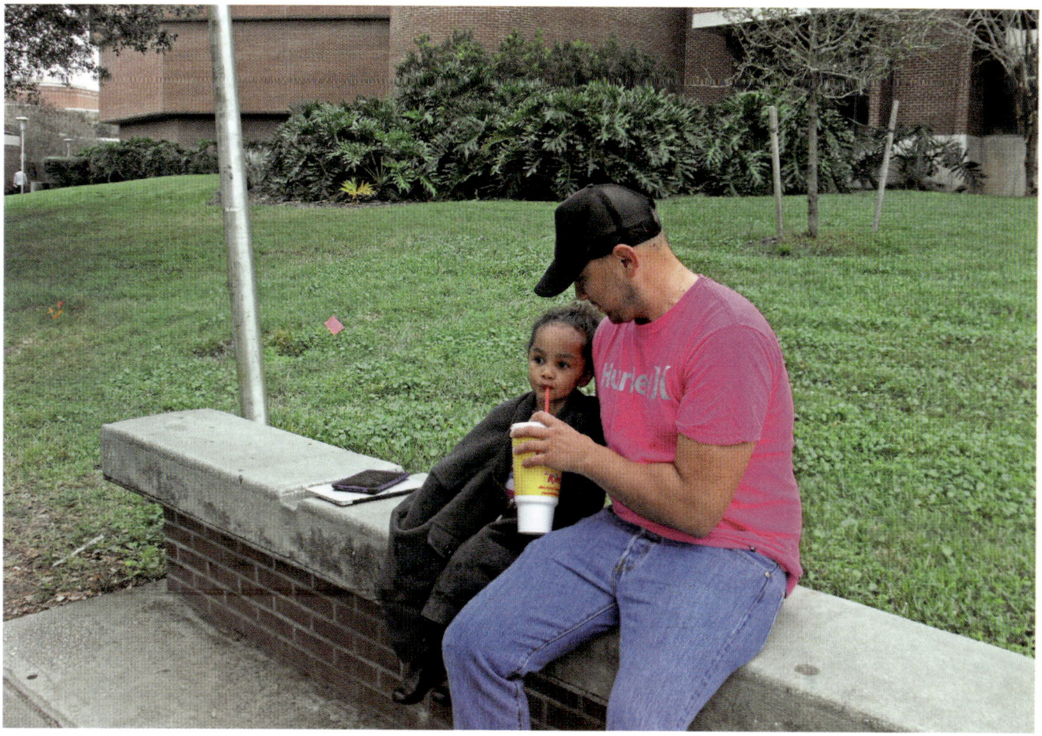

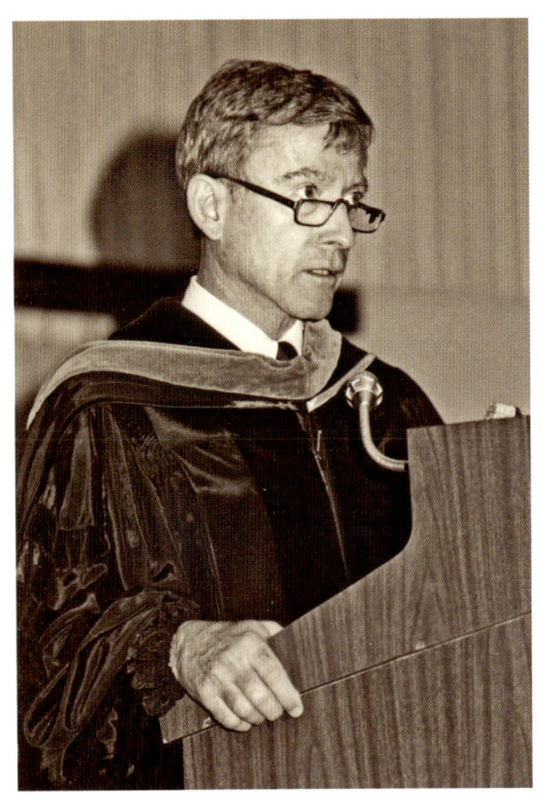

UNIQUE COMMUNITY: UCF enjoys
the distinction of a close association
with the National Aeronautics and Space
Administration; NASA. Astronaut John
Young has addressed graduating classes
at both FTU and UCF, and NASA gave FTU
its first research grant in 1968. Students
gather at the reflecting pond in a sobering
memorial to Americans who died aboard
the Space Shuttle Challenger.

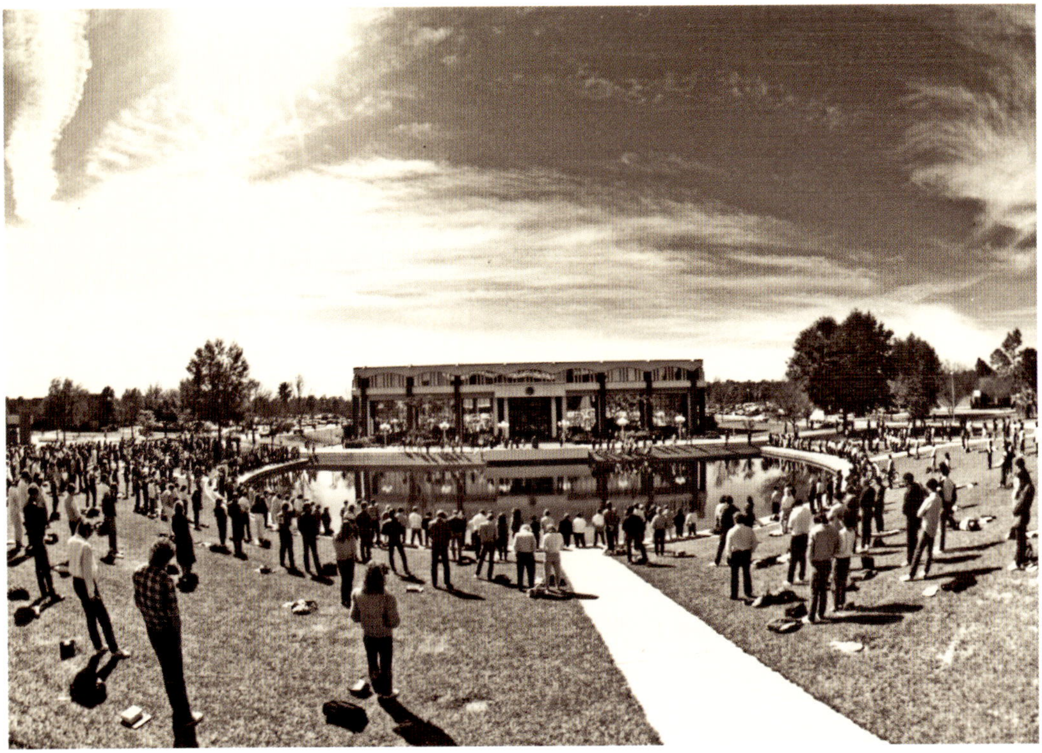

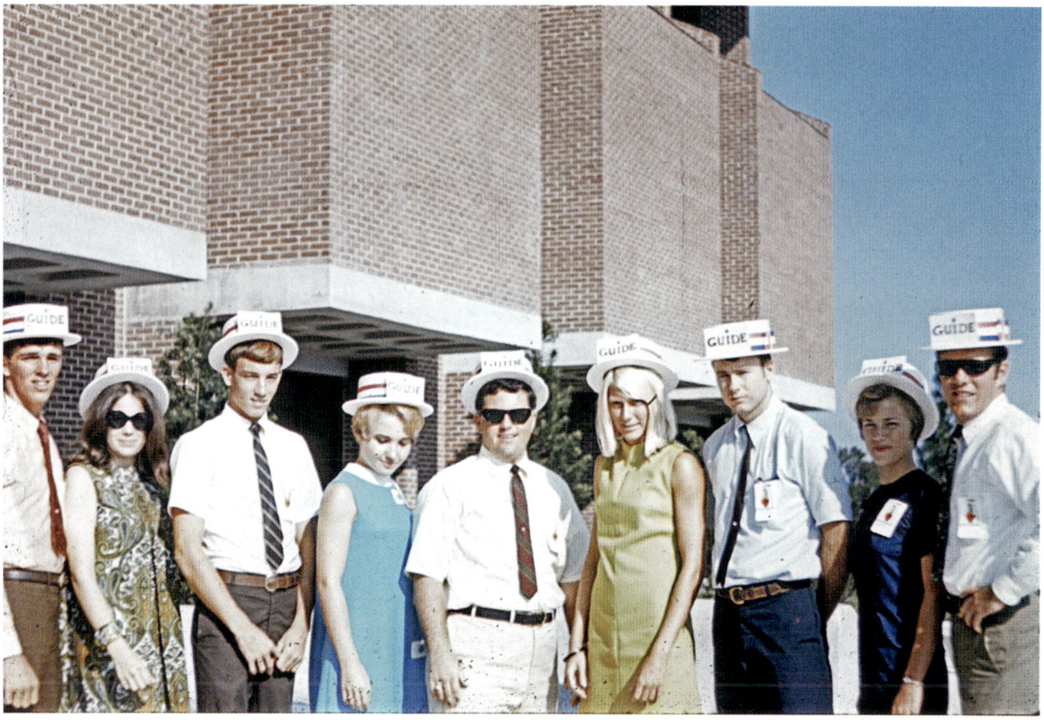

WORK AND STUDY: Many UCF students work on campus and some take jobs here after graduation. Volunteering is also an important part of this educational community; eight students assemble to assist with the university's first orientation.

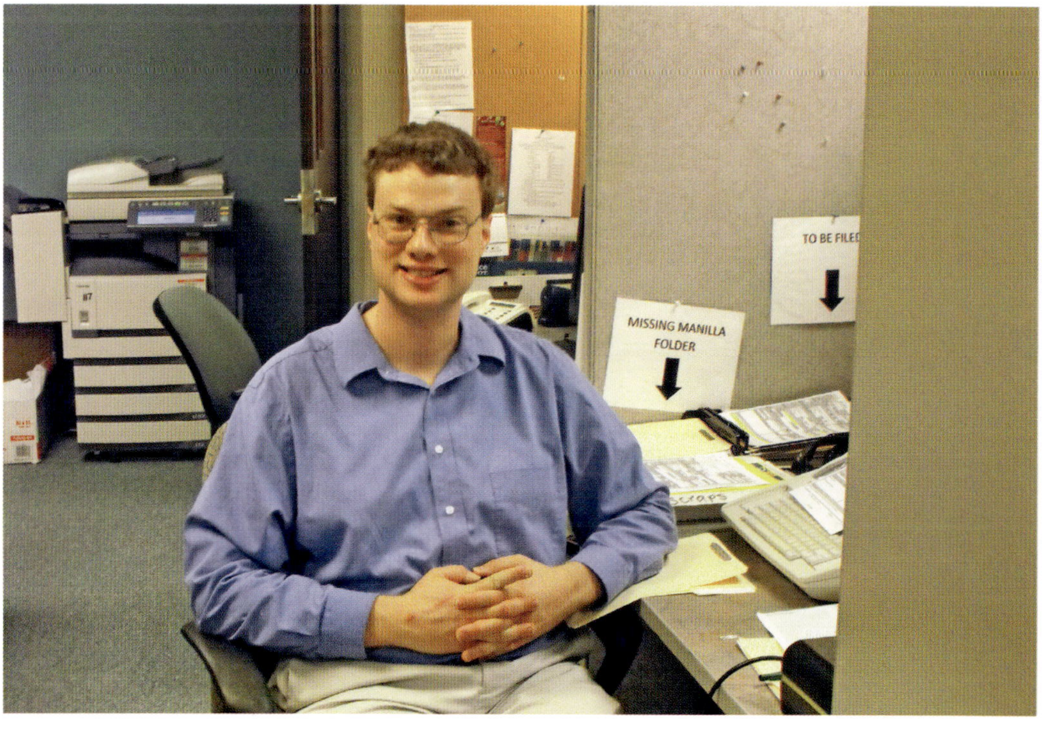

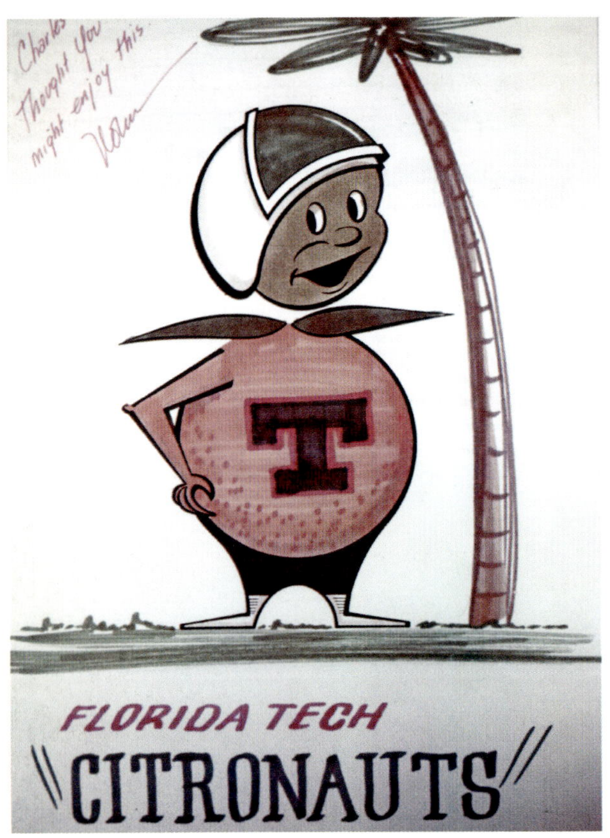

President Millican chose the first FTU mascot; the Citronaut, a cross between an orange and an astronaut. It proved unpopular with students and in 1971 students voted for a new mascot and selected the Knight of the Pegasus, which remains to this day UCF's official mascot.

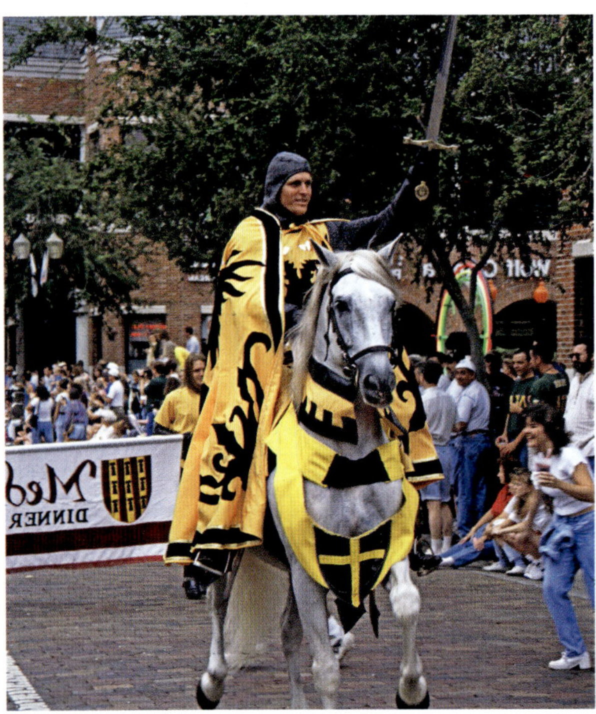

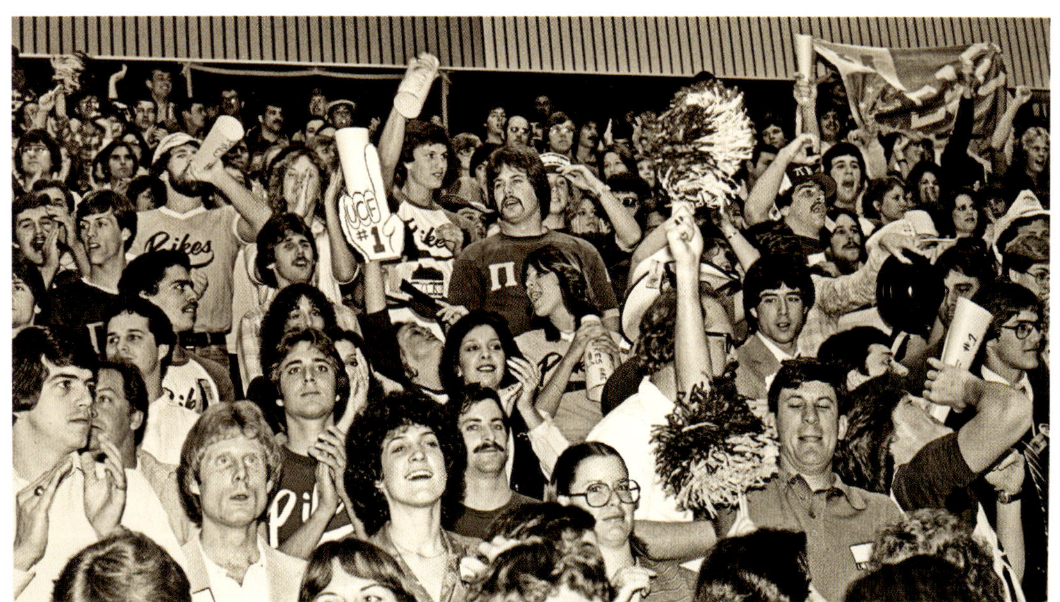

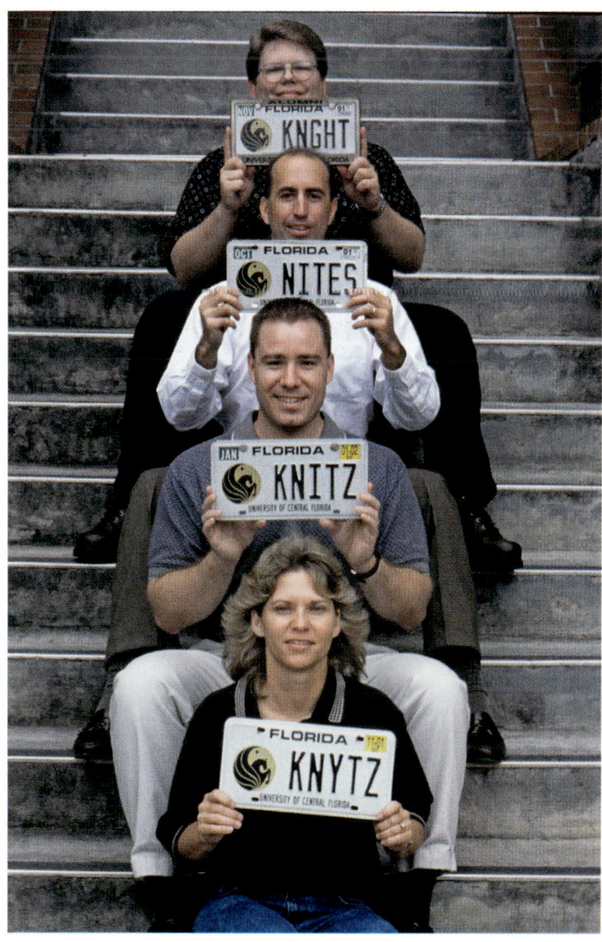

ALL IN GOOD CHEER: School spirit is reflected not only at football games, other sporting events, and in UCF gear, but on local license plates. It is common to see UCF clothing and gear throughout Central Florida and it is also big business.

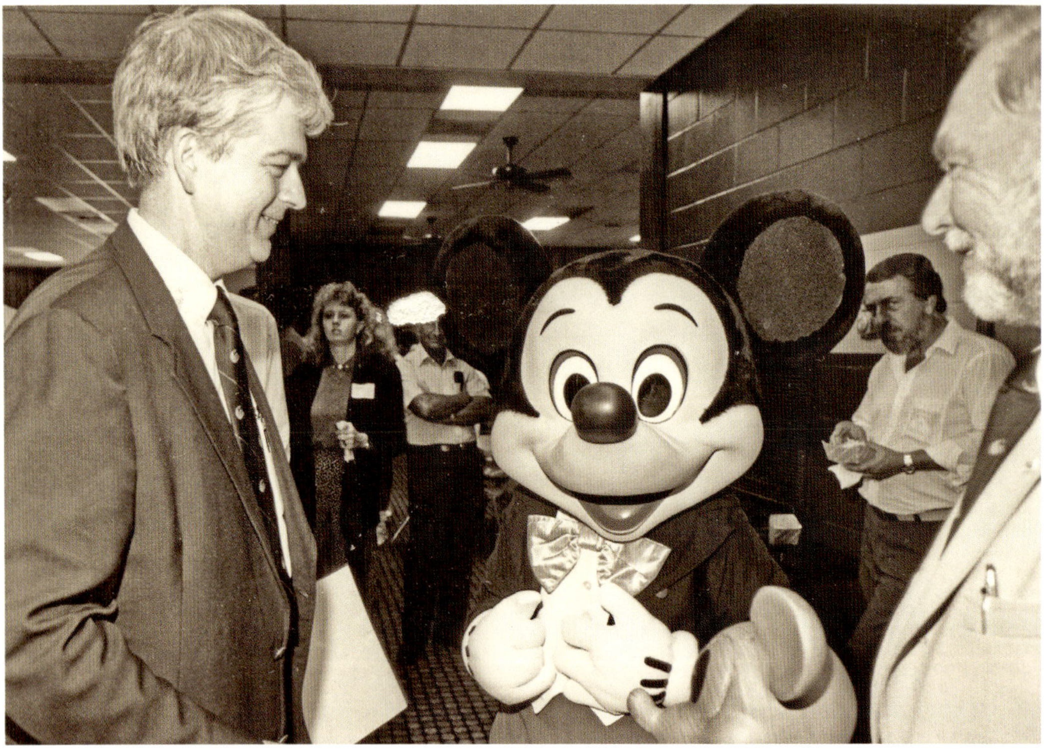

THEN AND NOW: Dignitaries pose with a local celebrity. Orlando has become a world-wide tourist destination and the area continues to experience rapid growth as Americans move south. A variety of international foods are available for busy students throughout campus.

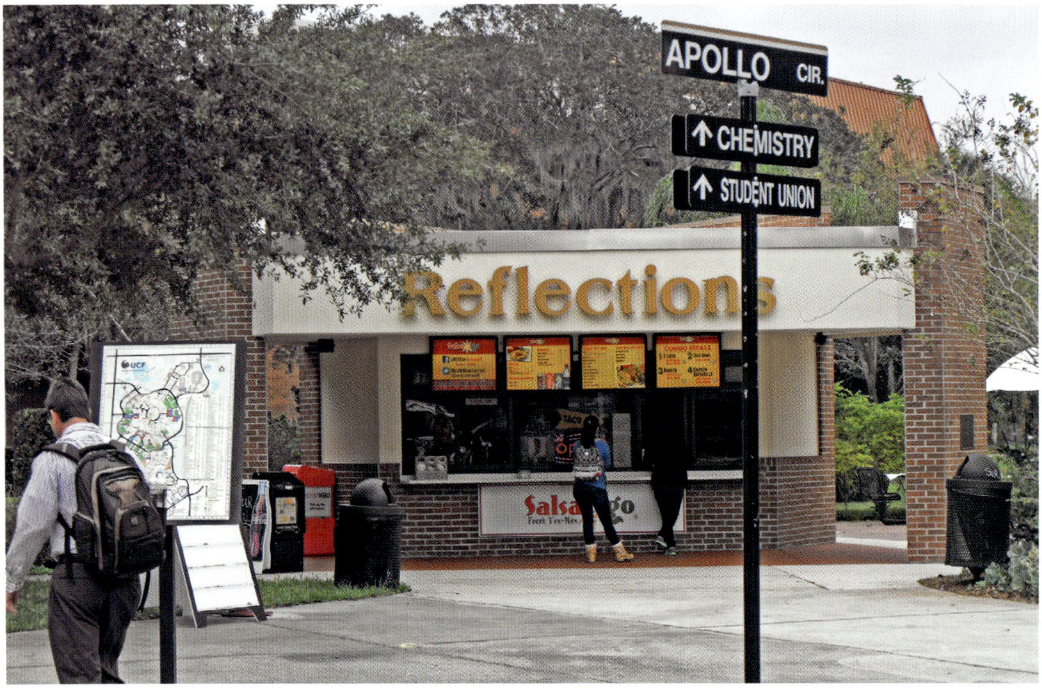

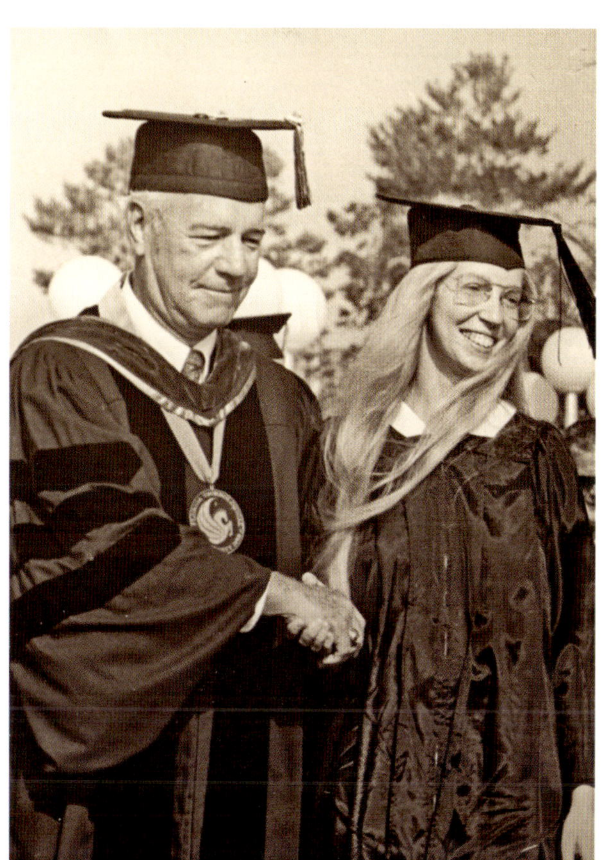

ONWARD: UCF's 10,000th graduate, Cynthia Annemarie Niemi poses with President Millican at her 1976 graduation ceremony. A school which, just half a century ago, was a dream to be realized has become a place steeped in tradition.

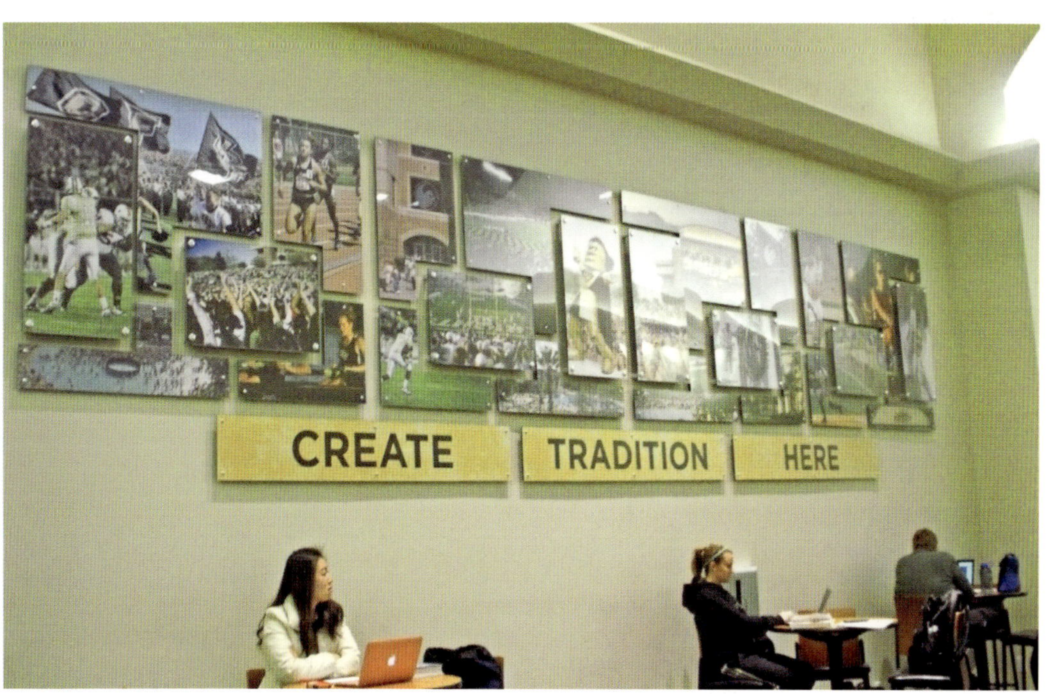

CREATE TRADITION HERE

ACKNOWLEDGMENTS

Laila Miletic-Vejzovic, of the University of Central Florida's Special Collections and University Archives, has been of invaluable help. Without her kindness, intelligence, willingness, and patience, this book would not be. Angie Vallafane and Mary Rubin in Special Collections gave patient assistance to this project as well. My work family at the Center for Autism and Related Disabilities, particularly Dr. Teresa Daly, has been encouraging and enthusiastic about this project. A low bow to all; they do vital work with grace and heart and strength for those who cannot speak for themselves. Under the direction of the inimitable Mel Rogers, Associate Dean of the College of Health and Public Affairs and chair of the Diversity Committee, I have learned what makes UCF a unique and lovely place. Finally, I am most grateful to my husband, Mikel, our sons, and to my mother Anne Davis.

All of the historic photos come from the University Photograph Collection, Special Collections & University Archives, University of Central Florida Libraries, Orlando, Florida.

All new photographs by Aaron Hausman and Kate Cumiskey.